The History of the Jews in the Greco-Roman World

The Jews of Palestine from Alexander the Great to the Arab Conquest

The History of the Jews in the Greco-Roman World examines Judaism in Palestine throughout the Hellenistic age, from Alexander the Great's conquest in 334 BC to its capture by the Arabs in AD 636. Under the Greek, Roman and finally Christian supremacy which Hellenism imposed, Judaism developed far beyond its biblical origins into a form which was to influence European history from the Middle Ages to the present day. The book focuses particularly on social, economic and religious concerns, and the political status of the Jews as both active agents and passive victims of history.

The author presents a straightforward chronological survey of this important period through analysis and interpretation of the existing sources. With its accessible style and explanation of technical terms, the book provides a useful introduction for students and those with an interest in Jewish history.

Peter Schäfer is Professor of Religion and Ronald O. Perelman Professor of Jewish Studies at Princeton University, and University Professor of Jewish Studies and Director of the Institut für Judaistik at Freie Universität Berlin. His most recent book is *Mirror of His Beauty: Feminine Images of God from the Bible to the Early Kabbalah* (2002).

The History of
the Jews in the
Greco-Roman World

Peter Schäfer

Routledge
Taylor & Francis Group

LONDON AND NEW YORK

First edition (German language) published
1983 by Stuttgart Katholisches Bibelwerk
© 1983 Stuttgart Katholisches Bibelwerk

Revised English language edition published
1995 by Harwood Academic Publishers GmbH
© 1995 by Harwood Academic Publishers GmbH

Revised edition with correction published 2003
by Routledge
2 Park Square, Milton Park, Abingdon, Oxon, OX14 4RN

First published in paperback 2003

Simultaneously published in the USA and Canada
by Routledge
270 Madison Ave, New York NY 10016

Routledge is an imprint of the Taylor & Francis Group

Transferred to Digital Printing 2005

© 2003 by Routledge

British Library Cataloguing in Publication Data
A catalogue record for this book is available from the British Library

Library of Congress Cataloging in Publication Data
A catalog record for this book has been requested

ISBN 0–415–30587–X

Printed and bound by Antony Rowe Ltd, Eastbourne

For Ruth, Eva and Simon

CONTENTS

Preface   xi

Preface to English Edition   xv

Preface to the Reprint of the English Paperback Edition   xvi

List of Abbreviations   xvii

Chapter 1   Alexander the Great and the Diadochi   1
Alexander the Great   1
The Samaritan Schism   2
Alexander's Visit to Jerusalem   5
The Diadochi   7

Chapter 2   Palestine Under Ptolemaic Rule (301–200 BCE)   13
Ptolemaic Government and Economy   13
Political History: The First Syrian Wars   15
Palestine Under the Ptolemies: Government, Economy, Social
    Relations   15
Political History: The Third Syrian War   18
The Rise of the Tobiad Family   18
Political History: The Fourth Syrian War   21
The Break-up of the Tobiad Family   22
The Fifth Syrian War   23

**Chapter 3   Palestine Under Seleucid Rule
    (200–135/63 BCE)**   27
Seleucid Government and Economy   27
Palestine as a Seleucid Province   28
Oniads and Tobiads   32
The Heliodorus Affair   34
The "Hellenistic Reform" under Antiochus IV   35
The "Religious Edicts"   41
The Maccabean Revolt   44

Chapter 4   The Hasmonean Dynasty   65
Government and Economy of the Hasmonean State   65
John Hyrcanus I (135/34–104 BCE)   67
The Pharisees   69
Aristobulus I (104–103 BCE)   73

Alexander Jannaeus (103–76 BCE)   74
Salome Alexandra (76–67 BCE)   76
Aristobulus II (67–63 BCE)   76

Chapter 5   Herod the Great (37–4 BCE)   81
Herod's Rise to Power   81
Government and Economy Under Herod   87
A Summary of the Events of Herod's Reign   91
Assessment   97

Chapter 6   From Herod to the First Jewish War   101
The Settlement of the Succession   101
Philip (4 BCE to 33/34 CE)   102
Herod Antipas (4 BCE–39 CE)   103
Archelaus (4 BCE–6 CE)   104
Judaea under Roman Rule (6–41 CE)   105
Agrippa I (37–44 CE)   112
Agrippa II (50?–92/93 CE)   113
The Roman Procurators (44–66 CE)   114

Chapter 7   The First Jewish War (66–74 CE)   121
The Beginnings   121
The War in Galilee (67 CE)   123
The Years 68 and 69 CE   124
The Conquest of Jerusalem (70 CE)   127
The End of the War   128

Chapter 8   Between the Wars: From 74 to 132 CE   131
The Consequences of the War   131
The Rabbis   133
Johanan ben Zakkai   135
Jabneh   137
The Revolt Under Trajan (115–117 CE)   141

Chapter 9   The Bar Kochba Revolt (132–135 CE)   145
The Causes of the Revolt   145
Bar Kochba   148
The Revolt   154
The Consequences   158

Chapter 10 From the Bar Kochba Revolt to the Arab Conquest of Palestine 163
Usha and Beth Shearim 163
The Crisis of the Roman Empire in the Third Century 170
Judaism and Christianity 176
The Persian Conquest 190

Bibliography 199

Index 227

Chronological Table 233

PREFACE

A "History of the Jews in Antiquity" requires some explanation. First, let us be clear what the present history does not aim to be. It is not intended as a piece of research covering every aspect of ancient Judaism. The cultural history of ancient Judaism is entirely ignored, and little attention is paid to literary and religious history: these areas are already covered by a number of authoritative handbooks. Geographically, the focus is solely on Judaism in Palestine; no mention is made of the major Jewish centres in the so-called diaspora.

The main emphasis of this book is on the political history of the Jews in Palestine, where "political" is to be understood not as the mere succession of rulers and battles but as the interaction between political activity and social, economic and religious circumstances. A particular concern is the investigation of social and economic conditions in the history of Palestinian Judaism.

At the centre stand the Jews of antiquity as both subject and object of history; as a people who are politically both agents and passive victims, attempting to realize their political ideals and goals in a variety of changing circumstances. This implies three things: firstly, the fundamental recognition of the legitimacy of the political activity of ancient Judaism. In view of the confusion caused by the policies of the current representatives of Judaism in the modern state of Israel, this certainly does not seem to be something that everyone automatically takes for granted. Secondly, this means that the only applicable criterion must be the Jews themselves in their own intrinsic historic significance and not their function in a Christian narrative of redemption, however this may be defined. And finally, this means that the identity of whatever is signified by "Judaism" in antiquity is subjected to numerous radical transformations which do not permit the history of this Judaism to be described simply as the self-assertion of a constant "idea" in a hostile environment.

Nor is it a simple matter to specify a precise period for the consideration of the Judaism of antiquity. In the present instance, the period chosen is that characterized by the global domination of Hellenism, extending from the conquest of Palestine by Alexander the Great in the second half of the fourth century BCE until the seizure of the land by the Arabs in the seventh century CE. In the encounter (sometimes fruitful, sometimes repudiative, but always significant) with Hellenism in the widest sense, which confronted the Jews of Palestine in the form of Greek, Roman, and finally Christian supremacy, a Judaism developed which had far outgrown its biblical origins and which was to influence the history of Europe from the Middle Ages up until the modern era. A survey of such a colossal period of time, almost one thousand years, must follow its own literary laws. It should neither exhaust itself in sweeping generalization nor become bogged down in tiresome detail. Great care was taken in the present study to make the reader aware, at least in part and at important points, of the relationship between the author's account, which is always condensed and (inevitably) biased, and the original source; that is, to show how much the account depends on the interpretation of by no means unambiguous sources. Although there are naturally severe limits on this within the framework of a historical summary, an attempt was nevertheless made (more than in previous surveys) to cite sources and thus account for how specific judgements were arrived at. Likewise, reference was made to the relevant sources as often as possible, at least in the notes, so that the reader can look these up for him- or herself and check the information provided against the source material.

Unfortunately, the source material for the period in question is highly inconsistent. Whereas there is an abundance of information available for the early period (the Books of the Maccabees, Josephus), there is a striking lack of historically useful material for the Rabbinic period. This should not be papered over, as is frequently the case in the literature, by excessive recourse to rabbinic texts, which can only be turned to use for the historical events in question through the expenditure of a great deal of imaginative effort. The present survey takes this imbalance into account and is more thorough in its depiction of the period up to about 70 CE than the Rabbinic period. Despite the worthy efforts of M. Avi-Yonah, the fundamental research into the period of so-called Rabbinic Judaism on which a summary account like this one could be based still remains to be done. A really solid history of Rabbinic Judaism (and this means one that subjects its sources to critical examination) is one of the urgent desiderata of Judaic research.

This book is not aimed at experts. It is intended to be accessible to anyone interested in Judaism, as well as students of theology and Jewish studies in particular. A comprehensive bibliography at the back of the book should assist further study. The notes, on the other hand, have been kept largely free of references to the literature and primarily serve the purpose of indicating the sources in question. Similarly, no attempt was made (bar a few exceptions) to discuss dissenting opinions in the secondary literature or to specify in every case which opinions originated from or were influenced by which author. The informed reader will know this anyway, while it will be an unnecessary encumbrance for the laymen. I should, however, like to emphasise that I am especially indebted to the work of Martin Hengel, Hans G. Kippenberg and Abraham Schalit.

The transcriptions of Hebrew and Greek terms do not lay claim to any scientific justification, but have deliberately been kept simple. Technical terms are explained in the text as far as possible; I would also refer the reader to the *"Kleines Lexikon des Judentums"* (Little Encyclopaedia of Judaism) edited by Johann Maier and myself (Stuttgart/Constance, 1981). One particular problem was to find a neutral designation for the whole of the area populated by Jews which constitutes the subject of the book. The term "Judaea" was out of the question as its meaning is already ambivalent and it is used to designate both the Jewish province and a particular (but not precisely defined) geographical area ("Judaea" as distinct from "Galilee", for instance). Although fully aware of its inadequacy, I decided on the term "Palestine", by which I mean the area in the Near East, variously defined at various times, where the political activities in the period under consideration took place.

I would like to thank everyone who helped in the writing of the book, above all my colleagues Michael Krupp (Jerusalem), Alex Carmel (Haifa) and Yoram Tsafrir (Jerusalem) for their assistance in acquiring the illustrations.

Peter Schäfer
Cologne, April 1982

PREFACE TO THE ENGLISH EDITION

The English translation is based on the German original published in 1983. Apart from the correction of obvious mistakes only minor additions have been made. For technical reasons, the illustrations in the German edition (as well as in the French translation) could unfortunately not be included.

I would like to thank David Chowcat for his translation and Ulrike Hirschfelder for her generous assistance in preparing the book.

Peter Schäfer
Berlin, May 1995

PREFACE TO THE REPRINT OF THE ENGLISH PAPERBACK EDITION

Nearly twenty years after the publication of the original German version of this book (*Geschichte der Juden in der Antike*, 1983) and seven years after the English translation was issued (*The History of the Jews in Antiquity*, 1995), Routledge approached me about publishing a new edition of the English translation. I am delighted that they have decided to reissue this book in paperback form, under the new and more fitting title, *The History of the Jews in the Greco-Roman World*.

The text remains the same as in the 1995 edition, apart from the correction of minor typographical mistakes. Fortunately enough, however, the chronological table found at the end of the German version, which was omitted from the first English edition, could now be included. I know from my students in Germany that this is the part of the book which they like most, and I thank the press for agreeing to print an English version of it in the present edition.

In the last 20 years, research has obviously made much progress, and it goes without saying that I myself have changed my mind on quite a number of issues. Nevertheless, my students and colleagues in Germany and in the US keep telling me that the book works well as a textbook in a variety of courses. Particularly since the German version is now out of print, I trust that the present edition will prove helpful. I do hope, however, that in the not too distant future I will be able to revise the book and to publish a completely new edition.

Peter Schäfer
Princeton, August 2002

ABBREVIATIONS

AASOR	Annual of the American School of Oriental Research
AAST	Atti della reale accademia delle scienze di Torino
Ab	Tractate Abot
AC	L'Antiquité classique
Acts	Acts of the Apostles
Adv. haer.	Epiphanius, Adversus haeresium
Adv. jud.	Tertullian, Adversus Judaeos
AIPh	Annuaire de l'institut de philologie et d'histoire orientales et slaves
AJP	American Journal of Philology
ALUOS	Annual of Leeds University Oriental Society
Am.	Amos
Anab.	Arrian, Anabasis Alexandrou
AnGr	Analecta Gregoriana
ANRW	Aufstieg und Niedergang der römischen Welt
Ant.	Josephus, Antiquitates
Apol.	Justin, Apologia
ARNA	Aboth de-Rabbi Nathan, Version A
ARNB	Aboth de-Rabbi Nathan, Version B
ASNSP	Annali della Scuola Normale Superiore di Pisa
AZ	Tractate 'Abodah Zara
b	Babylonian Talmud
b.	ben (son of)
BA	Biblical Archaeologist
BASOR	Bulletin of the American School of Oriental Research
BB	Tractate Baba Bathra
Bell.	Josephus, Bellum
Ber	Tractate Berachot
BerR	Bereshith Rabbah
Bibl	Biblica
Bibl. Hist.	Diodorus, Bibliotheke Historike
BM	Tractate Baba Metzia
BZ	Biblische Zeitschrift
CAH	Cambridge Ancient History
CBQ	Catholic Biblical Quarterly

CCL	Corpus Christianorum, Series Latina
CD	Damascus Rule
CHM	Cahiers d'histoire mondiale
Chr.	First and Second Book of Chronicles
Chron.	Sulpicius Severus, Chronica
CI	Codex Iustinianus
CIL	Corpus Inscriptionum Latinarum
CP	Classical Philology
CSEL	Corpus Scriptorum Ecclesiasticorum Latinorum
CT	Codex Theodosianus
Dan.	Daniel
DBS	Dictionnaire de la bible, Supplément
Deut.	Deuteronomy
Dial. c. Tryph.	Justin, Dialogus cum Tryphone
Diss.	Arrian, Dissertationes Epikteti
Eccles.	Ecclesiastes
Ecclus.	Ecclesiasticus
EchaR, Pet.	Echa Rabba, Peticha
EchaRB	Echa Rabba, ed. S. Buber
Ed	Tractate Eduyot
EI	Eretz Israel
Ep.	Ambrose, Epistulae
Ezek.	Ezekiel
GCS	Die griechischen christlichen Schriftsteller der ersten Jahrhunderte
Gen.	Genesis
Git	Tractate Gittin
HA	Historia Augusta
Hab.	Habakkuk
HAW	Handbuch der Altertumswissenschaft
HE	Eusebius, Historia Ecclesiastica
Hist	Historia
Hist.	Curtius Rufus, Historiae Alexandri Magni
Hist.	Tacitus, Historiae
Hist. eccl.	Rufinus, Historia ecclesiastica
Hist. eccl.	Sozomenos, Historia ecclesiastica
Hist. Jud.	Historia Judaica

Hor	Tractate Horayot
Hos.	Hosea
HR	Dio Cassius, Historia Romana
HR	History of Religions
HSCP	Harvard Studies in Classical Philology
HTR	Harvard Theological Review
HUCA	Hebrew Union College Annual
IEJ	Israel Exploration Journal
INJ	Israel Numismatic Journal
Isa.	Isaiah
j	Jerusalem Talmud
JBL	Journal of Biblical Literature
JEOL	Jaarbericht van het vooraziatisch-egyptisch Genootschap "Ex oriente lux"
JITL	Jahresbericht der israelitisch-theologischen Lehranstalt, Vienna
JJS	Journal of Jewish Studies
JNG	Jahrbuch für Numismatik und Geldgeschichte
JPOS	Journal of the Palestine Oriental Society
JQR	Jewish Quarterly Review
JR	Journal of Religion
JRH	Journal of Religious History
JRS	Journal of Roman Studies
JSJ	Journal for the Study of Judaism
JSS	Journal of Semitic Studies
JTS	Journal of Theological Studies
Judg.	Judges
Ket	Tractate Ketubbot
Kgs	Kings
Lev.	Leviticus
m	Mishnah
Macc.	First and Second Book of Maccabees
Matt.	Matthew
Meg	Tractate Megillah
MegTaan	Megillat Ta'anit

MGWJ	Monatsschrift für die Geschichte und Wissenschaft de Judentums
MH	Museum Helveticum
Mic.	Micah
MQ	Tractate Mo'ed Qatan
MSh	Tractate Ma'aser Sheni
Mur.	Murabba'at Dokumente, ed. J. T. Milik
Nah	Nahum
Nat. Hist.	Pliny, Naturalis Historia
Ned	Tractate Nedarim
Neh.	Nehemiah
Nov.	Justinian, Novellae
NT	New Testament
NTS	New Testament Studies
Num.	Numbers
Orat. adv. Iud.	Chrysostom, Oratio adversus Iudaeos
Orat. V.	Gregory of Nyssa, Oratio V contra Iulianum
PEQ	Palestine Exploration Quarterly
Pes	Tractate Pesachim
PesR	Pesiqta Rabbati
PG	Migne, Patrologiae Cursus Completus, Series Graeca
Ph.S.	Philologus, Supplement
PIASH	Proceedings of the Israel Academy of Sciences and Humanities
PJB	Palästinajahrbuch
PRK	Pesiqta deRab Kahana
Qid	Tractate Qiddushin
1QpHab	Commentary on Habakkuk
4QpNah	Commentary on Nahum
1QSb	Blessings
RB	Revue biblique
RdQ	Revue de Qumran
REJ	Revue des études juives
RHD	Revue historique de droit français et étranger
RHR	Revue de l'histoire des religions
RHSh	Tractate Rosh ha-Shanah

RIDA	Revue internationale des droits de l'Antiquité
RivBib	Rivista Biblica
RMP	Rheinisches Museum für Philologie
RN	Revue numismatique
San	Tractate Sanhedrin
SBFLA	Studii biblici Franciscani liber annuus
SchM	Schweizer Münzblätter
SCI	Scripta Classica Israelica
ScrHie	Scripta Hierosolymitana
Shab	Tractate Shabbat
Shebi	Tractate Shebi'it
Sot	Tractate Sotah
StC	Studii Clasice
StTh	Studia Theologica
Suk	Tractate Sukkah
Syr.	Appian, Syriake
t	Tosefta
Taan	Tractate Ta'anit
TCAAS	Transactions of the Connecticut Academy of Arts and Sciences
ThLZ	Theologische Literaturzeitung
ThZ	Theologische Zeitschrift
TO	Targum Onkelos
TPsJ	Targum Pseudo-Jonathan
VT	Vetus Testamentum
WHJP	World History of the Jewish People
WThJ	Westminster Theological Journal
Yad	Tractate Yadayim
Yeb	Tractate Yebamot
Yom	Tractate Yoma
ZAW	Zeitschrift für die alttestamentliche Wissenschaft
ZDPV	Zeitschrift des deutschen Palästinavereins
Zech.	Zechariah
Zeph.	Zephaniah
ZNW	Zeitschrift für die neutestamentliche Wissenschaft
ZPE	Zeitschrift für Papyrologie und Epigraphik

1. ALEXANDER THE GREAT AND THE DIADOCHI

1.1. Alexander the Great

The Palestine in which we find ourselves at the beginning of the Hellenistic period was anything but a homogeneous economic and cultural entity. The dominant power before the conquest by Alexander the Great had been the Persians, an oriental empire that had long since gone into decline. The western regions of this Persian empire (and above all Phoenicia, that is, the maritime coastal towns) had long been oriented toward Greece and exposed to the economic, cultural and also the military influence of the Greeks. Numerous individual findings in Palestine have shown that Greek ceramics, Greek artworks and even Greek coins were widespread in this region, and that entire cities (especially on the coastal plain) might well be designated as "Greek" even prior to the country's conquest by Alexander.

Nevertheless, the triumphant campaign of the young Alexander (he was twenty-three years old), starting with the celebrated battle of Issus (333 BCE), opened a new chapter in the history of the Near East. The Orient, which had previously known the Greeks primarily as traders and artists, now came to know them and the ethnically related Macedonians as hard and brutal conquerors. After the victory at Issus, the general Parmenion advanced as far as Damascus and conquered Syria, while Alexander proceeded along the coast and was paid homage by the Phoenician cities of Aradus, Marathus, Byblos and Sidon, all of which surrendered without a fight. Only the reputedly impregnable Tyre (which had previously been laid siege to by Sanherib and Nebuchadnezzar for many years without success) refused the king access to city and temple. Alexander, who wanted both to make an example and to deprive the Persian-Phoenician fleet operating in the Aegean of a base, besieged the city for seven months before conquering it in August 332 with the aid of an artificial dam and his fleet. Classical historians report that two

1

thousand able men were crucified and thirty thousand survivors sold as slaves.[1] The city (as usually happened with Alexander's conquests) was converted into a Macedonian colony and settled by Greek colonists.

From Tyre, the campaign on the Phoenician-Palestinian coastal strip then proceeded further south. Alexander did not meet with any further significant resistance until reaching Gaza, one of the most important Arabian trading centres (Gaza was where one of the old caravan routes from the east reached the sea: in particular, trade with the Nabataeans was conducted via Gaza). Gaza fell after two months, the able men, as in Tyre, were killed, and the women and children sold into slavery.

While Alexander's campaign advanced south along the coast to Egypt, what was happening in the meantime in the Syro-Palestinian hinterland, and particularly in the province of Yehud (= Judah) which had remained autonomous under the Persians? Naturally, the classical historians had little interest in the fate of this provincial corner of the world. They concentrated mostly on the great conquests of the king and give the impression that most of the Palestinian cities had already submitted to Alexander either before or during the siege of Tyre. Nowhere is there mention of a special campaign by Alexander in the Palestinian hinterland.

Contrary to this consensus of opinion by the classical historians, the Jewish tradition reports a visit by Alexander to Jerusalem, as well as connecting the final separation of the Samaritans from the Jewish cult community (the so-called Samaritan schism) with the events surrounding Alexander's conquest of Palestine.

1.1.1. The Samaritan schism

The main source for the separation of the Samaritans and the founding of a (in Jewish eyes) schismatic sanctuary on Mt. Gerizim is Josephus.[2] According to him, Manasseh, a brother of the High Priest Jaddus, married Nikaso, the daughter of the Persian governor of Samaria, Sanballat. This Manasseh fled—still under Persian jurisdiction—to Samaria, as they could not tolerate his "mixed marriage" with Nikaso in Jerusalem. Sanballat promised to build a temple on Mt. Gerizim and to appoint him High Priest of this new sanctuary. Alexander, preoccupied with the siege of Tyre, demanded of the Jewish High Priest military support and the tribute which had up to then been paid to the Persian king, Darius. This was, however, refused him by the Jewish High Priest on the grounds of his oath of allegiance to Darius. Sanballat, on the other hand, saw his opportunity, hurried to Alexander's assistance with eight thousand Samaritan soldiers (that is, defectors from

Darius) and was rewarded with permission to build the temple. Shortly afterward, Sanballat died. This version of the story can perhaps be supplemented by Josephus' later note: "But the soldiers of Sanballat he [Alexander] ordered to accompany him to Egypt; there, he said, he would give them allotments of land".[3]

So much for Josephus. To evaluate this source, one may turn first of all to a parallel in the biblical book of Nehemiah (12:10–22; 13:28). Many researchers suppose that Nehemiah (particularly Nehemiah 13:28) is the basis of Josephus' report, which was then "elaborated into the legend of the origin of the Samaritan community".[4] This assumption is certainly problematic, even from a purely methodological point of view: biblical texts do not develop into legends in a vacuum, within the confines of the author's room, as it were. Moreover, there is a difference in genealogy between Nehemiah and Josephus; i.e. one must ask why, if he wanted to spin out the report in Nehemiah, Josephus decided to alter the genealogy in particular. It is more likely that both reports reflect a historical fact, although the relation between these two sources must remain an open question. Perhaps there were also links between them of which we are not aware.

As regards the historical basis, the papyri found in the so-called Cave of Death in Wadi ed-Daliyeh, north of Jericho, would seem to establish that a third governor called Sanballat ruled in Samaria at the time of Alexander's campaign.[5] If there was a governor called Sanballat at the time of Alexander's campaign, then there is little reason to doubt Josephus when he goes on to report that this same Sanballat submitted to Alexander along with the other local rulers of Syria and Palestine and also—as a sign of this submission—offered his assistance in the conquest of Tyre. Josephus' abovementioned note, that Sanballat's soldiers accompanied Alexander to Egypt, is thus also not improbable.

But what are we to make of the report of the founding of the temple on Mt. Gerizim which, according to Josephus, was both connected with these political events as well as being the result of an internal dispute within the Jerusalem priesthood? It must first of all be pointed out that Josephus' report is the only relevant source for the founding of the temple on Mt. Gerizim, that is, the actual Samaritan schism. Reference has indeed been made to biblical passages for this schism,[6] but it is very unlikely that these passages, which refer originally to a conflict between the northern and the southern kingdoms, were written with the Samaritans in mind. Archaeological digs have produced some confirmation of the fact that there was a temple on Mt. Gerizim; the archaeologists (above all R. J. Bull) suspect that the remains of the building found under Hadrian's temple on Mt. Gerizim date from this Samaritan sanctuary. The Greek ceramics found in this building would seem to support this.

So we are left with Josephus' report, which probably stems from a propaganda story of Samaritan origin from the second century BCE. Its historical core seems to consist in an internal dispute among the Jerusalem priesthood over the mixed marriage question following the rebuilding of the Temple and the restitution of the Jewish city state. A group of priests had evidently seen a danger for the new Jewish order in such mixed marriages, and in the wake of such quarrels certain parties (including the Manasseh mentioned by Josephus) may have left Jerusalem and resettled in an area under Samaritan rule. Whether the building of the temple was approved by Alexander is, however, quite another matter. It would seem much more likely that we see here the understandable concern of the Samaritans to establish that the construction of the temple on Mt. Gerizim was authorized by the great king Alexander, i.e. this particular aspect of the narrative is almost certainly unhistorical.

This is further confirmed by a second report by Josephus which probably stems from another source.[7] Here the Samaritan temple is presumed to be already in existence, even though Sanballat (according to the first report by Josephus) had received permission to build from Alexander only a few months earlier. Moreover, relations between Alexander and the Samaritans are much cooler here than one would expect in view of Sanballat's defection to Alexander as described in the first text. It is therefore not unlikely that this second source stems from a Jewish, and thus anti-Samaritan original. Historically, this means that Alexander certainly had nothing to do with the building of the temple by the Samaritans, and so neither had he authorized it (as the first text will have us believe), nor was the temple already built during his stay in Palestine.

The conflict between Alexander and the Samaritans and the preferential treatment of the Jews, only hinted at by Josephus, is dealt with more thoroughly in other sources. As well as a legendary story in the Talmud,[8] Curtius Rufus mentions in his biography of Alexander that the inhabitants of Samaria had burnt alive (*vivum Samaritae cremaverant*) Andromachus, the governor of Syria appointed by Alexander.[9] Alexander is said to have hurried immediately from Egypt to Samaria to avenge his death, to have put the perpetrators of the crime to death and to have appointed Menon successor to Andromachus. This report is supplemented by the Chronicle of Eusebius, which states:

> Alexander laid siege to Tyre and took Judaea; exalted by the Jews, he made sacrifice to God and honoured the high priest. He appointed Andromachus governor of the province, who was killed by inhabitants of the Shamyrtaean city (= Samaria). Alexander punished them, after returning from Egypt and occupying the city, by settling Macedonians there.[10]

According to this version of events, then, Alexander personally destroyed Samaria and turned the city into a Macedonian military colony. Admittedly, the historical value of the last point of this report (the transformation into a military colony) must be qualified by another remark in Eusebius to the effect that it was not until Perdiccas was governor (296/95) that the city was resettled.

This contradiction has still not been settled, but does not play a decisive role. What is important, and backed up by the findings in Wadi ed-Daliyeh (aside from documents, the remains of two hundred and five persons were found there, apparently eminent Samaritans who had gone into hiding and had been thoroughly smoked out by the pursuing Macedonians), is the fact that Samaria was destroyed at an early date (probably already under Alexander). Such a finding fits in with the history of the settlement of the city of Shechem, which had been unpopulated between 480 and 330 BCE, but experienced a new period of growth from 330 onward, peaking in 300 BCE. The resettlement of Shechem and the building of the Samaritan temple on Mt. Gerizim are in all probability related to the destruction of Samaria and its subsequent re-establishment as a Macedonian military colony.

1.1.2. Alexander's visit to Jerusalem

There are references in both Josephus and rabbinical literature to a visit to Jerusalem by Alexander.[11] According to these, the High Priest Jaddus marched out of the gates of Jerusalem to confront Alexander and prevent him plundering the city. When Alexander saw the High Priest he prostrated himself before him since, according to Josephus, he recognized in him the figure which had once appeared to him in a dream and encouraged him to wage war against the Persians. Finally

> he gave his hand to the high priest and, with the priests running beside him, entered the city. Then he went up to the temple, where he sacrificed to God under the direction of the high priest, and showed due honour to the priests and to the high priest himself. And, when the book of Daniel was shown to him, in which he (scil. Daniel) had declared that one of the Greeks would destroy the empire of the Persians, he believed himself to be the one indicated; and in his joy he dismissed the multitude for the time being, but on the following day he summoned them again and told them to ask for any gifts which they might desire. When the high priest asked that they might live in accordance with the

laws of their fathers and in the seventh year be exempt from tribute, he granted all this.[12]

This story is for the most part a legend without any historical foundation.
The motif of the unexpected reverence of the heathen conqueror before the
Jewish representative can also be found in other historical contexts and, like
the visit to Jerusalem and the sacrifice in the Temple, serves to confirm the
superiority of the Jewish God: that is, it belongs to the realm of religious propaganda. However, this does not imply that no contact at all took place
between Alexander and the Jews of the former Persian province of Yehud. It is
quite possible that the Jews asked Alexander for the right to live according to
the "laws of their fathers", just as they had done in the case of the Persian and,
later, the Hellenistic kings. As Alexander had also granted such a right to their
own laws to other peoples, we must take this point to be the historical core of
Josephus' account. As regards the details of such an encounter, it should be
noted that the Talmudic report does not speak of the king visiting Jerusalem,
but relates that the Jewish High Priest and his retinue met Alexander at Kefar
Saba (later known as Antipatris) on the coastal plain. This version has much to
commend it, especially in view of its claim that the Jews called on the king
and not vice versa, and that the meeting with the king took place during his
campaign of conquest through the coastal plain, and thus Alexander would
not have had to diverge from this natural southerly course (which the Greek
historians were only aware of) in order to arrive at Jerusalem.

A further problem is the question as to whether and to what extent
Alexander intervened in the administration of the conquered territories (in this
case, Syria and Palestine). We merely learn the names of a variety of different
satraps, amongst whom was said to be a Persian called Bessos in the period
329–325 BCE. This would suggest a high degree of tolerance and indicates
that Alexander had recourse to competent local officials and did not substantially alter the administrative structure of this very diverse country with its
numerous more or less independent cities and provinces. For the formerly
autonomous Persian province of Yehud this meant that the changeover of
political power was unlikely to have resulted in any sudden radical changes
and that Alexander was not going to intervene directly in Jerusalem affairs.
He was probably satisfied with the recognition of Greek sovereignty by the
High Priest acting as the representative of the people, and otherwise left the
organizational structure of Judaea untouched, allowing the High Priest and
the Council of Elders to remain the heads of state. His only intervention was
in the autonomy of the currency of the local city states, where he put new
Alexander coins into circulation as the standardized currency, no doubt with
the intention of facilitating trade and thereby stimulating the economy.

However, Alexander was unable to enjoy the fruits of his campaign of conquest and the associated economic measures. He died aged thirty-three in Babylon on the 10th June 323 BCE, soon after his return from India. His brief period of influence met with little positive resonance in Judaeo-Palestinian literature. The apocalyptic Book of Daniel, for instance, calls him a "heroic" king (*melech gibbor*), but a critical tone is clearly struck in the very same verse: "And a heroic king shall stand up, that shall rule with great dominion, and do according to his will" (Dan. 11:3). Above all, the kingdom founded by him, the "fourth kingdom" of the Macedonians and Greeks, is depicted as an incarnation of sheer evil:

> After this I saw in the night visions, and behold a fourth beast, dreadful and terrible, and strong exceedingly; and it had great iron teeth: it devoured and brake in pieces, and stamped the residue with the feet of it (Dan. 7:7).

Or in the animal vision of the Ethiopic Book of Enoch:

> After that I saw with my own eyes all the birds of heaven—eagles, vultures, kites, and ravens—coming; the eagles[13] were the ones who were leading all the birds; and they began to eat those sheep,[14] to dig out their eyes, and to eat their flesh.[15]

And finally, the First Book of the Maccabees, which begins its report with a characterization of Alexander that could not be clearer:

> And he fought many battles, and won many strongholds, and slew the kings of the earth, and went through to the ends of the earth, and took spoils of a multitude of nations. And the earth trembled before him. And he became arrogant and his heart got above itself.[16]

1.2. The Diadochi

1.2.1. Political background

When Alexander the Great died in Babylon in 323 at the height of his military successes, a power struggle began between his generals for the succession. Palestine, which, in its exposed position, had long been the subject of dispute between the two great cultural centres in the north (Syria-Mesopotamia) and in the south (Egypt), once more became the focus for competing interests.

In Egypt, initial success (from the end of 322) could be claimed by the energetic and ambitious Ptolemy (son of Lagus), the founder of the Ptolemaic dynasty. He not only took control of Cyrenaica, but also of Alexander's corpse, which he recognized as a politically valuable relic and, in the time-honoured tradition of the Pharaohs, immediately laid claim to Phoenicia and Coele-Syria,[17] the possession of which guaranteed control of the most important trade routes and naval bases. His first venture in 320 BCE against Laomedon, Syria's satrap, was successful, but he was soon faced with a much more powerful rival. His main opponent was Antigonus Monophthalmus ("the One-Eyed", together with his son Demetrius Poliorketes, "the Besieger"), the leading advocate of the idea of unity of empire and therefore the bitter enemy of the other satraps. Antigonus drove out Seleucus, the satrap of Babylon, and in 315 BCE occupied Syria/Palestine, which Ptolemy (together with the expelled Seleucus) was unable to win back until 312 BCE (at the Battle of Gaza) and then only for a few months. When Antigonus marched back into Syria/Palestine that very same year, Ptolemy avoided a military confrontation and gave up the province without a fight to his rival, who retained uncontested control over it for the next ten years.

In 302 BCE the events of 312 BCE repeated themselves; Ptolemy of Egypt (upon acceptance of the title of king he now called himself Ptolemy Soter) conquered Syria/Palestine for the third time and withdrew in the same year, this time following a rumour of the defeat of the coalition of allied Diadochian kings against Antigonus and his son Demetrius. This retreat was premature, as in 301 BCE Antigonus was defeated by his adversaries. The victors handed over Syria/Palestine to Seleucus (who had already regained possession of Babylon in 312 and thereby founded the Seleucid dynasty), but through his rapid occupation of the province, Ptolemy achieved a *fait accompli*; he calculated correctly that Seleucus was unlikely to take action against his former comrade-in-arms, to whom he also owed the reconquest of his Babylonian province. Seleucus did indeed refrain from armed confrontation, but did not relinquish his claims on this important southern province of his kingdom. Here lay the seeds of the conflict between the Seleucids and the Ptolemies which was to play such a crucial role in the politics of these two kingdoms and the eventual fate of Palestine.

1.2.2. Palestine under the Diadochi

The classical historians make practically no mention of Palestine and the Jews at the time of the struggles among the Diadochi. One can only conclude "that the politico-economic significance of the small Jewish temple state in the mountains between the Dead Sea and the coastal plain was too small to attract the attention of the historians".[18] But Josephus, too, has relatively little to report about this period. The first mention of any interest in Josephus is supposedly taken from a work entitled "On the Jews" by Hecataeus of Abdera. However, this work is very probably a Jewish forgery from the middle of the second century BCE, although this does not necessarily entail that the forger had not himself made use of historically relevant information:

> Hecataeus goes on to say that after the battle of Gaza Ptolemy became master of Syria, and that many of the inhabitants, hearing of his kindliness and humanity, desired to accompany him to Egypt and to associate themselves with his realm.
>
> Among these (he says) was Ezechias, a high priest of the Jews, a man of about sixty-six years of age, highly esteemed by his countrymen, intellectual, and moreover an able speaker and unsurpassed as a man of business. ...[19]

We may suppose that this statement has a core of historical truth. We must assume that at the time of the struggles amongst the Diadochi, in view of the unclear and constantly changing political situation in Jerusalem, there were two rival parties, one of which sympathized with Ptolemy and one with Antigonus Monophthalmus. If the dates in Pseudo-Hecataeus are correct, we are in the year 312 BCE, when there was indeed a battle south of Gaza between Ptolemy and Antigonus/Demetrius.[20] Less probable is the benevolence of Ptolemy and the wish to allow the Jews to participate in the government of the kingdom in Egypt, which Pseudo-Hecataeus gives as the reason for the departure of the High Priest and his compatriots for Egypt. It must be remembered that Ptolemy retreated that same year before Antigonus and surrendered the province of Syria/Palestine to him without a struggle. This would seem a much more probable occasion for the departure of Ezechias/Hiskia and his colleagues. Hiskia probably had good grounds for fearing that he would be accused by the victorious Antigonus of pro-Ptolemaic leanings and therefore preferred to leave the country and evade Antigonus' clutches. This same Hiskia is also associated in the research with coins bearing the inscription (in ancient Hebrew script) *Yechezqiyo/ah hapechah* ("Hiskia the Governor") which might indeed refer to the High Priest Hiskia. It may be supposed that the designation *pechah* ("governor") on these coins signals the continuity of government between the Persian era (*pechah* was originally a Persian word) and the beginnings of the Ptolemaic era and that Hiskia was possibly Judaea's last governor at the end of Persian rule, who then decided in 312 BCE that he would rather go into Egyptian exile with Ptolemy. This hypothesis of the continuity of government between the end of Persian and the beginnings of Ptolemaic rule is further supported by other coins which, instead of the Persian ruler, bear the portrait of Ptolemy I and whose inscription differs merely insofar as the word *yehud* (the Aramaic name of the province commonly used by the Persians) is replaced by the Hebrew word *yehudah*.

A further statement by Josephus regarding the constantly changing situation during the struggles among the Diadochi is based on the geographer and historian Agatharchides of Cnidus (second century BCE):

> [So] all of Syria at the hands of Ptolemy, the son of Lagus, who was then called *Soter* (Saviour), suffered the reverse of that which was indicated by his surname. And this king seized Jerusalem by resorting to cunning and deceit. For he entered the city on the Sabbath as if to sacrifice, and, as the Jews did not oppose him—for they did not suspect any hostile act—... he became master of the city without difficulty and ruled it harshly. This account is attested by Agatharchides of Cnidus ... in these words: "There is a nation called Jews, who have a strong and great city called Jerusalem, which they allowed to fall into the hands of Ptolemy by refusing to take up arms and, instead, through their untimely superstition submitted to having a hard master." This, then, was the opinion which Agatharchides expressed about our nation. Now Ptolemy, after taking many captives both from the hill country of Judaea and the district round Jerusalem and from Samaria and those on Garizein, brought them all to Egypt and settled them there.[21]

This report of a conquest of Jerusalem by Ptolemy on a Sabbath is not contested as such. The practice is familiar enough and was also used, for instance, by the Seleucids at the beginning of the Maccabean Revolt. Agatharchides' report is confirmed by the so-called *Letter of Aristeas*, which likewise relates that Ptolemy had abducted numerous Jews to Egypt and selected some of them to be soldiers.[22] The date of Jerusalem's seizure by Ptolemy is contested, however, but there is considerable evidence in favour of 302 BCE for the third conquest of Syria/Palestine. The ruling classes of Jerusalem seem to have sided with Antigonus and to have paid for this with an armed attack by Ptolemy and other drastic penalties as well. The Jews who emigrated voluntarily to Egypt or were deported there by Ptolemy then formed the core of the subsequent Jewish Diaspora, especially in Egypt (and Alexandria in particular).

The struggles of the Diadochi in Palestine were also reflected in Jewish literature. Many researchers interpret Zechariah 14:2 as referring to the conquest of Jerusalem by Ptolemy:

> ... and the city shall be taken, and the houses rifled, and the women ravished; and half of the city shall go forth into captivity, and the residue of the people shall not be cut off from the city.

And Zechariah 9:13 f. may reflect the resistance and the hatred shown by the inhabitants of Jerusalem towards the foreign conquerors:

> For my bow is strung, O Judah;
> I have laid the arrow to it, O Ephraim;
> I have roused your sons, O Zion,
> against your sons, O Javan,[23]
> and made you into the sword of a warrior.

The much later First Book of the Maccabees (written in about 120 BCE) passes judgement on Alexander's successors as follows:

> And Alexander reigned twelve years, and he died. And his servants bare rule, each one in his place. And they did all put diadems upon themselves after that he was dead, and so did their sons after them many years: and they multiplied evils in the earth.[24]

Notes

1. Arrian, Anab. II, 24 f.; Diodorus, Bibl. Hist. XVII, 46.4; Curtius Rufus, Hist. IV, 4.17.
2. Ant. XI, 8. 2–4 § 302 ff.
3. Ant. XI, 8.6 § 345.
4. Kippenberg, Garizim und Synagoge, p. 52.
5. A distinction should probably be made between the following: Sanballat I, Nehemia's antagonist (b. approx. 485 BCE); Sanballat II (b. approx. 435 BCE): his name was found on a seal in the cave in Wadi ed-Daliyeh; and Sanballat III as mentioned here by Josephus (b. approx. 385 BCE): this third Sanballat is not mentioned in the papyri, but Josephus' testimony gains in plausibility following the discovery of evidence of the existence of Sanballat II, of whom nothing had previously been known either.
6. Cf. Judg. 5:14; Hos. 13:1; Mic. 6:9–16; Trito-Isa.; 2 Chr. 13:4–12; Zech. 11:14.
7. Ant. XI, 8.6 §§ 340–344.
8. b Yom 69 a.
9. Hist. IV, 8.9–11.

10. Armenian version, ed. J. Karst, p. 197 (GCS XX); Latin version of Jerome, ed. R. Helm, pp. 123, 128 (GCS XLVII).
11. Ant. XI, 8.4–5 §§ 326–339; b Yom 69 a; cf.also MegTaan, ed. Lichtenstein, HUCA 8–9, 1931/32, p. 339.
12. Ant. XI, 8.5 §§ 336–338. Quotations from the *Antiquitates* and *Contra Apionem* are based on the English translations by H. St. J. Thackeray, Ralph Marcus and Louis H. Feldman in *Josephus: Jewish Antiquities* and *Against Apion* (Loeb Classical Library, London/Massachusetts, 1926–1965) and *The Jewish War* tr. G. A. Williamson, rev. E. Mary Smallwood (Middlesex, rev. ed. 1981). The original Greek and other translations were consulted for difficult or controversial passages.
13. They symbolize the Macedonians and the Greeks.
14. = Israel.
15. Eth. Enoch 90:2. The English translation is taken from The Old Testament Pseudepigrapha, Vol. I: Apocalyptic Literature and Testaments, ed. James H. Charlesworth (London, 1983).
16. I Macc. 1:2 f.—Quotations from the two Books of the Maccabees are based on the Revised Version in The Apocrypha (rev. 1926, OUP London, 1960).
17. Palestine and southern Syria: official designation of the province from approx. 200 BCE (that is, under the Seleucids).
18. Hengel, Juden, Griechen und Barbaren, p. 31.
19. Josephus, Contra Apionem I, 22 §§ 186–189.
20. See p. 8 above.
21. Ant. XII, 1.1 § 5 f.; Contra Apionem I, 22 §§ 208–211; cf. also Appianus, Syr. 50.
22. Letter of Aristeas 4.12 ff., 23.
23. = Greece.
24. I Macc. 1:7–9.

2. PALESTINE UNDER PTOLEMAIC RULE (301–200 BCE)

The occupation of Syria-Palestine by Ptolemy I (305–283/82) inaugurated the almost exactly one hundred years of Ptolemaic rule in Palestine which, despite numerous wars, was a time of peace and economic growth for Palestine. Initially, the entire province of "Syria and Phoenicia" (the official designation) was not yet in the hands of Ptolemy. By 286 BCE, however, he had succeeded in taking control of the Phoenician coastal cities as well (Tyre and Sidon in particular) and thus ruled over the entire province. The border of the Seleucid kingdom in the north ran from the coastal plain along the river Eleutherus (= Nahr el-Kebir) across the fertile Biqaᶜ north of Baalbek in an arc going south-east to Damascus, thus incorporating Coele-Syria and the most important Phoenician coastal towns.

2.1. Ptolemaic government and economy

Unlike the Seleucid kingdom, the Ptolemaic state, incorporating "Syria and Phoenicia" as a northern province, was a self-enclosed and rigidly centralized governmental organism. At the head of the state stood the all-powerful king, accredited with divine attributes, who, like all Hellenistic monarchs, appeared to his subjects as a "saviour" and a "divine manifestation". The country and all its produce were his personal possession. The state was his "house", the national territory his "estate": "So the king managed the State as a plain Macedonian or Greek would manage his own household".[1]

The country was divided up into various administrative units (*nomoi* = administrative districts in Egypt, hyparchies in the provinces) at whose head stood in each case a politico-military *stratēgos* and an *oikonomos*, who was in charge of the economic and fiscal administration. The chief governmental

13

official of the kingdom was—apart from the king—the *dioikētēs* ("Minister of Economics and Finance") whose prototype we encounter under Ptolemy II in the Zenon papyri as the *dioikētēs* Apollonius.

The main function of the Ptolemaic administrative apparatus was to increase economic productivity. The fundamental defining concept of the state, the identity of king and country, required the absolute obedience of the population. Not only the king's land in the narrow sense (*gē basilikē*), which was leased to the king's farmers, but also the land allocated to the Egyptian Greek cities Alexandria, Ptolemais and Naucratis, was only held on trust (*en aphesei*) by the cities and belonged legally to the king. The Temple land was also controlled by the state, as we can see from an office probably created by the Ptolemies, that of the *epistatēs*, or "Temple President", who was responsible for the taxes paid by the Temple to the state. Cultivation of the land could not in most cases be carried out independently, but the tenants had to act in accordance with the centralized planned economy of the state. The state had also claimed a monopoly on the most important economic goods, such as vegetable oils, salt, linen, and beer. Foreign trade was strictly controlled and high duties were imposed.

To the revenue from the leases on the land, the state monopolies and the duties must be added not inconsiderable direct taxes. No poll tax was levied, at least under the early Ptolemies, but there were taxes on property (e.g. houses, slaves), on legal deeds in connection with property, on domestic trade and the use of roads and waterways (tolls), and so on. Overall, the system of taxation seems to have been devised to perfection and was apparently very oppressive in effect. One special feature of this tax system was the engagement of private middlemen between the tax-paying population and the government, a practice introduced from Greece. These middlemen were tax farmers (*telōnai*) who guaranteed the king a specified amount in taxes (money or goods) for the raising of which they were responsible. If the actual tax collected exceeded the fixed sum, then this surplus was the tax farmers' profit; on the other hand, they accepted liability with their property (and that of their guarantors) if the tax collected was less. This complicity between the government authorities and the desire for profit of the tax farmers (who were of necessity recruited from amongst the well-to-do) guaranteed the greatest possible exploitation of the tax-paying population, and especially of the indigenous Egyptian underclass. This highly developed state capitalist economic and fiscal policy provided the state (and that meant the king) with massive wealth and was the basis for the dominance of the Ptolemies not only over the Seleucids, but in the eastern Mediterranean region as a whole.

2.2. Political history: the first Syrian Wars

Following the first generation of Diadochi in Syria and Egypt (Ptolemy I died in 283 and Seleucus I in 281) the active Ptolemy II Philadelphus came to power in Egypt (283–246 BCE). In 280/279 the first confrontation took place in the so-called Syrian War of Succession, which led to the Ptolemies gaining territory along the coast of Asia Minor. Shortly afterwards, Ptolemy II conquered the Nabataeans and thus brought the spice trade under Egyptian control; this was now channelled through the Ptolemaic stronghold of Gaza rather than through Syria. Ptolemy II was also able to hold on to his Phoenician and Syrian possessions in the so-called First Syrian War[2] against Antiochus I (274–271 BCE). The same applies for the Second Syrian War (260–253 BCE) which took place almost exclusively in Asia Minor and the Aegean and thus hardly affected Palestine.

2.3. Palestine under the Ptolemies: government, economy, social relations

The tried-and-tested administrative and economic system of the Egyptian mother country was also applied by the Ptolemies to the kingdom's provinces. The tax organization resembled that of Egypt, that is, the country was divided up into administrative units (hyparchies = *nomoi* in Egypt). At the head of each administrative unit stood a *stratēgos* for military matters and an *oikonomos* for the fiscal administration. The smallest economic and tax unit was the village, which was probably leased to a general tax farmer (*kōmomisthōtēs*), one of whose main duties was to secure the royal income. As in Egypt, the native population (*laoi*) were considered as (semi-) independent lessees of the plot of land which they had leased from the king through the *kōmomisthōtēs*.

Essentially the same administrative system would also have been employed in "Syria and Phoenicia", of which Judaea was part. The entire land was considered a "territory won by the spear", and thus essentially the property of the king. At all events, this province was anything but a homogeneous ethnic and geographical entity, and so in practice certain local discrepancies have to be expected. A special position was doubtless enjoyed by the old Phoenician coastal cities (Sidon, Tyre, Acco-Ptolemais) and the large cities of the coastal plain (Gaza, Ascalon, Joppa, Dor), as well as the newly established military settlements with their various "independent" or "semi-independent" *polis* constitutions. The taxes for these Greek cities were put on offer in Alexandria and collected by local tax farmers.

Whether and to what extent the Jewish *ethnos* in Judaea, the heartland of the province of Syria-Phoenicia, was granted a special semi-autonomous status is a matter of some controversy. It is, however, most unlikely that the Ptolemies made an exception in this case to their normal administrative policy. Judaea, which was essentially a temple state (with the High Priest at the head and an increasingly influential Council of Elders, comprising high-ranking priests and laymen from the wealthy aristocracy), was more likely to have been treated like the other temple cities in Egypt and the provinces. This will also have meant that, in addition to the High Priest, an official was appointed with a function similar to that of the *epistatēs* in other holy places, being responsible for the fiscal administration and, above all, for taxes due to the king.

There is no precise information concerning taxation in Judaea, but this was unlikely to have differed very much from the tax system operating elsewhere in the province of "Syria and Phoenicia". This means that, as well as a fixed tribute, new taxes payable to the king were demanded. This can be deduced indirectly from the decree of Antiochus III[3] who, upon his accession to the throne, exempted certain groups amongst the Jewish population from the poll tax, the wreath tax and the salt tax (that is, from personal taxes) and waived a third of the tribute for the entire population. This means that the above-mentioned taxes—as well as the tribute and the direct lease duties from the royal domains[4]—had previously been exacted by the Ptolemies. Nothing is known as to the nature and amount of the tribute in the Ptolemaic era. In all probability, it was exacted from the rural population in the form of produce, that is, a proportion of the crop yield. Thanks to the perfect administrative system of the Ptolemies and the enormous increase in productive capacity of the land, the revenue from tax and rent will have been considerable and, under Ptolemaic rule, seems to have reached the maximum possible that could be "squeezed out" of the province. The Rainer papyrus, in which a variety of fragmentary decrees (*prostagmata*) issued by Ptolemy II are preserved, expressly forbids the sale of native free peasants (*sōmata laika eleuthera*) as slaves:

> And also in future shall no-one under any circumstances be permitted to buy free native inhabitants or allow them to give themselves in pledge.[5]

This shows the dire straits in which the indigenous peasantry must have found themselves as a result of the Ptolemaic tax system and, at the same time, the state's interest in the retention of an independent or semi-independent peasantry to facilitate the smooth functioning of the Ptolemaic economic system.

The so-called Zenon papyri afford us some insight into the situation in Palestine and the economic activity under Ptolemy II and his *dioikētēs* Apollonius. These papyri (they constitute an entire archive) were discovered in 1915 in Faiyum in Egypt. The archive comprises approximately two thousand documents, of which about forty refer to the situation in Syria/Palestine. The eponymous Zenon travelled for about one year (from January 259 until February 258 BCE) through Syria/Palestine on behalf of the Ptolemaic *dioikētēs*. His itinerary took him from Straton's Tower (subsequently known as Caesarea) via Jerusalem and Jericho into Transjordan to the stronghold of the local Jewish prince Tobiah in Araq el-Emir; from there he travelled north to the sources of the Jordan and back via Galilee (where, in Beth Anath, Apollonius possessed a large vineyard) to Acco/Ptolemais on the coast. The main purpose of the journey was probably inspection and improvement of the fiscal administration, as well as the development of economic relations between the Egyptian motherland and its northern province (Zenon was accompanied by numerous high-ranking officials, officers and economic and business specialists). The journey was evidently successful, as it can be deduced from the papyri that the returns from the province were increased. So, for example, new plants were introduced (vines from the island of Kos in Apollonius' vineyards, for instance), and technical improvements made (such as artificial irrigation, sowing with a plough, etc.). The balsam plantations of Jericho and En Gedi, famous throughout the ancient world, were owned by the king ("royal estate") and were exploited more efficiently than in the Persian era. The administration was expanded; Acco became the capital of the province and was renamed Ptolemais in 261 (that is, shortly before Zenon's journey); numerous new fortresses were erected to secure the borders (e.g. the new expansion of Samaria), new military settlements and cities were founded, old ones renamed.[6]

On the Jewish side, it would seem that the family of the aforementioned Tobiah, who had originally settled on the east bank of the Jordan and whose head had been visited by Zenon on his journey, took particular advantage of the new economic possibilities. At any rate, the Zenon papyri contain two letters from Tobiah to Apollonius giving notice of presents for Apollonius and the king himself.[7] There seems to have been a lively correspondence between the Jewish local prince and his master in Egypt. The pro-Ptolemaic leanings of the Tobiad family, which date from this time and were based on their common business interests, were to become an important long-term factor in Jewish politics. As regards the Greek influence at this time in Palestine, it may be regarded as typical that the correspondence was held in Greek as a matter of course (Tobiah had a Greek secretary) and that even the mercenaries in Tobiah's fortress (Araq el-Emir) were Jews and Macedonians.

Whereas the upper classes in particular were active participants in and beneficiaries of the new economic order, the simple rural population (*laoi*) were exploited even more intensively than before. As in Egypt, they served "primarily as objects of exploitation for which one only had to show consideration to the extent of ensuring that their economic productivity did not suffer";[8] unlike Egypt (where the tax farmers were for the most part members of the Greek bourgeoisie), an *indigenous* upper class interposed itself between the rural population and the state apparatus, comprising aristocratic owners of large estates and the priestly nobility (the very groups which Nehemia had fought with his reforms) who "collaborated" with the Ptolemies in the exploitation of the people on the basis of common economic interests.

2.4. Political history: the Third Syrian War

After the Second Syrian War had shattered the supremacy of Egypt in the Aegean, Ptolemy II performed a volte-face and pursued a policy of peace. He offered Antiochus II his daughter Berenice's hand in marriage, which Antiochus accepted, disowning his previous wife Laodice and her sons. However, this attempt at introducing marriage into politics as a replacement for war did not achieve the desired result. The rejected Laodice naturally did not want to forgo the succession of her sons and persuaded Antiochus II to reinstate her as his lawful wife, thus ensuring the succession of her son Seleucus (II). This in turn proved unacceptable to the Ptolemaic Princess Berenice, who had meanwhile also borne a son and—as she hoped—an heir. The situation was aggravated when the two peacemakers Antiochus II of Syria and Ptolemy II of Egypt died in the same year (246 BCE) and Ptolemy III Euergetes found himself forced to march on Syria in order to protect his sister Berenice and her young son. This triggered the Third Syrian War, the so-called Laodicean War (246–241 BCE). Berenice and her son were murdered in Syria, and her brother Ptolemy III had to retreat after some initial successes due to an uprising in Egypt. Seleucus II Callinicus (the son of the originally rejected and subsequently reinstated Laodice) likewise had little success in his attempt to conquer Coele-Syria and also had to withdraw on account of internal difficulties. So a peace treaty was concluded on terms which, on the whole, were again much more favourable for the Ptolemies than for the Seleucids.

2.5. The rise of the Tobiad family

What was the situation in Jerusalem during this Third Syrian War? We may refer here to Josephus who, in *Contra Apionem*, recounts a visit to Jerusalem by Ptolemy III and a sacrifice made by the king in the Temple.[9] It is quite possible that this is a reference to the conclusion of the struggles between

Ptolemy III and Seleucus II and that Ptolemy did indeed make a thanks-offering in Jerusalem in honour of his victory.

A further reference to the events of the Third Syrian War can be found in the Book of Daniel (Dan. 11:5–9). It does not contain any new information, but nevertheless shows the interest of apocalyptic circles in the political events of this time, events which exerted a direct influence on the fate of Palestine.

More light is shed on the situation in Jerusalem during the conflict between the Ptolemies and the Seleucids in the Third Syrian War by the so-called "Tobiad novel", which is only preserved in Josephus.[10] The account commences:

> At this time the Samaritans, who were flourishing, did much mis-chief to the Jews by laying waste their land and carrying off slaves; and this happened in the high-priesthood of Onias. ... This Onias was small-minded and passionately fond of money and since for this reason he did not render on behalf of the people the tribute of twenty talents of silver which his forefathers had paid to the kings out of their own revenues, he roused the anger of King Ptolemy Euergetes, the father of Philopator. And the king sent an envoy to Jerusalem to denounce Onias for not rendering the tribute, and threatened that, if he did not receive it, he would parcel out their land and send his soldiers to settle on it. Accordingly, when the Jews heard the king's message, they were dismayed, but Onias was not put out of countenance by any of these threats, so great was his avarice.[11]

The dating of this account in Josephus is erroneous (he sets it in the period of Antiochus III), but there can be no doubt as to its historical relevance. It is, however, highly unlikely that the High Priest Onias (that is, Onias II, the brother-in-law of the local prince Tobiah who is mentioned in the Zenon papyri) really refused to pay the tribute to Ptolemy III due to his own greed. The real reason was probably that he—and not he alone, but a specific group in Jerusalem—was hoping that the Seleucids would capture Palestine and that power would change hands. It would therefore seem that, as on other occasions, there was a pro-Seleucid party in Jerusalem which was anticipating a Seleucid victory in the Third Syrian War. That this was precisely Ptolemy's evaluation of the situation is demonstrated by his threat to turn Jerusalem into a cleruchy, that is, to establish a military colony in Jerusalem and thus put an end to the limited degree of autonomy that existed at that time.

It was in this dangerous political situation that the rapid rise of the Tobiad family began. They originally came from Transjordan, but Joseph, the son of

Tobiah and nephew of the High Priest Onias II, already spent most of his time in Jerusalem. Evidently, the Jewish "landed gentry" lived increasingly in the capital itself. Joseph became spokesman for the opposition to the High Priest and demanded that he abandon his anti-Ptolemaic policies and seek reconciliation with the king. Onias II had to bow to the opposition, which apparently also had strong popular support, and thus in effect gave up the political leadership of the people.[12] He remained nominally the High Priest, but could not prevent the office of *prostasia*, that is, of political representation of the people before the king, from being transferred to Joseph. At the same time, Joseph received money "from his friends in Samaria (!)" for the trip to Alexandria and went in person to see the king.[13] There, by outbidding all the competition and promising double the amount in taxes, he managed to acquire for himself the position of "head tax-collector" for the entire province of Syria and Phoenicia, as well as command over two thousand soldiers for effective support in carrying out this function.[14]

According to Josephus, Joseph carried out this office of *prostatēs* and tax-collector for twenty-two years,[15] that is, from approximately 240 to 218 BCE, or until the outbreak of the Fourth Syrian War when—in anticipation of the success of Antiochus III—his loyalty to the Ptolemies began to dwindle.

Joseph knew how to make radical use of the instruments of power at his disposal in order to financially exploit his people. So, according to Josephus,[16] he captured the cities of Ascalon and Scythopolis when they refused to pay higher taxes and had the leading (and wealthiest) citizens put to death and their property confiscated. In this way, he not only raised the promised taxes but also, according to Josephus,

> made great profits ... [which] he used ... to make permanent the power which he now had, thinking it prudent to preserve the source and foundation of his present good fortune by means of the wealth which he had himself acquired ...[17]

Behind this circumlocution we might well detect a shrewd power politician looking after his own interests rather than the representative "of the young enterprising forces who endeavoured to break through the constraints of their native land and pave the way for the new spirit which was now beginning to stir in Jerusalem as well".[18] It may indeed be the case that "backward Jerusalem gained considerably in political and economic significance"[19] as a result of Joseph's policies, but such progress could only have benefited the small but powerful upper classes and certainly not the great majority of poorer inhabitants. That Joseph of all people "was able to protect his countrymen from excessive exploitation"[20] is in any case highly unlikely. There is certainly no reason to believe that he only used the methods described by

Josephus to extort the doubled tax revenue from pagan cities like Ascalon and Scythopolis and spared his Jewish co-religionists. On the contrary, it must be assumed that the policies of the Tobiads played a significant role in the intensification of social conflict in Palestine and the consequent emergence of apocalyptic tendencies and revolutionary currents. We might also wonder whether it was only the "Ptolemaic governmental bureaucracy" which was being attacked in texts such as Eccl. 5:7 (cf. also 4:1 ff., 5:9 f.), where it states:

> If thou seest the oppression of the poor, and violent perverting of judgment and justice in a province, marvel not at the matter: for he that is higher than the highest regardeth; and there be higher than they.

This might equally well refer to exploitation by the Ptolemies and their accomplices, the Jewish priests and lay nobility, headed by the Tobiad family. It was doubtless in the Ptolemaic period that the fateful equation of "poor" with "pious" and "rich" with "Hellenized" originated, a mixture of social with religious categories which was subsequently to prove dangerous. "The piety of the poor which developed mainly in apocalyptic circles thus implied a clear protest against the changes to the social structure brought about by the foreign Hellenistic rulers and their aristocratic accomplices".[21] At the same time, the long-standing enmity between the urban and the rural population would have intensified, since—as we can see from the example of the Tobiad family—the upper classes were concentrated mainly in Jerusalem, while the poorer people lived mainly in the country (the extent to which an urban petty bourgeoisie had already developed cannot be determined from the sources).

2.6. Political history: the Fourth Syrian War

A new chapter in the political history of Syria/Palestine was opened with the accession to the throne of the young Antiochus III (later known as "the Great") in 223 BCE in Syria following the murder of his brother Seleucus III Soter. Antiochus III set out with new vigour to conquer the province of Syria and Phoenicia, in which endeavour he was to prove successful (although not as quickly as he had hoped). He carried out an initial attack in 221 BCE, soon after the death of Ptolemy III and the accession of a successor, the seventeen-year-old Ptolemy IV Philopator, who showed little interest in military undertakings, but was repulsed by the Ptolemaic general Theodotus. He tried again in the spring of 219, during the so-called Fourth Syrian War (221 or 219–217 BCE), and was now able, with the help of various defectors (amongst them the general Theodotus), to conquer a large area of Coele-Syria. Ptolemy IV was totally unprepared for this advance, but acted skilfully to bring about a cease-fire and peace negotiations, which were in fact an opportunity for him to equip himself militarily.

He finished his preparations by the spring and met with Antiochus III for the decisive battle on the 22nd June 217 at Raphia on the southern border of Palestine (south of Gaza). Although the Syrian troops were superior in number, the battle was won by Ptolemy IV, who owed his victory not least of all to the Egyptian "natives" who were employed for the first time in a Ptolemaic battle (it had previously been the custom to employ only Macedonian mercenaries; the ensuing increase in self-confidence amongst the native Egyptian population was to cause a lot of problems for the Ptolemies later on). Antiochus III had to flee and withdraw from Coele-Syria. Meanwhile, the peaceable Ptolemy IV did not take any further advantage of his victory but, although he could have made much greater demands, he essentially merely restored the former borders. Then he toured the reconquered province, reorganised the administration and let himself be celebrated as victor together with his sister-wife Arsinoë (we know of honorary inscriptions from Marissa, Joppa and from the vicinity of Tyre). The Third Book of the Maccabees even reports a visit to Jerusalem and to the Temple[22]—following in the footsteps of Ptolemy III—and the apocalyptic prophecies in the Book of Daniel also make mention of the battles of the Fourth Syrian War.[23]

2.7. The break-up of the Tobiad family

The intensifying struggle for the province of Syria and Phoenicia and—despite the victory at Raphia—the ever more apparent weakness of the Ptolemaic kingdom led finally to the break-up of the effective rulers of Judaea, the Tobiad family, and even to a division in the nation as a whole. The Tobiad novel as given in Josephus reports that Joseph the *prostatēs* and head tax-collector sent his youngest son Hyrcanus to Egypt for the birthday celebrations of the heir to the throne—it was probably the later Ptolemy V Epiphanes, born 210 BCE—where he followed in the family tradition (cf. the behaviour of his father in Egypt) and took advantage of the opportunity to buy his way into the king's favour by making him presents of large sums of money.[24] When, according to Josephus, the king "in admiration of the young man's magnanimity" wanted to give him a present in return,

> Hyrcanus asked that the king do no more for him than to write to
> his father and brothers about him. And so the king, after showing
> him the highest honour and giving him splendid presents, wrote

to his father and brothers and to all his governors and administrators, and sent him away.[25]

Josephus does not mention exactly what the king was to write to Hyrcanus' father and brothers. As Ptolemy IV would hardly have wanted to inform Hyrcanus' father and brothers, let alone the royal governors and administrators, merely of Hyrcanus' generosity, there must have been another reason for writing the letters. Many researchers suspect (and with justification) that in reality Hyrcanus bought the office of *prostasia* with his gifts and that this was what the king informed the family and all the royal officials in the province of Syria and Phoenicia. Otherwise, neither the presents nor the king's letters seem to make sense. With this tactic, Hyrcanus would only have been imitating his father Joseph, who had himself used it to gain political advantage over the High Priest Onias II. This explanation also fits in best with the enmity of his brothers towards Hyrcanus:[26] they apparently already suspected the worst and therefore wanted to have him murdered in Alexandria, and, as Josephus goes on to recount, did not even abandon this scandalous plan when Hyrcanus returned home basking in the glow of royal favour:

> And when Hyrcanus' brothers encountered him in battle, he killed many of the men with them and also two of the brothers themselves, while the rest escaped to their father in Jerusalem. Hyrcanus therefore went to that city, but as no one admitted him, he withdrew in fear to the country across the river Jordan, and there made his home, levying tribute on the barbarians.[27]

As the conclusion of the account shows, Hyrcanus was unable to take up his office in Jerusalem and had to withdraw to the family estate at Araq el-Emir in Transjordan. There he stood his ground against his family as a faithful adherent of the Ptolemies even when Palestine finally fell to the Seleucids and the remaining major branch of his family in Jerusalem had long since undergone the necessary conversion to the Seleucid cause. Only with Antiochus IV did he lose control of Transjordan, whereupon he committed suicide (in 168 BCE?).

2.8. The Fifth Syrian War

Notwithstanding the victory at Raphia over Antiochus III, the Ptolemaic kingdom became ever weaker. The self-confidence of the indigenous population was constantly increasing, due in no small part to the Egyptian priesthood. Consequently, the king had to accede more and more to the wishes of the "natives" after Raphia, one result of which was the steady increase in the importance of the old Egyptian religion and its ancient traditions.

The position in the Seleucid kingdom of the loser at Raphia, Antiochus III, looked quite different. After his defeat at Raphia, Antiochus had concentrated on the eastern part of his kingdom, and had marched through the whole of Asia to India and created a system of dependent vassal states. This campaign, a sort of *imitatio Alexandri*,[28] hugely increased his standing, so that he could afford to take on the title of "Great King" (*basileus megas*) and to institute a royal cult. When the five-year old Ptolemy V Epiphanes acceded to the throne in Egypt in 205 BCE, Antiochus realized his hour had come. He made a secret agreement with Philip V of Macedonia concerning the division of the Ptolemaic kingdom after the death of Ptolemy IV and, in 201 BCE, he started the so-called Fifth Syrian War. Within a short time, he had taken the whole province. In the winter of 201/200 BCE, the Ptolemaic general Scopas attempted a counterattack. He succeeded in retaking the southern part of the province and apparently also reached Jerusalem which, following Hyrcanus' retreat, was a pro-Seleucid stronghold and so could hardly have been spared. Scopas' counterattack took him as far as Panion (Paneas, Banias) near the sources of the river Jordan where, in 200 BCE, he was crushingly defeated by Antiochus III. Antiochus occupied Syria-Phoenicia once again, this time for good. Jerusalem was likewise retaken permanently by the Syrians, and the Jews appear to have submitted willingly to their new masters, from whom (as always when power changed hands) they anticipated a marked improvement in their conditions:

> But not long afterwards Antiochus defeated Scopas in a battle near the sources of the Jordan, and destroyed a great part of his army. And later, when Antiochus took possession of the cities in Coele-Syria which Scopas had held, and Samaria, the Jews of their own will went over to him and admitted him to their city and made abundant provision for his entire army and his elephants; and they readily joined his forces in besieging the garrison which had been left by Scopas in the citadel of Jerusalem.[29]

Notes

1. Rostovtzeff, Gesellschafts- und Wirtschaftsgeschichte, p. 209.
2. It was actually the second if one counts the Syrian War of Succession. I shall, however, keep to the traditional designation.
3. See p. 29 below.
4. That crown estates, and thus royal land existed outside of Judaea can be seen from Apollonius' estate in Galilee, but their existence within Judaea itself is

disputed (cf. Hengel, Judentum und Hellenismus, p. 48, note 167), although Ein Gedi with its balsam plantations, for example, might be taken as evidence to the contrary.

5. H. Liebesny, "Ein Erlaß des Königs Ptolemailos II Philadelphos über die Deklaration von Vieh und Sklaven in Syrien und Phönikien", Aegyptus 16, 1936, l. 15–18; translation p. 263.

6. Renaming: e.g. the former Beth-Shean became Scythopolis = city of the Scyths (probably mercenaries from the region around the Bosphorus). Newly-founded cities: perhaps a large Hellenistic city which was excavated at Tel Anafa in the Hule basin and whose name is as yet unknown.

7. V. A. Tcherikover/A. Fuks, Corpus Papyrorum Judaicarum, vol. 1, Cambridge, Mass. 1957, Nos. 4 and 5. Tobias even uses a "pagan" Greek salutation: "Many thanks to the gods (tois theois)"!

8. Hengel, Judentum und Hellenismus, p. 93f.

9. Contra Apionem II, 5 § 48.

10. Ant. XII, 4.1 § 158–4, 11 conclusion.

11. Ant. XII, 4.1 §§ 156–159.

12. Ant. XII, 4.2 § 160 ff.

13. Ant. XII, 4.3 § 168.

14. Ant. XII, 4.4 f. § 175 ff.

15. Ant. XII, 4.6 § 186.

16. Ant. XII, 4.5 § 181 ff.

17. Ant. XII, 4.5 § 184.

18. Hengel, Judentum und Hellenismus, p. 106.

19. Hengel, Judentum und Hellenismus, p. 53.

20. Hengel, ibid.

21. Hengel, Juden, Griechen und Barbaren, p. 51.

22. III Macc. 1:8–2:24.

23. Dan. 11:10–12.

24. Ant. XII, 4.7 § 196 ff.

25. Ant. XII, 4.9 § 219 f.

26. Ant. XII, 4.7 § 202.

27. Ant. XII, 4.9 § 222.

28. Hengel, Juden, Griechen und Barbaren, p. 60.

29. Ant. XII, 3.3 § 132 f.

3. PALESTINE UNDER SELEUCID RULE (200–135/63 BCE)

The victory of Antiochus III at Panion ended almost one hundred years of Ptolemaic sovereignty over Palestine. Palestine fell to the Seleucids and remained in the Seleucid sphere of influence until the Roman conquest in 63 BCE (although Seleucid rule was all but nominal in the final days).

3.1. Seleucid government and economy

Unlike the Ptolemaic kingdom in Egypt, the Seleucid state was anything but a homogeneous political and economic entity. The legacy of the diffuse Persian kingdom was a multitude of different religious, political and economic circumstances which, unlike Egypt, could not be united in a centralized form of organizational structure.

One thing the Seleucids had in common with the Ptolemies, however, was a state doctrine tailored to the person of the king. The king claimed to be a descendant of Alexander as well as the gods (Apollo). The cult of the king was institutionalized under Antiochus III and, together with the worship of Zeus Olympius as the supreme "God of the Empire", seems increasingly to have been regarded as a uniting force for the divergent parts of the empire. However, the Seleucids attached great importance (initially at least) to respecting and even strongly encouraging the various religious cults under their dominion. The evidence for this comes mainly from Babylon, but the same situation was likely to have applied for Syria and Phoenicia as well.

Very little is known about the economic organization of the Seleucid kingdom. The main source is the pseudo-Aristotelian treatise *Oeconomica*, which can indeed be dated to the early Hellenistic period, but is also very probably applicable for conditions in the Seleucid state. According to this, there were

four administrative departments *(oikonomiai)* which can be sub-
divided into types...: that of the king, that of the satrap, that of
the *polis* and that of the private citizen.[1]

The royal department was in charge of the mint, exports and imports and
public spending. The administrative functions of the satrap (= provincial governor) were mainly to do with revenues from the province, which were as
follows: from agriculture *(ekphorion* or *dekatē—*"tithes" = revenue from
land, which probably meant a tax on produce); from special products such as
gold, silver and copper; from the domestic and foreign trade of the satrapy
(tariffs, market levies etc.); from tolls (?) and from sales taxes; from income
from cattle *(epikarpia* or *dekatē);* and finally, from personal taxes *(epikepha-
laion—*"poll tax" and *cheirōnaksion—*"trade tax" on the artisans and tradesmen). The *polis* received its revenues from the real estate on its territory,
from business taxes (markets, roads), commercial transactions and public services. Finally, the administration for the private citizen covered, amongst
other things, revenue from land and interest charges.

Of particular interest are the revenues from the satrapies, or provinces. It is
striking that, while noting the revenues from land, the *Oeconomica* does not
make specific mention of the tribute *(phoros)* that the communities in the
provinces no doubt had to pay as well. The relationship between land taxes
and tribute cannot be determined with any certainty from the sources and
may well have varied from province to province.

3.2. Palestine as a Seleucid province

It took Antiochus III about another two years (until 198) before he had the
former province of Syria and Phoenicia completely under his control. We are
relatively well informed in a variety of documents as to the legal position of
the Jewish population in the Seleucid empire.

The first document is a letter from the king to Ptolemy, the new governor
of Syria and Phoenicia, which, according to the research carried out by
Bi(c)kerman(n), may be regarded as an authentic decree. In the first part of
this decree the king promises to assist in the rebuilding of the destroyed
Jerusalem and the Temple, "as the Jews, ... when we came to their city, gave
us a splendid reception and met us with their senate ... and also helped us to
expel the Egyptian garrison in the citadel".[2] The construction materials for
the restoration of the Temple were exempted from taxation, which probably
refers to customs duties.[3] At the same time, the king decided "on account of
their piety" *(dia tēn eusebeian)* to grant the Jews an allowance for their sacri-

fices, part of which was to be in cash (twenty thousand silver drachmas) and part in natural produce.[4] It is unclear whether this was for the daily burnt offering (the *tamid*) in the name of the Jewish community or a special offering for the king (or both?); at all events, the decree confirms the concern of the Seleucids to encourage local cults. The text then continues:

> And all the members of the nation shall have a form of government in accordance with the [laws of their fathers], and the senate, the priests, the scribes of the temple and the temple-singers shall be relieved from the poll-tax and the crown-tax and the salt-tax which they pay. And, in order that the city may the more quickly be inhabited, I grant both to the present inhabitants and to those who may return before the month of Hyperberetaios exemption from taxes for three years. We shall also relieve them in future from the third part of their tribute (*tōn phorōn*), so that their losses may be made good. And as for those who were carried off from the city and are slaves, we herewith set them free, both them and the children born to them, and order their property to be restored to them.[5]

This part of the decree is particularly informative regarding the economic and political situation of the Jews under Seleucid rule.

The economic arrangements are typical of Hellenistic administrative practice. Permanent tax exemption is accorded to the cult officials and attendants (priests, temple scribes and singers), as is appropriate for a state-approved place of worship. What is new, perhaps, is that the *Gerousia*, that is, the senate or council of elders, is mentioned together with the temple officials (and what is more, *before* them). The senate recruited chiefly from the aristocracy at this time (whether exclusively from the lay nobility or also from the priestly nobility is disputed; if the priestly nobility did *not* belong to the *Gerousia*, one might already be seeing here the "beginning of the emancipation of the aristocracy from the hierocracy"[6]). At the same time, the population of Jerusalem (but not the Jewish *ethnos* as a whole!) is exempted from all taxes for three years. The purpose of this measure was doubtless to reinvigorate the economy of a Jerusalem which had apparently suffered large-scale destruction.

The text mentions two types of taxes, namely the poll-, crown- and salt-tax, i.e. all personal taxes, and the tribute. Of the personal taxes, we know most about the salt tax, which seems to have been one of the state's most important sources of income. Nothing is known regarding the type and the mode of collection of the poll tax. However, as it is also mentioned in the *Oeconomica*, it seems to have been one of the standard taxes imposed on the provinces in the Seleucid empire. The "crown" was originally a voluntary gift from the people on the occasion of a visit by the ruler, but was apparently turned into a fixed annual tax under the Seleucids.

Finally, the inhabitants of Jerusalem were excused payment of one-third of the tribute (*phoroi*) which every community in the Seleucid state was obliged to pay as a sign of subjection. The size and nature of this tribute (natural produce or a fixed sum) is not known, but we may suppose that it amounted to a lump sum of three hundred talents,[7] which Antiochus III had reduced by one-third, that is, to two hundred talents. Neither do we know exactly how the tribute was collected. As shortly afterwards, in a tax agreement between Antiochus III and Ptolemy V Epiphanes of Egypt, Josephus mentions "the prominent men" who "purchased the right to farm the taxes in their respective provinces" and pay it to the kings,[8] the system of intermediary tax farmers will have been similar to that at the time of the Ptolemies. The tribute might perhaps have consisted in part of produce (from the rural population, at any rate) and in part of a specific sum of money. The tax farmers guaranteed the specified amount and paid this in cash to the king.

The sentence which introduces the tax relief characterizes the political situation:

> All the members of the nation (*hoi ek tou ethnous*) shall live as citizens in accordance with the laws of their fathers (*kata tous patrious nomous*).

The term *ethnos* is no doubt used in a technical sense to designate the population of Judaea, i.e. of the Jewish temple state comprising Jerusalem and its environs, but not all the Jews of the Diaspora communities in the Seleucid empire. This Jewish *ethnos* as a political entity is accorded the right to live according to the "laws of their fathers", which can only refer to the Torah of Moses, i.e. the traditional Jewish law in its political and religious dimensions. This concession implies recognition of the Torah as "royal law", thus granting the people of Judaea autonomous or semi-autonomous status. However significant this quasi-constitutional act may have been for the Jewish people (especially in comparison to the prior situation under the Ptolemies), two things must not be overlooked. On the one hand, this procedure was by no means unusual for Antiochus, but accorded with standard practice for Hellenistic rulers following the conquest of a city; in other known cases concerning Greek cities, the privileges went far beyond those granted the Jews. On the other hand, "the legal validity of the Torah depended on an act of volition by a pagan ruler"[9] and thus contained an element of the arbitrary and unstable, which would have been especially dangerous if the balance between the religious and the political aspects of the Torah was upset and the political forces in Judaea associated themselves directly with the intentions of the pagan state.

Directly after this letter, Josephus reports a further decree by the king:

> And out of reverence for the temple he also published a procla-
> mation throughout the entire kingdom, of which the contents
> were as follows. "It is unlawful for any foreigner to enter the
> enclosure of the temple which is forbidden to the Jews, except to
> those of them who are accustomed to enter after purifying them-
> selves in accordance with [the laws of their fathers]. Nor shall
> anyone bring into the city the flesh of horses or of mules or of
> wild or tame asses, or of leopards, foxes or hares or, in general, of
> any animals forbidden to the Jews. Nor is it lawful to bring in
> their skins or even to breed any of these animals in the city. But
> only the sacrificial animals known to their ancestors and neces-
> sary for the propitiation of God shall they be permitted to use.
> And the person who violates any of these statutes shall pay to the
> priests a fine of three thousand drachmas of silver."[10]

So here non-Jews are forbidden on the one hand to enter the Temple courtyard, and on the other, to import or rear ritually unclean animals. It has been
suggested (with justification) that behind the second prohibition we can find
the influence of the "conservative" priesthood, and that this prohibition
would lead to the restriction of trade in and with Jerusalem. This prohibition
was, perhaps, even aimed (at least indirectly) at the economic power and con-
nections of the Tobiad family, since they had profited the most from the economic upturn under the Ptolemies.

And finally, we know of a third document regarding the situation in
Palestine both during and directly after the conquest of the province by the
Seleucids. This is a stele discovered at Hefzibah in Lower Galilee (west of
Beth-Shean or Scythopolis) on which various letters and memoranda have
been chiselled in Greek concerning the possessions of a general called
Ptolemy in the Plain of Jezreel. This Ptolemy had originally been a general
under the Ptolemies and then gone over to the Seleucids in the Fourth (or
Fifth?) Syrian War. He may well be identical with that Ptolemy to whom
Antiochus addressed the above-mentioned letter. The memoranda on the stele
concern the protection of the inhabitants of the estates of this Ptolemy during
the turmoil of the Fifth Syrian War and immediately afterwards, when under
occupation by the Seleucid troops.

On the whole, the change in government doubtless met with a positive
response from the inhabitants of the conquered province, the Jews included.
The tax exemptions and, above all, the permission to live according to the

"laws of their fathers", which may be attributed to the federalistic power structure adopted by the Seleucids, will initially have won over the majority of the population. That this would not remain so—even the tax concessions were repealed—was soon to become apparent.

3.3. Oniads and Tobiads

The High Priest during the Syrian conquest of Palestine was Simon II, the son of Onias II. Simon II had sided relatively early with the Seleucids and had been confirmed in this policy by the victory of Antiochus II at Panion. The pro-Jewish decrees of the king were therefore due in no small measure to Simon's skilful politics, which are praised in the Book of Ecclesiasticus[11] and which later earned him the epithet "the Just" (*Shim^con ha-tsaddiq*):

> The greatest among his brothers and the glory of his people, the high priest Simon, the son of Onias!... It was he that took thought for his people that they should not fall, and fortified the city against besieging: how glorious was he when the people gathered round him at his coming forth out of the sanctuary! As the morning star in the midst of a cloud, as the moon at the full: as the sun shining forth upon the temple of the Most High, and as the rainbow giving light in clouds of glory ...[12]

The powerful Tobiad family became increasingly the High Priest's bitterest enemy. Although they had originally been committed supporters of the Ptolemies and had close economic ties with "Ptolemaic high finance",[13] the head of the family, Joseph, had gone over in good time to the Seleucids. However, through his skilful use of political tactics and as a result of the family disputes between the sons of Joseph, the High Priest Simon II was able to consolidate his power and was perhaps even able to regain his role as the people's political representative (*prostatēs*) to the new king.

Following the death of Simon II shortly after the final conquest of Palestine by Antiochus III, a naked power struggle broke out between the Oniad dynasty of High Priests and the Tobiads. Simon II's successor was Onias III, who evidently did not possess his father's competence in dealing with the tangled web of political, economic and religious affairs. He seems to have quickly fallen out with his more Hellenistically orientated brother, Jason/Joshua, and was perhaps also unable to deal effectively with the influence of the pro-Seleucid and more politically skilful sons of Joseph at the Seleucid court.[14]

An important factor affecting the situation in Jerusalem was the change in the balance of power abroad, the significance of which cannot be emphasized enough. Rome was well on its way to becoming a great power. In 197 BCE, at Cynoscephalae in Thessaly, it defeated Philip V of Macedonia in the Second Macedonian War, and in 196 BCE at the Isthmian Games proclaimed the "freedom of the Hellenes". Thus commenced the slow decline of the Hellenistic monarchies, bringing with it a decisive turn in the fortunes of Palestine, namely the change (to use the later Rabbinic terminology) from *malchut yawwan* (Greek rule) to *malchut edom* (Roman rule), although this was only to reach its conclusion in 63 BCE with the conquest of Palestine by Pompey. Antiochus III refused to comply with the Roman demand for the freedom of the Greek cities, in return for which the Romans offered their services as mediators in the Ptolemaic-Seleucid conflict, but tried to settle matters on his own by employing the politics of marriage, an approach which had already failed so miserably under his grandfather, Antiochus II. He made peace with the seventeen year-old Ptolemy V Epiphanes and in 194/193 BCE gave him his daughter Cleopatra's hand in marriage. According to Josephus,[15] he also ceded to Ptolemy part of his income from "Coele-Syria, Samaria, Judaea and Phoenicia" in the form of a dowry. As a result of this peace agreement with his "arch-enemy", Antiochus thought he had a free hand for new activities in Asia Minor and Greece, which was tantamount to a provocation of Rome. An expedition by Antiochus to Greece met with an immediate counter-attack by the Romans, and Antiochus had to flee and leave open the way to Asia. His army was defeated at a decisive battle at Magnesia (end of 190) and Antiochus had to submit to the terms dictated by the Romans in the peace treaty of Apamea (188 BCE). He lost all his possessions in Asia Minor (they went to the kingdom of Pergamon), had to hand over his combat elephants and almost his entire fleet, and in addition was forced to pay unusually high reparations (namely twelve thousand talents, payable within twelve years). This initial restriction of the Seleucid empire to the Syrian, Mesopotamian and western Iranian territories not only put an end to Antiochus III's long-term plans, but also initiated the decline of the Seleucid empire. The extent of the reparations plunged the empire into a desperate state, necessitating new and ever more unscrupulous methods of acquiring the money, and taking as a first victim the king himself, who died during the looting of the temple of Bel in Susa or, to be more precise, was killed like a common thief by the outraged population.[16]

Antiochus' successor was his son, the somewhat less dynamic Seleucus IV Philopator (187–175 BCE). During his reign new pro-Ptolemaic factions arose in Jerusalem, to which the High Priest Onias III evidently attached himself. The reason for this may have been the frustration of the hopes raised when power changed hands, the internal power struggle between the Tobiads and the Oniads and, above all, the simple fact that the financial burden placed upon the Seleucid state would certainly have left its mark on Jerusalem, and little would have remained of Antiochus III's tax concessions.

3.4. The Heliodorus affair

The most important evidence for the deteriorating situation in Jerusalem is the so-called Heliodorus affair:

> But one Simon of the tribe of Benjamin, having been made guardian of the temple (*prostatēs tou hierou*), fell out with the high priest about the ruling of the market in the city (*agoranomia*).[17]

This text is interesting for a number of reasons. First of all, we learn something about the administrative structure of Judaea under Seleucid rule. Simon was in charge of the Temple assets and so was probably responsible to the king for the regular payment of taxes. We can therefore see here the same division of supreme political power which had already seemed to apply in the Ptolemaic period. If this Simon was now also claiming control of the market, this would inevitably have met with firm resistance from the High Priest. As a supporter of the Tobiad family and thus of the lay aristocracy, such control would have considerably increased Simon's political influence. He might also have been hoping for a repeal of the trade restrictions imposed in Antiochus' decree, which had been to the priesthood's advantage.[18] Simon did not attain his immediate objective (to bring both offices under his personal control); on the other hand, the High Priest was not strong enough to force Simon's removal, even though he must have found him intolerable. The text thus contains the traces of a power struggle between the hierocracy and the lay aristocracy, which can certainly be attributed to "attempts by a section of the Jewish aristocracy to emancipate itself".[19]

After having been rebuffed by the High Priest, Simon denounced Onias to the Seleucid governor, Apollonius, claiming that Onias was hoarding untold riches in the treasury of the Temple, a claim that was bound to arouse interest in view of the chronic financial difficulties of the state. The denunciation proved effective, for Seleucus IV immediately sent his chancellor, Heliodorus, to Jerusalem with orders to confiscate the money or a part of the wealth. When Heliodorus arrived in Jerusalem and inquired about the funds in the Temple treasury, the High Priest told him

> that there were in the treasury deposits of widows and orphans, and moreover some money belonging to Hyrcanus the son of Tobiah, a man in very high place ...[20]

This passing mention of Hyrcanus was without doubt political dynamite. Upon being expelled from Jerusalem, the Tobiad Hyrcanus had fled to his estates in Transjordan,[21] where he made no secret of his good relations with the Ptolemies. So if the High Priest Onias was keeping assets belonging to Hyrcanus in the Temple, this throws some light on his political position (Hyrcanus would certainly not have entrusted his money to a true supporter of the Seleucids). If one also takes into account the fact that the main branch of the Tobiad family, with which Hyrcanus had fallen out, were committed advocates of the Seleucid cause and were engaged with the High Priest in a struggle for supremacy in Jerusalem, the suspicion of an anti-Seleucid (and thus pro-Ptolemaic) plot between the High Priest Onias III and the Tobiad Hyrcanus in Transjordan cannot easily be dismissed. Unfortunately, we do not know precisely how the Temple affair turned out, since the intervention of divine forces, as depicted so dramatically in II Maccabees,[22] is doubtless mere legend. At all events, it does appear to be the case that Heliodorus' attempted theft from the Temple proved unsuccessful, whatever the real reason for this may have been. The Temple warden Simon seemingly remained unimpressed by the divine miracle and denounced the High Priest to the king as a "conspirator against the state",[23] a further clear indication that massive political interests were at stake. Jerusalem was apparently on the brink of civil war, and Onias felt himself compelled to intervene in person at the Seleucid court.[24] This desperate attempt by the High Priest was, however, overtaken by political events. Seleucus IV was assassinated by that same chancellor Heliodorus whom he had sent to Jerusalem to confiscate the Temple treasury, and his brother Antiochus returned from Rome to become head of state in 175 BCE as Antiochus IV Epiphanes.

3.5. The "Hellenistic reform" under Antiochus IV

The landed aristocracy represented by the Tobiad family took advantage of the confusion during the change of sovereigns and, step by step, seized power in Jerusalem. First, they promised the new king to increase the tribute to three hundred and sixty silver talents (Seleucus IV had probably already rescinded his predecessor's reduction of the tribute to two hundred talents and demanded the former amount of three hundred talents to help ease his chronic financial situation) and to pay an additional eighty talents if the king appointed Jason, the brother of Onias, to the position of High Priest.[25] Antiochus IV, whose own position was not yet fully secure, acceded to this request, particularly as the appointment of officials on financial grounds was established in the system of tax farming and so was a completely normal procedure for him. The Jewish landed aristocracy thus merely made logical use of an instrument at their disposal under the tax farming system in order to place one of "their" men in the office of High Priest. The fact that this led to increased economic oppression of the people was certainly a matter of little concern. In circles which remained true to the traditional faith of the Torah, however, this changeover of power took on a quite different aspect. In the eyes of the orthodox Jews—and that meant the majority of the people—the appointment of Jason while the legitimate High Priest was still alive represented a high-handed governmental encroachment on the autonomy of the Jewish Temple state. This was the first evidence of the inherent danger which lay in the dependency of the Torah as a constitutional basis on the recognition and sympathy of the pagan ruler.

The full extent of this dependency made itself felt when the Hellenizers in Jerusalem (that is, the lay nobility and presumably some of the priestly nobility as well), with the new High Priest Jason at their head, systematically set about the preparation of a constitutional reform and proposed to the king that Jerusalem be turned into a Hellenistic *polis*,[26] a proposal backed up by a special payment of one hundred and fifty talents:

> and beside this, he [= Jason] undertook to assign a hundred and fifty more, if it might be allowed him through the king's authority to set him up a Greek place of exercise (*gymnasium*) and form a body of youths to be trained therein (*ephebeum*), and to register the inhabitants of Jerusalem as citizens of Antioch.[27]

Gymnasium and *ephebeum*, that is, institutions for the physical and spiritual training of young people, served as the outstanding symbols of Greek culture in the Hellenistic era. The wish "to register the inhabitants of Jerusalem as citizens of Antioch" meant nothing other than to accord political status to the members of the *gymnasium* and the *ephebeum*. The king gladly agreed to this request. Apart from the welcome special payment, it was certainly in his interests if the indigenous population of his inhomogeneous state were to follow the Hellenistic way of life, the most important single unifying factor of the empire. This was especially true for Judaea, whose incorporation in the Seleucid empire was constantly endangered by neighbouring Egypt.

Admission to *gymnasium* and *ephebeum* was regulated by means of membership lists, which were under the exclusive control of Jason and his followers. The "conservatives" who remained faithful to the Torah, consisting mainly of the urban and especially the rural poor, were no doubt excluded from Greek education and the future *polis*, and so virtually disenfranchised. So even though it was a gradual process rather than something that happened overnight, Jerusalem was nevertheless transformed step by step into a *polis* on Greek lines. Josephus, whose account of the process is probably chronologically incorrect (i.e. he has it take place under Menelaus),[28] nevertheless gets right to the heart of the matter:

> They [= the Hellenizing party] informed him [= the king] that they wished to abandon the laws of their fathers and the corresponding constitution (*politeia*) and to follow the king's laws and adopt the Greek way of life. Accordingly, they petitioned him to permit them to build a gymnasium in Jerusalem.[29]

So the transformation of Jerusalem into a *polis* led to the invalidation of the Torah as the constitution of the Jewish *ethnos* and meant the abrogation of the decree issued by Antiochus III (which was in essence only a confirmation of ancient rights dating from the Persian era) and thus a total renunciation of the Jewish temple state as it had existed for centuries. The religious and ritual significance of the Torah remained unaffected (for the time being), but the original unity of the Torah as a national constitution *and* a religious norm was split up for the first time into a "purely" religious aspect and a political one.

According to II Macc. 4:12, the *gymnasium*, the germ cell of the new *polis*, was built near to the Temple (we still do not know exactly where it stood), and even the priests were said to have preferred to take part in the athletic activities in the *gymnasium* rather than attend the altar:

> so that the priests had no more any zeal for the services of the altar: but entirely taken up with the new thinking, they neglected the sacrifices and hastened to take part in the unlawful games in the palæstra when the discus-throwing was announced.[30]

The followers of the traditional faith will have been outraged that, following Greek custom, athletic sports were of course performed naked, many of the ephebes even going so far as to restore their foreskins by means of epispasm,[31] not to mention the fact that, as elsewhere, sporting activities in Jerusalem were closely associated with the cult of Hercules and Hermes, the tutelary gods of the *gymnasium*. A typical episode was that of the pagan games in Tyre, to which the "Antiochenes of Jerusalem" sent a delegation with a cash offering for Hercules. Upon arrival, the emissaries could not bring themselves to spend the money on sacrifices to Hercules, and instead made a diplomatic request that, contrary to their orders, the money be used to equip Tyrian warships.[32]

Things became even more critical following a further change of High Priest about three years after the appointment of Jason. Jason had sent Menelaus, the brother of the above-mentioned Temple official Simon,[33] to deliver the tribute to Antioch. Menelaus, an extreme Hellenizer and probably an even more faithful devotee of the Seleucid dynasty than Jason, took advantage of the opportunity to buy the office of High Priest from the king for an immense increase in the tribute (from three hundred and sixty to six hundred and sixty talents).[34]

According to Josephus (who possibly refers back to a Seleucid source),[35] the Tobiad party were behind this second and even more momentous changeover of power, and with the fall of the still moderate Jason, they finally succeeded in ousting the Oniads. This not only meant a break with the internal succession to the High Priest's office, as had already been the case with Jason, but Menelaus was the first non-Zadokite (as an Oniad, Jason still came from the Zadokite line, the ancient dynasty of High Priests) and thus complete "outsider" to be appointed High Priest. Jason had to leave Jerusalem and flee to Transjordan, probably to the pro-Ptolemaic Hyrcanus.[36] Once more we see the reality of power politics at work: as soon as Jason lost the support of the pro-Seleucid Hellenizers who had brought him to power, he had practically no alternative but to go over to the pro-Ptolemaic party. The political dividing line between adherents of the Seleucids and the Ptolemies thus ran (for the first time) right through the Hellenizers in Jerusalem and probably weakened their movement considerably.

When Menelaus openly embezzled the Temple treasury in order to finance the high tribute payments, there was an uprising in Jerusalem, in the course of which his brother and representative Lysimachus was murdered.[37] Menelaus was at the court in Antioch at the time and, in order to secure his power in Jerusalem, he bribed the king's deputy and high official, Andronicus, to assassinate the deposed and exiled High Priest Onias III.[38] In both cases (that is, the murder of Onias and his brother Lysimachus' plundering of the Temple on his behalf) Menelaus escaped unscathed. Although the king had the guilty official, Andronicus, executed for Onias' murder, the instigator, Menelaus, was left alone;[39] and when the Jerusalem senate (the *Gerousia*) sent three delegates to Antioch after the Lysimachus affair to lay their case against Menelaus before the king, Menelaus managed to bribe his way out, and the king had the delegates summarily executed.[40]

Further developments were once more decisively influenced by political events abroad. The weak tutelary government of the boy-king Ptolemy VI Philometer of Egypt gave Antiochus IV the opportunity he was looking for to invade Egypt at the end of 170 BCE (Sixth Syrian War). His victory at Pelusium gave him control of the whole of Egypt up to Alexandria, and after signing a treaty with Ptolemy on very favourable terms (for him), he could regard himself as practically the ruler of Egypt. Antiochus IV's withdrawal from Egypt was possibly occasioned by events in Jerusalem.[41] Acting on the rumour that the king had been killed in his Egyptian campaigns, the deposed

High Priest Jason had invaded Jerusalem with over one thousand men and forced Menelaus, the usurper of the High Priest's office, to seek refuge in the citadel.[42] According to Josephus,[43] this uprising was in the first instance a power struggle between the once more openly pro-Ptolemaic Oniads and the pro-Seleucid Tobiads. Jason who, together with his followers, had again turned to the religious and political "conservatives", drove the Seleucids from the city, in which action he was probably supported by the majority of the orthodox population, who were heartily sick of the regime of the extreme Hellenizer and out-and-out Seleucid supporter, Menelaus, and who once again must have hoped that the political upheaval would lead to the fulfilment of their religious aspirations. This, however, provoked an attack by the king. Even before Antiochus IV entered Jerusalem, Jason had to leave the city and flee to Egypt via Ammanitis and Nabataea;[44] the Transjordanian tribes had apparently also gone over to the Seleucids, and the Tobiad Hyrcanus had committed suicide in Araq el-Emir. In the autumn of 169 BCE, Antiochus IV captured Jerusalem, took a gruesome revenge on the inhabitants and plundered the Temple. Just how closely the "solid basis of a common interest in money"[45] united the king and the reinstated Menelaus can be seen from the fact that Menelaus assisted with the plundering in person:

> He presumed to enter into the most holy temple of all the earth, having Menelaus for his guide (him that had proved himself a traitor both to the laws and to his country).[46]

The First Book of the Maccabees is also indignant at the sacrilege committed by the king and, above all, his avarice:

> [He] entered presumptuously into the sanctuary, and took the golden altar, and the candlestick of the light, and all that pertained thereto, and the table of the showbread, and the cups to pour withal, and the bowls, and the golden censers, and the veil, and the crowns, and the adorning of gold which was on the face of the temple, and he scaled it all off. And he took the silver and the gold and the precious vessels; and he took the hidden treasures which he found.[47]

Upon his withdrawal from Jerusalem, besides the hated High Priest Menelaus, Antiochus left behind two *epistatai* (commissioners), one in Jerusalem (Philip) and one on Mt. Gerizim (Andronicus), together with an occupying army.[48]

In the spring of 168 BCE Antiochus had to undertake a second Egyptian campaign as Ptolemy VI had come to an understanding with his siblings and co-regents, Ptolemy VII/VIII and Cleopatra II. He got as far as Alexandria where, in Eleusis, his expansionism came to an abrupt end. The Romans had decisively defeated the last Macedonian king in June 168 at Pydna and won a free hand over the Seleucids. The Roman legate Popillius Laenas met Antiochus in Eleusis and conveyed to him in a humiliating fashion the Roman Senate's ultimatum that he should end the war and leave Egypt immediately. So just as had happened previously to Antiochus III in the north, Antiochus IV was now decisively prevented from carrying out his political plans in the south of his empire by the Roman great power. The ensuing escalation of events in Jerusalem leading up to full-scale religious persecution would appear to have been a direct consequence of this collapse of the king's plans for Egypt. This was the case according to the Book of Daniel:

> At the time appointed he shall return, and come toward the south; but it shall not be as the former, or as the latter. For the ships of Kittim shall come against him: therefore he shall be grieved, and return, and have indignation against the holy covenant: so shall he do; he shall even return, and have intelligence with them that forsake the holy covenant.[49]

In all probability, Antiochus did not travel himself from Egypt to Jerusalem, but attempted to restore order in the Phoenician coastal cities, where the situation had now also become turbulent (there are reports of unrest in Aridus).[50] Early in 167, he dispatched the "Mysarch" Apollonius, who entered the city by deceit on the Sabbath, carried out a massacre among the inhabitants, tore down the city walls and, above all, erected a citadel in the old city of David,[51] the so-called Akra.[52] In the citadel he garrisoned a non-Jewish occupying army, "a sinful nation, transgressors of the law":[53]

> And they stored up arms and victuals, and gathering together the spoils of Jerusalem, they laid them up there, and they became a sore snare: and it became a place to lie in wait in against the sanctuary, and an evil adversary to Israel continually.[54]

The Akra, this "sore snare", was for a long time the centre of the Seleucid presence in Jerusalem. The city itself became a kind of cleruchy, that is, a military colony with a mixed pagan-Jewish population.[55] In concrete terms, this meant that the land belonging to all the departed supporters of Jason (i.e. the pro-Ptolemaic Oniads) was seized and given to non-Jewish military farmers. Menelaus was still nominally High Priest, but real power in the Jerusalem *polis* lay in the hands of non-Jews, above all the *epistatēs*, Philip. The Temple certainly also became the common property of all the citizens of the *polis*, including non-Jews. So in this way there came to pass what not even the most extreme "Hellenizers" in the Jerusalem upper classes (including the Tobiads) had wished or striven for, that is, the end of Jewish self-government, the complete absorption into a Hellenistic-Oriental absolutist multi-racial state and, above all, the end of religious "self-determination" or "freedom".

3.6. The "religious edicts"

The last and decisive phase of the attempts at Hellenization and thus the culmination of this process was reached when the king—soon after Apollonius' campaign—issued his notorious decrees against the free practice of the Jewish religion. Apollonius' campaign had probably already resulted in the desecration of the Temple and the discontinuation of the *tamid* offering.[56] The order, initially promulgated throughout the whole kingdom, "that all should be one people, and that each should forsake his own [special religious] laws"[57] was followed up by the special decree for Jerusalem and Judaea:

> And the king sent letters by the hand of messengers unto Jerusalem and the cities of Judah, that they should follow laws strange to the land, and should forbid whole burnt offerings and sacrifice and drink offerings in the sanctuary; and should profane the sabbaths and feasts, and pollute the sanctuary and the holy ones; that they should build altars, and temples, and shrines for idols, and should sacrifice swine's flesh and unclean beasts, and that they should leave their sons uncircumcised, that they should make their souls abominable with all manner of uncleanness and profanation; so that they might forget the law, and change all the ordinances. And whosoever shall not do according to the word of the king, he shall die.[58]

Overseers were employed everywhere to ensure that the pagan sacrifices were offered up, forcibly if need be; whoever had their children circumcised or followed the Torah and secretly observed the Sabbath were condemned to death.[59] With the erection of a pagan altar on the great sacrificial altar in the Temple—the "abomination of desolation" according to Daniel[60]—and the consecration of the Jerusalem Temple to "Olympian Zeus" (= Baal-Shamem, "Baal of Heaven") on 6th December 167 BCE, the Seleucid measures reached their peak:

> And on the fifteenth day of Chislev, in the hundred and forty and fifth year, they builded an abomination of desolation upon the altar, and in the cities of Judah on every side they builded idol

altars. And at the doors of the houses and in the streets they burnt incense. And they rent in pieces the books of the law which they found, and set them on fire. And wheresoever was found with any a book of the covenant, and if any consented to the law, the king's sentence delivered him to death.[61]

Any assessment of the character of Antiochus IV and the background to the escalation of events in December 167 BCE, an almost inseparable amalgam of Jewish attempts at Hellenization and royally ordained religious persecution, must be highly controversial. Already in antiquity, the opinion of pagan authors, to whom the king appeared as an upholder of civilization and fighter against the superstitious barbarism of the Jews, conflicted with the view of Jewish historians, to whom Antiochus was the pure embodiment of evil and religious hubris.[62] The main area of dispute in the modern research is the question as to which side the main initiative came from, the king or the Jews: in other words, whether the religious edicts were largely an internal Jewish affair, the logical consequence, as it were, of the Hellenization aimed at and initiated by certain Jewish circles, or whether they were a political measure stemming from the Seleucids. The thesis that they were a local, internal Jewish matter, in which the king merely played a role without a precise knowledge of the rules of the game, as it were, was first put forward by E. Bickermann. Bickermann conjectures: "As the persecution was territorially restricted, it seems reasonable to suppose that it originated with the local authorities",[63] and finds evidence for this in the fact that Menelaus is already branded the "cause of all the evils" in the Second Book of the Maccabees.[64] Bickermann concludes: "Like the unspoilt children of nature of Greek theory, the 'sons of the Akra', Menelaus and his supporters, worshipped the heavenly god of their forefathers without temple pillar or statue, under the open sky at the altar which stood on Mt. Zion, free from the yoke of the law, at one with the pagans in a state of mutual toleration. What could be more human, more natural, than the desire to impose this toleration on their still benighted co-religionists? *Such was the nature of Epiphanes' persecution.*"[65]

The counter-thesis to this (indeed, its exact antithesis) was put forward by V. Tcherikover. Unlike Bickermann, Tcherikover holds that Antiochus' religious edicts must be understood as a reaction by the king to a rebellion—probably instigated by the "pious" (*chasidim*)—against the measures introduced by the "Mysarch" Apollonius. The erection of the Akra, the conversion of Jerusalem into a *polis* and the consequent opening up of the Temple to the pagan citizens of this *polis* were all, in the eyes of pious Jews faithful to the Torah, a direct threat to the very roots of their existence: "The Jewish faith was faced, not *after* Antiochus' decree, but *before* it, with the alternative of renouncing its existence or of fighting for its life."[66] So: "It was not the revolt which came as a response to the persecution, but the persecution which came as a response to the revolt".[67] According to Tcherikover, then, Antiochus' persecution was actually a punishment following the revolt by the pious Jews, and one aimed specifically at religion, for its chief target was the existence of the Jewish faith.

Finally, M. Hengel has taken up Bickermann's thesis again and elaborated it further. For Hengel, "Bickermann's view that the impetus for the extreme escalation of events in Judaea came from the extreme Hellenizers in Jerusalem itself seems highly probable. ... Menelaus and his Tobiad supporters therefore appear to be the spiritual authors of the edict of persecution".[68] Taking their essential inspiration from the Jewish Hellenizers in this way, the edicts had two main aims: on the one hand, the "complete *abolition* of the Mosaic *law*", and on the other, a radical *reform of religious practice.*[69] The detailed knowledge of the Jewish religion betrayed by the edicts of Antiochus are a clear indication of their actual authors, namely the "determined Jewish reformers" who saw separation from the pagans as the cause of all misfortune.[70]

In support of this interpretation, Hengel again follows Bickermann by pointing to the events in Samaria. The Samaritans in Shechem had received a royal commissioner at the same time as Jerusalem,[71] from which we may conclude that the Seleucids ranked them alongside the Jews for administrative purposes. However, according to Josephus, when they "saw the Jews suffering these misfortunes, they would no longer admit that they were their kin". They sent a letter to Antiochus[72] in which they designated themselves the "Sidonians in Shechem" and asked not to be accused of "the charges of which the Jews are guilty" and to be allowed to dedicate their temple to "Zeus Hellenios".[73] Antiochus agreed to this request. As it can hardly be assumed that the Samaritans had in mind a total abrogation of the Torah, in Shechem "the Torah of Moses and the accompanying religious practices such as the keeping of the Sabbath remained in force, [whereas] in Jerusalem it was forbidden on pain of death and was subject to bloody persecution. ... The Samaritans ... retained law and rite, although they differed in this respect from their pagan neighbours no less than did the Jews".[74]

A further viewpoint in the discussion of the causes of Antiochus' persecution was contributed by G. Bunge. Bunge[75] calls attention to the previously overlooked significance of political events elsewhere in the world for the actions of Antiochus IV. He emphasises the connection between events during the king's last Egyptian campaign and in Jerusalem and speculates that the erection of the "abomination of desolation" was connected with "a kind of total seizure of power" by the Hellenizers in Jerusalem on the occasion of the invitation to the demonstrative "victory celebrations" (*pompē*) of the king after his humiliation by the Romans. On the 25th of Kislev (= 15th December) in 167 BCE, a sacrifice was offered up to Epiphanes, thereby officially inaugurating the ruler cult in Jerusalem. "This sacrifice in honour of the king does not seem to have been carried out on the initiative of the fervent Hellenizers in Jerusalem, but at the command of the king's envoy."[76] The refusal by many Jews to carry out the sacrifice then led the king to his notorious actions. The introduction into the argument by Bunge of the king's demonstrative victory celebrations after his humiliation by the Romans is certainly problematic and largely hypothetical. However, it is to Bunge's credit that he points out the connection between events in Egypt and those in Jerusalem; at all events, the initiative came *at least in part* from the king.

The exact sequence of events in the religious persecution carried out by Antiochus is not perfectly clear and assessments are always likely to remain controversial, even if the viewpoint proposed by Bickermann and Hengel remains dominant in the current research. Supplemented by the wider political perspective of the king's confrontation with the eastern policy of Rome, it would seem to do most justice to the complexities of the source material. It should also be pointed out that the opposing viewpoints are based on fundamental preconceptions which are hardly capable of objective substantiation (which should not, however, stop their proponents from formulating them and bringing them into the discussion as consciously made preliminary decisions).

3.7. The Maccabean Revolt

3.7.1. The beginnings under Mattathias and Judas

Intentionally or not, the measures ordered by the king against the Torah (as state and religious law) and Jewish rites and observances had hit Judaism on a vital nerve. Not too much must be made, therefore, of statements such as those contained in I Macc. 1:52 and 2:16 ("And from the people were gathered together unto them many ... and they did evil things in the land"), that is, that many Jews were willing followers of the Seleucid officials. In the population as a whole, it will only have been a relatively small number of Hellenizers that opposed the majority of faithful adherents of the Torah. The account of the martyr's deaths of the grey-haired Eleazar and the mother with her seven sons is certainly apocryphal,[77] but nevertheless contains a core of truth in reflecting the resistance of the people, even if this was initially passive.

This passive resistance gave way to active rebellion when the priest Mattathias, from the village of Modein, intervened with his five sons (Judas, Jonathan, Simon, John and Eleazar). According to the similarly tendentious, but essentially historically accurate account given in I Macc. 2:1 ff., Mattathias refused to obey an order to make a pagan sacrifice, killed both a Jew who was willing to do so and a royal officer, and destroyed the altar:

> And Mattathias answered and said with a loud voice, If all the nations that are in the house of the king's dominion hearken unto him, to fall away each one from the worship of his fathers, and have made choice to follow his commandments, yet will I and my sons and my brethren walk in the covenant of our fathers. ... We will not hearken to the king's words, to go aside from our worship, on the right hand, or on the left.

> And when he had left speaking these words, there came a Jew in the sight of all to sacrifice on the altar which was at Modein, according to the king's commandment. And Mattathias saw it, and his zeal was kindled, and his reins trembled, and he shewed forth his wrath according to judgement, and ran, and slew him upon the altar. And the king's officer, who compelled men to sacrifice, he killed at that time, and pulled down the altar. ... And Mattathias cried out in the city with a loud voice, saying, Whosoever is zealous for the law, and maintaineth the covenant, let him come forth after me. And he and his sons fled into the mountains, and forsook all that they had in the city.[78]

As well as the religious and political motives of the revolt addressed here, it is also essential to take the social background into account as one of the causes of the struggle against the Seleucids initiated by the Maccabees. A clear reference to this can be found in Daniel, where it states of Antiochus:

> Who acknowledges him shall be increased with glory: and he shall cause them to rule over many, and shall apportion land to them as reward.[79]

Antiochus IV probably regarded the entire province of Judaea as royal land, that is, as his own personal possession, and used the land as an instrument of his policies by confiscating land owned by his political opponents and giving it to his supporters. The reference to Mattathias fleeing with his sons into the mountains and forsaking all that they had in Modein might likewise be understood in this sense. And finally, Antiochus will have imposed even heavier taxes than before on the orthodox population as a punishment for their obstinacy. This can be seen from the tax exemption which Demetrius I was later to promise and Demetrius II finally implemented.[80] If we may assume that the taxes in question go back to Antiochus IV, then these were indeed considerable and would have represented a good reason for a large part of the population to support the rebels.[81]

Right from the start, his son Judas seems to have played a prominent role in the guerilla war organized by Mattathias, for it is he alone who is mentioned in II Macc. 5:27 and who is later given the nickname *Maccabee* (aram. *maqqaba*—"the Hammer") which was to become the name of the entire dynasty. The pious Chasidim, who had initially fled to virtually inaccessible wasteland, were soon to join forces with the Maccabee family[82] After a group of these Chasidim, to whom observance of the Sabbath was more important than their own lives, was attacked by Syrian troops on the Sabbath and massacred without putting up any opposition, the necessity of active resistance was recognized even in their circles.[83]

This is the first time that we encounter the "Assembly of the Pious" (*synagōgē Asidaiōn* = Hebr. *ʿadat chasidim*) as a clear-cut group. The origins of this group are obscure, but probably go back to the period of the Hellenistic reform of about 175–170 BCE. They are often regarded as the fathers of apocalyptic thought; the early apocalypses of the Book of Daniel and the oldest sections of the Ethiopic Book of Enoch, in particular the animal vision in chapters 85–90 and the ten-week apocalypse in chapters 93:1–10 and 91:12–17, can probably be traced back to them. They can also be seen as the forerunners of the later groupings of the Essenes and the Pharisees.

Not long after the beginning of the uprising, probably in 166 BCE, the head of the family, Mattathias, died after appointing his son, Judas, commander-in-chief in the battle against the Syrians.[84] Judas, who avoided open engagement with the Syrians and preferred surprise attacks, won a whole series of victories. First, he defeated a Syrian army under Apollonius, killing Apollonius himself in the process.[85] Shortly after, he subjected a second Syrian army under the command of Seron to a crushing defeat at Beth-Horon.[86] Finally, the Syrian army suffered a third defeat at Emmaus under the generals Nicanor and Gorgias, as Judas was able to play the individual divisions of the huge Syrian army off against each other in the most skilful fashion. While Gorgias was preparing to attack the Jewish camp with his cavalry, Judas made a surprise attack on the main forces and put them to rout.[87]

In Syria, meanwhile, Antiochus IV had started out in 165 BCE on a campaign against the Parthians (according to I Macc. 3:31, this was mainly in order to replenish the treasury), leaving Lysias as viceroy and guardian of the young Antiochus V. In the very same year,[88] Lysias intervened personally in the crisis and marched on Judaea from the south via Idumaea.[89] The two armies clashed in the vicinity of Beth-Zur, south of Jerusalem, and Lysias was crushingly defeated (according to both I Macc. 4:34 f. and II Macc. 11:10–12). After this victory, Lysias seems to have undertaken a revision of

Seleucid policy, acting initially on his own responsibility.[90] At any rate, the Second Book of Maccabees records a letter originating from Lysias in which he promises to represent the best interests of the Jews.[91] A little while later, probably early in 164, this was followed by a letter from the king himself to the Jewish people:

> King Antiochus to the senate of the Jews and to the other Jews, greeting. If ye fare well, we have our desire: we ourselves also are in good health. Menelaus informed us that your desire was to return home and follow your own business. They therefore that depart home up to the thirtieth day of Xanthicus [April] shall have our friendship, with full permission that the Jews use their own proper meats and observe their own laws, even as heretofore; and none of them shall be in any way molested for the things that have been ignorantly done. Moreover I have sent Menelaus also, that he may encourage you. Fare ye well. Written in the hundred forty and eighth year, on the fifteenth day of Xanthicus.[92]

With this letter, the three-year-old ban on the Torah was repealed and the constitution of the *polis* practically annulled. Judas conquered Jerusalem (with the exception of the Akra), purified the Temple and, on the 25th of Kislev 148 (= 14th December 164 BCE), restored the Temple service. This ceremony of reconsecration of the Temple is still celebrated by Jews today as the feast of Hanukkah.[93]

However, despite the king's concessions and the reconquest of Jerusalem, the peace was not yet won. The insurrectionary movement of the Maccabees had meanwhile developed its own dynamic which went beyond the immediate objectives originally pursued. Judas now set out to consolidate his own authority. He fortified the Temple Mount and the important stronghold of Beth-Zur.[94] He then carried out military campaigns in the areas adjoining Judaea. Responding to a call for help by Jewish communities in Galilee and Transjordan, Judas himself went to Transjordan and his brother Simon to Galilee in order to assist their distressed fellow-believers. Both achieved numerous victories in battle and brought the Jewish population of these largely pagan areas safely to Judaea.[95] A campaign against the coastal city of Jabneh/Jamnia carried out during the absence of the two brothers by their deputies Joseph and Azariah went wrong, and they were beaten off by the Syrian general Gorgias.[96] Upon his return, Judas himself then went south again, conquering Hebron and destroying the altars and statues of the pagan gods in Ashdod/Azotus.[97]

Note should be taken here of the escalation of events, or rather, the skilful dramaturgy of the author of the First Book of the Maccabees. After the reconquest of Jerusalem, the Maccabees initially take up the cause of their fellow-Jews in predominantly pagan areas, that is to say, their motives are thoroughly noble and imbued with the spirit of a war of faith; they are not simply interested in raiding and plundering. This is precisely what motivates their deputies Joseph and Azariah, and their attempt must fail, since they "were not of the seed of those men, by whose hand deliverance was given unto Israel".[98] That is, they did not have the necessary charisma and the benediction of a just cause. Judas, on the other hand, possessed this to excess and consequently could dare to venture south merely in order to attack the detested heathen, without any mention being made in this case of rescuing co-religionists in distress.

The court of the Seleucids in Antioch had initially kept aloof from these events, mainly because it was preoccupied with its own internal affairs. There had, in fact, been a changeover of power in Antioch and the situation at court was apparently still somewhat unstable. At the end of 164 BCE, Antiochus IV had died during his Persian campaign, and effective power in the empire passed to Lysias who, against the wishes of the deceased king, had set himself up as vice-regent and guardian of the still under-age Antiochus V Eupator. However, when Judas was on the point of taking the Akra as well,[99] Lysias had to intervene and, together with Eupator, set out on his second campaign to Judaea. The Syrian army first lay siege to Beth-Zur. A battle was fought at Beth-Zacharia, south of Bethlehem, where the Seleucids achieved their first major victory over the Maccabees.[100] After this victory, the Syrian army placed Jerusalem under siege, and here too, capitulation was imminent, when Lysias and Eupator had to withdraw suddenly to deal with a revolt led by Philip, who had originally been appointed vice-regent by Antiochus IV.[101] So there was an unexpected declaration of peace at the end of 163 BCE on very favourable terms for the Jews. Eupator gave them express permission to live "after their own laws, as aforetime"[102] and officially endorsed the return of the Temple which Judas had already won back at the end of 164 BCE. This is further confirmed in a letter from the king to Lysias cited in II Macc. 11:22–26:[103]

> King Antiochus unto his brother Lysias, greeting. Seeing that our father passed unto the gods having the wish that the subjects of his kingdom should be undisturbed and give themselves to the care of their own affairs, we, having heard that the Jews do not consent to our father's purpose to turn them unto the customs of the Greeks, but choose rather their own manner of living, and make request that the customs of their law be allowed unto

them,—choosing therefore that this nation also should be free
from disturbance, we determine that their temple be restored to
them, and that they live according to the customs that were in the
days of their ancestors.

This surprising peace of 163 BCE, approximately one year after the death
of Antiochus IV, put the seal on the virtual collapse of Hellenistic power in
Jerusalem. Menelaus was removed from office and executed for being "the
cause of all the evils".[104] His successor, probably still under Eupator, was the
moderate Hellenizer Alcimus, a Zadokite,[105] who at first was apparently recognized even by the pious.[106] According to Josephus, the legitimate High
Priest, Onias IV, the son of the assassinated Onias III, fled to Egypt following
the appointment of Alcimus, where he established the schismatic sanctuary of
Leontopolis.[107] However, Judas and his followers, for whom there was more
at stake than the appointment of a more or less legitimate High Priest, did not
give up their opposition. When, soon after taking office, Alcimus had sixty
adherents of the Chasidic pietists executed,[108] open conflict broke out
between the Maccabees and the new High Priest. Alcimus had to flee from
Jerusalem and brought a complaint against Judas before the king.[109]

Meanwhile Demetrius I Soter, a son of Seleucus IV Philopator, had come
to power in Antioch (162 BCE) and had his cousin Antiochus V and Lysias
murdered. Demetrius sent the general Nicanor to Judaea with an army to reinstate Alcimus. The decisive battle was fought on 13th Adar 161 BCE at
Adasa, where the Syrian army was once again crushingly defeated. Nicanor
fell in the battle, and from then on "Nicanor Day" was celebrated every year
in commemoration.[110]

Probably even before Nicanor's campaign (contrary to the chronology
given in I Macc. 8:1 ff.), Judas had sent a legation to Rome, at that time a
newly emerging great power and, as a natural opponent of the Hellenistic
kingdoms, a potential ally of the Jews, in order to request "amity and confederacy" with the Romans.[111] Since the Romans were no doubt interested in
increasing their influence in Syria-Palestine, a friendly alliance was formed
between Rome and Judaea:

> Good success be to the Romans, and to the nation of the Jews, by
> sea and by land for ever: the sword also and the enemy be far
> from them. But if war arise for Rome first, or any of their confed-
> erates in all their dominion, the nation of the Jews shall help them
> as confederates, as the occasion shall prescribe to them, with all
> their heart: and unto them that make war upon them they shall not
> give, neither supply, food, arms, money, or ships, as it hath
> seemed good unto Rome, and they shall keep their ordinances

without taking anything therefore. In the same manner, moreover, if war come first upon the nation of the Jews, the Romans shall help them as confederates with all their soul, as the occasion shall prescribe to them: and to them that are confederates with their foes there shall not be given food, arms, money, or ships, as it hath seemed good unto Rome; and they shall keep these ordinances, and that without deceit.[112]

The treaty took the legal form of a *senatus consultum*, that is, a resolution of the Senate. On the Jewish side, the agreement was negotiated by Eupolemus, son of John, and Jason, son of Eleazar. Behind Eupolemus, many suspect the Alexandrian-Jewish author of the same name, fragments of whose book about the kings of Judah have come down to us. Legally, the treaty belongs to the class of *foedera aequa*, that is, treaties establishing a friendly alliance concluded on the basis of the equality of status of the parties concerned (the parties become *socii*). The alliance did not, however, appear to treat both sides equally. This may be indicated by the occurrence of the phrase "as it hath seemed good unto Rome" in respect of both Judaea's obligation to Rome (v. 26) and Rome's obligation to Judaea (v. 28), as well as the similarly duplicated "as the occasion shall prescribe to them" in both parts of the treaty. It therefore seems that the Romans demanded absolute allegiance from the Jews while reserving their own judgement from case to case. Contracting parties were the Roman Senate and the *ethnos* of the Jews. This implies that the Romans classed the Jewish people as an independent legal entity and thus accorded them a certain degree of sovereignty vis-à-vis the Seleucids. This can also be seen from a letter written at the same time to Demetrius, in which they threaten him:

If therefore they [= the Jews] plead any more against thee, we will do them justice, and fight with thee by sea and by land.[113]

If and when Demetrius received this admonition is not known. Even without an explicit threat, Demetrius no doubt feared an intervention by Rome (who did not recognize him as king until the autumn of 160 BCE), and hurried to create a *fait accompli* in Judaea. So probably immediately after the collapse of Nicanor's campaign, he sent a new army to Judaea under Bacchides, which defeated the Jewish forces in autumn 161 BCE near Jerusalem. Judas himself was killed in the battle and was buried at Modein.[114] So the Hellenizers in Jerusalem had once again won a temporary victory. Alcimus was reinstated as High Priest and, with Bacchides' assistance, was able to suppress any resistance:

... the lawless put forth their heads in all the coasts of Israel, and
all they that wrought iniquity rose up...[115]

Here too, we can find further evidence of the social and economic background to the events in Judaea in the subsequent comment that there was in
those days "an exceeding great famine" and "the country went over with
them [i.e. became rebellious]".[116] The victory of Bacchides therefore meant
both a further redistribution of property in favour of the pro-Seleucid
Hellenizing party and increased exploitation of the disenfranchised rural
population:

And Bacchides chose out the ungodly men, and made them lords
of the country.[117]

3.7.2. Jonathan (161–142 BCE)

Soon after the death of Judas, the dispersed rebels succeeeded in regathering
their forces under his brother Jonathan and reorganizing the armed resistance.
Their first mission was against an Arab tribe in Transjordan that had attacked
and killed John, Jonathan's brother.[118] While returning from this successful
campaign, Jonathan was attacked by Bacchides but was able to flee to safety.

Bacchides consolidated the newly-won Syrian supremacy over the country
by fortifying many of the cities in Galilee and Judaea. Alcimus, firmly back
in the saddle in Jerusalem, ordered the demolition of the wall of the inner
court of the sanctuary in May 160, probably in order to give the pagans
access to the Temple. The stroke he suffered soon afterwards was interpreted
by the pious as an intervention by God. According to Josephus,[119] after
Alcimus' death the office of High Priest remained vacant for seven years until
Jonathan accepted the post in 152. It is possible that Josephus merely came to
this conclusion due to the lack of any reference to a new High Priest in his
sources. At any rate, his contradictory claim[120] that Judas became High Priest
after Alcimus' death is certainly incorrect, since according to the chronology
of I Maccabees, Judas died before Alcimus.

After the death of Alcimus, Bacchides left the country for two years, only
returning in 158. "The lawless",[121] that is, the Hellenizers in Jerusalem, had
requested his assistance, apparently because the power of the Maccabees was
clearly on the increase again. It soon became evident how justified the fears
of the Hellenizers were, as Bacchides was defeated by Jonathan and vented
his anger on those who "gave him counsel to come into the country".[122] He
made peace with Jonathan, "sware unto him that he would not seek his hurt

all the days of his life",[123] returned his prisoners and left Judaea forever. Jonathan settled in Michmas to the north of Jerusalem and "began to judge the people; and he destroyed the ungodly out of Israel."[124] From this remark we may conclude that, despite all his progress, Jonathan was not yet in a position to exercise power in Jerusalem himself.

The First Book of the Maccabees has nothing to say about the next five years, and the account only resumes in 153/52 BCE. In the meantime, however, the political scenery had been totally transformed. In Syria, the period of internal disputes for the throne began, and the renewed strength of the Maccabees in Judaea was a factor in the balance of power which had to be taken into account by the various pretenders to the Seleucid throne. The first usurper was Alexander Balas who, giving himself out as the son of Antiochus IV, laid claim to the throne and, with the combined support of the kings allied against Demetrius and the Roman Senate, landed at Ptolemais-Acco. The two rival kings both attempted to secure the support of Jonathan. Jonathan soon decided in favour of Alexander Balas, but not before accepting Demetrius' offer to allow him back to Jerusalem and to free the hostages held in the Akra.[125] He was also permitted to restore the fortifications of the city and the Temple Mount and was apparently even able to arrange for the withdrawal of all the Syrian garrisons, except for that in Beth-Zur. Soon afterwards, Alexander Balas outdid Demetrius' concessions and appointed Jonathan "the king's Friend" and High Priest of the Jewish nation.[126] Jonathan was installed as High Priest on the Feast of Tabernacles in 153 BCE, and thereby became official head of the Jewish nation with the sanction of the Seleucid court.

The transfer of the office of High Priest to the Maccabee family was an important turning-point in the history of the Maccabee movement, and one which was to have grave consequences. Insofar as Jonathan allowed the title of High Priest to be conferred on him by the Seleucid monarch, he gave clear precedence to the political over the religious objectives of the struggle. Originating from the lower ranks of the priesthood, the Maccabee family hardly had any more entitlement to this office than the so bitterly opposed Menelaus and certainly less than the Zadokite Alcimus, who had, after all, initially been recognized by the Chasidim. This is often taken by the research as providing the background to the emergence of a movement of pietists which Josephus later refers to as the "Essenes". They are also associated with the group mentioned in some of the Qumran writings, who withdrew into the desert under a Zadokite leader, apparently known as the "Teacher of Righteousness". Perhaps this group regarded Jonathan as a "wicked priest" and considered the official cult in Jerusalem of which he was High Priest to be impure:

And as for that which He said, *Because of the blood of the city
and the violence done to the land:*[127] interpreted, *the city* is
Jerusalem where the Wicked Priest committed abominable deeds
and defiled the Temple of God. *The violence done to the land*:
these are the cities of Judah where he robbed the Poor of their
possessions.[128]

Here we see evidence of social as well as religious tensions. Jonathan evidently already considered himself lord of the land who could do what he pleased. This is what may be referred to in I QpHab. 8:11: "He robbed and amassed the riches of the men of violence who rebelled against God", which probably means his opponents, the pro-Greek Tobiad party. When he is accused of robbing the poor of their possessions, groups of "orthodox" Jews must be intended, and specifically, perhaps, followers of the "Teacher of Righteousness". Thus, already under Jonathan there began a development in which the new ruling class in Jerusalem no longer had to fight merely against the Seleucids and their Hellenized Jewish supporters, but was also faced with growing opposition from the "pious". However, whether the Qumran writings, whose ideas are often at variance, can be attributed *in toto* to a "sect" resident there is currently just as open to dispute as their respective dating.

Jonathan continued to show great skill as a political tactician. A final and, if historically true, totally despairing attempt by Demetrius to win Jonathan's favour was ignored by him in a realistic assessment of the existing balance of power.[129] Alexander prevailed over Demetrius and, on the occasion of his marriage to Cleopatra, a daughter of Ptolemy VI Philometor, rewarded Jonathan with the office of military and civil governor (*stratēgos* and *meridarchēs*) of Coele-Syria;[130] envoys from the Hellenizing party who tried to bring suits against Jonathan were turned away by the king. In this way, claims by Jonathan extending beyond Judaea were recognized and sanctioned by the Syrian side for the first time. When in 148/47 Demetrius II, a son of Demetrius I, lay claim to the throne, Jonathan fought "loyally" against Apollonius, the governor of Coele-Syria, who had allied himself to Demetrius. He defeated Apollonius, conquered Jaffa/Joppa, burned down Ashdod and its Temple of Dagon and let himself be fêted by the inhabitants of Ascalon.[131] As Alexander also presented him with the city of Ekron in gratitude, Jonathan now had effective control of an important part of the coastal plain.

Meanwhile, Jonathan had become so powerful that he was able not only to survive a further change of power in Syria unscathed, but was even able to win further concessions. Ptolemy VI of Egypt had now withdrawn both wife and favour from Alexander Balas and allied himself with Demetrius II. Alexander was defeated and forced to flee to Egypt, where he was murdered.[132] Although he had initially opposed Demetrius II, Jonathan nevertheless felt strong enough to to lay siege to the Akra following his assumption of power (145 BCE) and so attempt to achieve full sovereignty.[133] When Demetrius summoned Jonathan to Ptolemais-Acco, the latter even initially let the siege continue and only complied with the will of the king once Demetrius had granted him wide-ranging concessions:

> We have determined to do good to the nation of the Jews, who are our friends, and observe what is just toward us, because of their good will toward us. We have confirmed therefore unto them the borders of Judaea, and also the three governments of Aphaerema and Lydda and Ramathaim (these were added unto Judaea from the country of Samaria), and all things appertaining unto them, for all such as do sacrifice in Jerusalem, instead of the king's dues which the king received of them yearly aforetime from the produce of the earth and the fruits of trees. And as for the other things that pertain unto us from henceforth, of the tenths [*tōn dekatōn*] and the tolls [*tōn telōn*] that pertain unto us, and the saltpits, and the crowns that pertain unto us, all these we will bestow upon them.[134]

This decree of Demetrius II must be seen together with that of Demetrius I,[135] which Jonathan had not accepted. Thus Jonathan achieved under Demetrius II what had seemed all too utopian under Demetrius I:

1. The edict mentions various taxes which are often difficult to interpret, but which nevertheless give us an insight into Seleucid taxation policy. The tolls are straightforward, as are the personal taxes, i.e. the salt- and the crown-tax. In contrast to the edict of Antiochus III,[136] the whole nation is now exempted from these taxes and not just the *Gerousia* and the Temple officials.[137] The dues from the produce of the earth and the fruit trees are specified in more detail in the edict of Demetrius I: in concrete terms, these amount to one third of the yield from sowing and half of the tree fruits.[138] This tax on produce will have constituted a land tax, which must be distinguished from the tribute.[139] As the figures show, it was considerable and must have been a great burden for the people, so that its abolition was a great success for Jonathan.

It is unclear whether Demetrius II also waived the tribute. The tribute is not mentioned in his edict, although it possibly is in the edict of Demetrius I.[140] However, it is not certain whether the term *hoi phoroi* in I Macc. 10:29 is to be understood as "tribute" in the technical sense. The parallel account of Demetrius II's edict in Josephus[141] specifically mentions that, in response to Jonathan's request to "let him pay three hundred talents for all Judaea and the three toparchies of Samaria and Peraea [or Joppa/Jaffa] and Galilee",[142] Demetrius gave his consent.[143] It is striking that this sum of three hundred talents corresponds precisely to the original tribute that was increased by Jason to three hundred and sixty and by Menelaus to six hundred and sixty talents.[144] It is also unlikely that Demetrius II agreed to go entirely without payment of a tribute, as then he would have given up any claim to Seleucid sovereignty over Judaea.

It is also unclear what the "tenth", or "tithe", refers to (as distinct from the land tax), and whether the poll tax was waived. The poll tax is not mentioned in either version of the edicts of Demetrius I and Demetrius II in the Book of the Maccabees, whereas Josephus makes specific mention of it in his version of the edict of Demetrius I together with the other taxes that were waived.[145] Antiochus III had also waived the poll tax for the Temple officials and the *Gerousia*, but not for the rest of the population, and it was probably compulsory for everyone again by the beginning of the Maccabean Revolt at the latest. As Josephus makes no mention of a waiver of the poll tax in his version of the edict of Demetrius II,[146] it would seem to have remained in force together with the tribute.

2. The ceding of the three Samaritan districts (= toparchies) Ephraim, Lydda and Ramathaim was also of great significance. These three toparchies did not form part of Judaea as such, but had evidently been occupied by Jonathan (Ephraim lay to the north-east, Ramathaim and Lydda to the northwest of Jerusalem). In officially placing these districts under the jurisdiction of Jonathan, the king was sanctioning for the first time a territorial expansion of the Jewish domain.

The outbreak of new disputes for the throne between Demetrius II and Tryphon, a former general of Alexander Balas, who wanted to install Antiochus (VI), a son of Alexander, on the throne,[147] was skilfully exploited by Jonathan so as to finally wrest the Akra as well away from the Syrian sphere of influence. Demetrius, who was in great trouble following an uprising by the population of Antioch, promised to fulfil his every wish if he came to his assistance with an army. Jonathan sent an army to Antioch and rescued the king from his precarious situation. When Demetrius then reneged on his promise, Jonathan made initial approaches to Tryphon and Antiochus VI, and they not only confirmed all previous privileges, but also appointed Jonathan's brother Simon commander of the coastal region stretching from the Ladder of Tyre to the Egyptian border.[148] The brothers then set about extending their domain (with the help of the Syrians, in some cases.) Jonathan conquered Ascalon and Gaza, and at Hazor defeated the army of Demetrius II, who had meanwhile been driven out of Antioch. Simon seized the fortress at Beth-Zur, the most important Syrian stronghold in Judaea apart from the Akra.[149]

At the same time, Jonathan did not fail to ensure the support of Rome and to establish relations with Sparta, which had become stronger following the defeat of the Achaean League (146 BCE). He sent an envoy to Rome "to renew ... the friendship and the confederacy, as in former time"[150] as well as a letter to the Spartans,[151] in which he harks back to earlier contacts between Sparta and the High Priest Onias (I ?).

After a fruitless campaign against Demetrius, which took him to Damascus, Jonathan arranged for Jerusalem to be further fortified and attempted to cut off the Akra from the rest of the city by a high wall.[152] Tryphon, who possibly himself harboured ambitions with respect to the Seleucid throne, followed the events in Jerusalem with growing misgivings, arranged a meeting with Jonathan at Beth-Shean/Scythopolis, enticed him without his army to Acco/Ptolemais and took him hostage.[153] While Tryphon made preparations to go to Jerusalem and take Jonathan's brother Simon prisoner as well, a national assembly elected Simon Jonathan's successor and authorized him to continue the struggle.[154] Simon continued the fortification of Jerusalem and finally won control of the coastal city of Jaffa/Joppa. Tryphon had to call off his campaign to Judaea, had Jonathan executed at the beginning of 142 BCE and retired to Syria.

3.7.3. Simon (142–135/34 BCE)

After the execution of Jonathan (and perhaps even earlier) Simon entered into further negotiations with Demetrius II, who needed the support of the Maccabees more than ever (Tryphon had meanwhile had the young Antiochus VI murdered and himself assumed his throne) and who honoured the renewed change of alliance with a decree of amnesty, the granting of full and final freedom from taxes and the recognition of the political status quo: in other words, the effective sovereignty of Judaea.[155] According to the First Book of the Maccabees, this year of 142 BCE, in which "the yoke of the heathen [was] taken away from Israel",[156] was the decisive turning-point in the history of the Maccabean Revolt:

> And the people began to write in their instruments and contracts,
> in the first year of Simon the great high priest and captain and
> leader of the Jews.[157]

Simon continued to systematically consolidate his power, conquered the strategically important Gezer/Gazara, expelled the pagan population and garrisoned the city with a Jewish force under his son John.[158] Immediately afterwards he was also able to capture the Akra in Jerusalem, the last Syrian stronghold in Judaea. At the beginning of June 141 BCE, he entered the Akra "with praise and palm branches ... because a great enemy was destroyed out of Israel".[159] The hymn I Macc. 14:4–15 praises Simon after this event in almost Messianic tones as the saviour of the nation and the prince of peace. Confirmation and culmination of this development was the decision of the Jerusalem "Great Assembly" in 140 to formally legitimize the Maccabean family and confer on Simon as hereditary titles the offices of sovereign ruler (*ethnarchés*), High Priest (*archiereus*) and commander of the army (*stratēgos*):

> ... the Jews and the priests were well pleased that Simon should be their leader (*hēgoumenos*) and High Priest for ever, until there should arise a faithful prophet; and that he should be captain (*stratēgos*) over them, and should take charge of the sanctuary, to set them over their works, and over the country, and over the arms, and over the strongholds; and that he should take charge of the sanctuary, and that he should be obeyed by all, and that all instruments in the country should be written in his name, and that he should be clothed in purple, and wear gold; and that it should not be lawful for any of the people or of the priests to set at nought any of these things, or to gainsay the words that he should speak, or to gather an assembly in the country without him, or to be clothed in purple, or wear a buckle of gold ...[160]

The decision by the Jerusalem Great Assembly was to be of far-reaching significance. The Maccabees had achieved their main political objective and freed Judaea *de facto* (though not *de jure*) from the Seleucid confederation. The constituted form of government was unique in Israel's history, insofar as the new High Priest did not derive his legitimation from his "special" (Zadokite) background but from the people, or more precisely: from the "great congregation of priests and people (*laos*) and princes of the nation (*ethnos*) [i.e. probably the Jerusalem *Gerousia*], and of the elders of the country [perhaps the rural aristocracy]".[161] As can be seen from the long account of Simon's heroic deeds[162] given by way of justification of the Great Assembly's decision, this all went to confirm one thing: the concentration of power in the hands of one dominant personality. The fact that this confirmation did not proceed quite so smoothly as the Book of the Maccabees would have us believe can be seen from the reservation made in respect of the future arrival of a "faithful prophet". Here can be heard the opposing voice of those circles for whom the legitimacy of the High Priest's office was as little dependent on the approval of the people as it had been on the authority of a heathen king. So in combining the office of High Priest with overall military and political power and making them dependent on popular consensus, this new political arrangement harboured a potential for conflict which was to prove crucial in times to come.

As regards foreign policy, Simon seems to have safeguarded his sovereignty by renewing relations with Sparta[163] and Rome. He sent an envoy to Rome who obtained a confirmation of the treaty of alliance. At the same time, the Romans sent letters to Ptolemy VIII (Euergetes II) and numerous other kings in which these were requested to hand over the fugitive supporters of the Hellenizing party to Simon.[164]

Meanwhile, Demetrius II had embarked on a campaign to Persia, where he had been taken captured in 139 BCE by Mithridates I.[165] His brother and successor, Antiochus VII Sidetes, initially reconfirmed to Simon all privileges and in addition granted him the right to mint his own coinage;[166] however, once he had fought off Tryphon[167] and won a free hand in internal affairs, he reneged on his promises. He demanded the return of the illegally seized cities of Jaffa/Joppa and Gezer/Gazara, as well as the Jerusalem Akra, and in addition taxes for all the cities and places under Jewish rule outside of Judaea, or else one thousand silver talents.[168] As Simon was only prepared to offer a payment of one hundred talents, Antiochus appointed the general Cendebaeus commander over the coastal region with orders to destabilize Judaea. Simon thereupon sent his two sons, Judas and John, into battle against Cendebaeus, and they inflicted a crushing defeat on him, burning down Ashdod for the second time in the process.[169]

If Simon had little to fear from outside during his reign, he was nevertheless to be the first Maccabee to succumb to intrigue from within. His son-in-law Ptolemy, the governor of Jericho, was ambitious for power and had Simon and his two sons, Mattathias and Judas, murdered treacherously at the beginning of 135 or 134 BCE during a banquet at the fortress of Dok, near Jericho.[170]

Notes

1. Oeconomica B II, 1.1, ed. B. A. van Groningen/A. Wartelle, Paris 1968.
2. Ant. XII, 3.3 § 138.
3. Ant. XII, 3.3 § 141.
4. Ant. XII, 3.3 § 140.
5. Ant. XII, 3.3 §§ 142–144.
6. Kippenberg, Religion und Klassenbildung, p. 84.
7. As specified in a note about Seleucus IV Philopator (?) in Sulpicius Severus, Chron. II. 17.4 f., ed. C. Halm, p. 73 (CSEL I).
8. Ant. XII, 4.1 § 155.
9. Bickermann, Gott der Makkabäer, p. 53.
10. Ant. XII, 3.4 § 145 f.

11. Ecclus. 50:1–24.
12. Ecclus. 50:1, 4–7.
13. Hengel, Judentum und Hellenismus, p. 492.
14. Hengel, Judentum und Hellenismus, p. 494 f.
15. Ant. XII, 4.1 § 154 f.
16. His rise and ignominious downfall is also alluded to in the Book of Daniel: cf. Dan. 11:15–19.
17. II Macc. 3:4.
18. See p. 31 above.
19. Kippenberg, Religion und Klassenbildung, p. 87.
20. II Macc. 3:10 f.
21. See p. 23 above.
22. II Macc. 3:23 ff.
23. II Macc. 4:2.
24. II Macc. 4:3–6.
25. II Macc. 4:7 f.
26. I Macc. 1:13; II Macc. 4:9.
27. II Macc. 4:9.
28. On the other hand, Josephus' chronology also shows that it must have been a lengthy process. It is often considered that this process came to an end and the new *polis* was officially constituted only upon the occasion of the king's visit to Jerusalem about two-and-a-half years after Jason's appointment (II Macc. 4:22). Others think that this only happened definitively with the erection of the Akra (cf. p. 40 below), although this is hotly contested by Bringmann, Hellenistische Reform, p. 84 f.
29. Ant. XII, 5.1 § 240 f.
30. II Macc. 4:14.
31. I Macc. 1:15; Ant. XII, 5.1 § 241.
32. II Macc. 4:18–20.
33. Josephus (Ant. XII, 5.1 § 237 ff.) makes Menelaus the brother of Jason and thus the youngest son of Simon II, apparently for apologetic reasons (just as he had already had Onias III die and Jason take up the office of High Priest in a legitimate fashion).
34. II Macc. 4:23–25.
35. Ant. XII, 5.1 § 239 ff.
36. II Macc. 4:26.
37. II Macc. 4:39–42.
38. II Macc. 4:32–34.
39. II Macc. 4:35–38.
40. II Macc. 4:43–50.
41. The chronology of the following events is extremely problematic. This is due to the detailed, but often contradictory accounts in the sources (I Macc. 1:20 ff.; II Macc. 5:1 ff.; Bell. 1,1.1 § 31ff., Ant. XII, 5.1 § 239 ff.; Dan. 11:28–31). There are basically two different versions given in the research, one assuming two visits to Jerusalem by the king (at the end of 169 BCE and in the summer of 168, following his return from his first and his second Egyptian campaigns respectively), and the other only one visit. I am of the latter opinion, and depict the chronology and the events accordingly.
42. II Macc. 5:5 f.

43. Bell. I, 1.1 § 32.
44. II Macc. 5:7–10.
45. Bickermann, Gott der Makkabäer, p. 67.
46. II Macc. 5:15.
47. I Macc. 1:21–24.
48. II Macc. 5:22 f.
49. Dan. 11:29 f.
50. Some researchers assume (see note 41 above) that Antiochus returned a second time to Jerusalem and that the following events were not only initiated, but also carried out by him.
51. The exact site is still not known: it was either south of the Temple mount or by the eastern Temple wall, where Hasmonean and Herodian masonry meet (the so-called "seam").
52. II Macc. 5:24–26; I Macc. 1:29–33; Ant. XII, 5.4 § 252.
53. I Macc. 1:34.
54. I Macc. 1:35 f.
55. I Macc. 1:38.
56. I Macc. 1:37, 39; Dan. 11:31.
57. I Macc. 1:41.
58. I Macc. 1:44–50.
59. I Macc. 1:51 f., 56–58, 60 f.; II Macc. 6:6–11.
60. Dan. 11:31; 12:11.
61. I Macc. 1:54–57; cf. also II Macc. 6:1–5.
62. Cf. Dan 7:25 f.; 11:21, 36–39.
63. Bickermann, Gott der Makkabäer, p. 126.
64. II Macc. 13:4.
65. Bickermann, Gott der Makkabäer, p. 133.
66. Tcherikover, Hellenistic Civilization and the Jews, p. 196.
67. Ibid., p. 191.
68. Hengel, Judentum und Hellenismus, pp. 525, 527.
69. Ibid., p. 533.
70. I Macc. 1:11.
71. See p. 39 above.
72. Ant. XII, 5.5 § 257 ff.
73. "Zeus Xenios" according to II Macc. 6:2.
74. Hengel, Judentum und Hellenismus, p. 537.
75. Bunge, Untersuchungen zum zweiten Makkabäerbuch, p. 469 ff.
76. Ibid., p. 477.
77. II Macc. 6:18 ff.
78. I Macc. 2:19–28.
79. Dan. 11:39.
80. See p. 54 below.
81. I Macc. 2:29 f., 42 f.
82. I Macc. 2:42.
83. I Macc. 2:29–48.
84. I Macc. 2:66.
85. I Macc. 3:10–12; Ant. XII, 7.1 § 287.
86. I Macc. 3:13–26; Ant. ibid. § 289.
87. I Macc. 3:38 ff.; 4:1 ff.; II Macc. 8:9–29; Ant. XII, 7.4 § 305 ff.

88. The dating is disputed, as the two Books of the Maccabees give different chronologies for all the events dealt with here. I follow the chronology of the first book.
89. I Macc. 4:29.
90. II Macc. 11:13–15.
91. II Macc. 11:16–21.
92. II Macc. 11:27–33. According to the internal chronology of the Second Book of Maccabees, this letter was not sent by Antiochus IV but by his successor, Antiochus V. However, current opinion based on recent research (to which I subscribe) is that it was written by Antiochus IV shortly before his death at the end of 164. This means that the about-turn in Seleucid policy was already decided on by Antiochus IV and not later by his young son under the influence of Lysias.
93. I Macc. 4:36–59; II Macc. 10:1–8; Ant. XII, 7.6 § 316 ff.
94. I Macc. 4:60 f.
95. I Macc. 5:45, 53 f.
96. I Macc. 5:55–62.
97. I Macc. 5:63–68.
98. I Macc. 5:62.
99. I Macc. 6:18–20.
100. I Macc. 6:31–47.
101. I Macc. 6:48–56.
102. I Macc. 6:59.
103. The letter is placed in the wrong order in II Maccabees. It cannot, like the following letter, be written by Antiochus IV as it presupposes that he is dead. The opening phrase would sound very unlikely coming from Antiochus IV, but would be highly appropriate for the young Antiochus V Eupator after the recent death of his father, Antiochus IV.
104. II Macc. 13:4–8; Ant. XII, 9.7 § 385.
105. I Macc. 7:5 ff.; II Macc. 14:3 ff.; Ant. XII. 9.7 § 385.
106. I Macc. 7:12 ff.
107. Ant. XII, 9.7 § 387.
108. I Macc. 7:16.
109. II Macc. 14:7 ff.
110. II Macc. 15:36.
111. I Macc. 8:17. According to the Second Book of the Maccabees (II Macc. 11:34–38), initial contact with Rome had already been made under Antiochus V Eupator. The authenticity of the letter from the Roman legates to the Jews is, however, disputed.
112. I Macc. 8:23–28.
113. I Macc. 8:32.
114. I Macc. 9:11 ff.
115. I Macc. 9:23.
116. I Macc. 9:24.
117. I Macc. 9:25.
118. I Macc. 9:35 ff.
119. Ant. XX, 10.3 § 237.
120. Ant. XII, 10:6 § 414.
121. I Macc. 9:58.

122. I Macc. 9:69.
123. I Macc. 9:71.
124. I Macc. 9:73.
125. I Macc. 10:4 ff.
126. I Macc. 10:18–20.
127. Cf. Hab. 2:17.
128. 1 QpHab. 12:6–10.
129. I Macc. 10:22 ff.
130. Ant. XIII, 4.1 f. §§ 80–85; I Macc. 10:51–66.
131. I Macc. 10:74 ff.
132. I Macc. 11:8 ff.
133. I Macc. 11:20 ff.
134. I Macc. 11:33–35.
135. I Macc. 10:22–31.
136. See p. 29 above.
137. It is improbable that the syntactically difficult phrase "for all such as do sacrifice in Jerusalem" is intended to refer merely to the priests.
138. I Macc. 10:30.
139. Unlike Kippenberg, Religion und Klassenbildung, p. 91.
140. I Macc. 10:29.
141. Ant. XIII, 4.9 § 125.
142. The three toparchies of Samaria in question are Ephraim, Lydda and Ramathaim (see below); "Peraea" and "Galilee" were added by Josephus.
143. Cf. also I Macc. 11:28: "And Jonathan requested of the king, that he would make Judaea free from tax [aphorologēton], and the three toparchies, and the country of Samaria; and promised him three hundred talents". The word aphorologēton can also mean "free from tribute", but as the tribute is not mentioned in the subsequent decree, it probably refers to the taxes specified therein. The three hundred talents might then be a total tribute for Judaea and the newly added Samaritan toparchies.
144. See pp. 35, 38 above.
145. Ant. XIII, 2.3 § 50.
146. Ant. XIII, 4:9 §§ 126–129.
147. I Macc. 11:39 ff.; Ant. XIII, 5.1–3 § 131 ff.; Diodorus, Bibl. Hist. XXXIII.4 a; Appianus, Syr. 68.
148. I Macc. 11:57 ff.
149. I Macc. 11:60 ff.; MegTaan, ed. Lichtenstein, HUCA 8–9, 1931/32, p. 281ff.
150. I Macc. 12:3.
151. I Macc. 12:5–18.
152. I Macc. 12:35 ff.; Ant. XIII, 5.10 f. § 179 ff.
153. I Macc. 12:41 ff.; Ant. XIII, 6:1 f. § 188 ff.
154. I Macc. 13:1 ff.
155. I Macc. 13:35 ff.
156. I Macc. 13:41.
157. I Macc. 13:42.
158. I Macc. 13:43 ff.
159. I Macc. 13:51.
160. I Macc. 14:41–44.
161. I Macc. 14:28.

162. I Macc. 14:29–40.
163. I Macc. 14:20 ff.
164. I Macc. 15:15 ff., but the precise circumstances of the letter remain problematic. The document recorded in Ant. XIV, 8.5 § 145 ff. probably belongs here and not in the time of Hyrcanus II.
165. I Macc. 14:1 ff.; Ant. XIII, 5:11 § 184 ff.; Appianus, Syr. 67.
166. I Macc. 15:1 ff.
167. I Macc. 15:10 ff., 25 ff., 37 ff.
168. I Macc. 15:25 ff.
169. I Macc. 16:1 ff.; Ant. XIII, 7.3 § 225 ff.
170. I Macc. 16:11 ff.; Ant. XIII, 7.4 § 228.

4. THE HASMONEAN DYNASTY

4.1. Government and economy of the Hasmonean state

Under Simon, the rule of the Maccabee family had stabilized both internally and externally. When the second generation came to power in the person of his son and heir, John Hyrcanus, the dynastic principle found full expression. From this point on, it is appropriate to speak of a "Hasmonean dynasty"[1] in the narrower sense.

The backbone of the Hasmonean state was the *military*. As *stratēgos*, Simon had full command over the national army; the Hasmoneans probably maintained a standing army of Jewish mercenaries right from the very beginning. This is evident from the fact that Jonathan was able to place thirty thousand Jews at the disposal of the king's forces,[2] or employ three thousand Jewish soldiers against the rebellious inhabitants of Antioch.[3] It is also reported that Simon sent the king (Antiochus VII Sidetes) two thousand soldiers to fight against Tryphon when he had him trapped in Dor.[4] John Hyrcanus took part in Antiochus VII's campaign against the Parthians[5] and appears to have been the first Hasmonean to recruit foreign mercenaries.[6] His son, Alexander Jannaeus, recruited mercenaries from Pisidia and Cilicia and employed them in the civil war.[7]

The increased self-confidence of the Hasmonean state found expression in an ever more expansionist *policy of conquest*, in which politico-economic motives were combined with religious ones. Jonathan had obtained the Samaritan toparchies of Ephraim, Lydda and Ramathaim, Simon the cities of Joppa and Gezer. John Hyrcanus and Alexander Jannaeus considerably extended the Jewish national territory, particularly by annexing non-Jewish territories.[8] The inhabitants of these latter were forcibly Judaized or expelled, or else made liable for payment of a regular tribute to the Jewish state. The territories with a large Jewish population which were incorporated directly into the Jewish state were included in the administrative system of the Hasmoneans, the land being divided up into toparchies.[9] It is possible that, at the height of Hasmonean power under Alexander Jannaeus, there were twenty-four such toparchies, a number which is not merely arbitrary, but corresponds to the old system of twenty-four classes of the priesthood.

The policy of conquest carried out by the Hasmoneans led to a major expansion of Jewish territory, achieved by expulsion and dispossession of non-Jewish population groups. In principle, these new territories became the property of the ruler, that is, the reigning Hasmonean family, just as was the case under the Hellenistic monarchies. It is unlikely that the legal position was different under the Hasmoneans than it was under the Ptolemies and the Seleucids. The Hasmonean state did, however, differ in one essential respect from Hellenistic rule, at least in its early days, insofar as it had made freedom from economic slavery a fundamental concern. The exemption from paying land tax achieved under Demetrius II was celebrated as a liberation from the "heathen yoke",[10] so it is hardly likely that the Hasmoneans leased the newly won land to Jewish farmers using the same system of "government leasing" as was employed under the Seleucids. Rather, the greater part of the land will have been handed over into the ownership of the farmers so that a free peasantry could emerge again. It is conceivable that, in return for the land, the rural population was liable for military service. This would explain why the Hasmoneans were constantly capable of large-scale military campaigns.

Certainly, not all the newly acquired land was given to the people, and the Hasmoneans themselves owned an immense amount of property. Jonathan had received the city of Ekron from Alexander Balas;[11] Simon possessed a palace near Jericho (in which he was murdered). The famous balsam plantations of Jericho had always formed part of the royal estate, and so it is more than likely that the Hasmoneans kept this productive region to themselves, as did their Hellenistic predecessors. The fertile Plain of Jezreel was likewise traditionally owned by Hellenistic royalty; upon being conquered by John Hyrcanus,[12] it doubtless came into the private ownership of the Hasmoneans. It is conceivable that the numerous Rabbinic references to the "Royal Mountain" of Alexander Jannaeus allude to this extensive private property of the Hasmoneans.[13]

A particular problem is posed by the question of *taxation* under the Hasmoneans. As there is no mention of this matter in the sources, we must rely mainly on supposition and inference. It goes without saying that the Hasmoneans did not impose a tribute on their Jewish subjects, as precisely this was the distinguishing characteristic of rule by foreign heathens. On the other hand, non-Jewish territories that had been incorporated into the Jewish state will have been treated in the same manner as under the Seleucids, and the payment of tributes will have been required of the inhabitants. The salt- and crown-tax, which Demetrius II had waived, no doubt remained abolished under the Hasmoneans. The land tax, that is, the *pro rata* payment of agricultural produce according to a specified quota, presumably only applied to the king's private estates. Whether Alexander Jannaeus later also demanded a land tax from the free peasantry remains an open question. If this was indeed the case, then it would indicate that economic factors were also at play in the opposition to him.[14]

So we are left with only customs duties and the poll tax as possible tax options. It may safely be assumed that the Hasmoneans imposed customs duties (these will have represented a considerable source of finance, especially in respect of the Nabataean caravans which had to pass through Jewish territory). As regards the poll tax, it has been supposed that John Hyrcanus collected part of the biblically prescribed tithe as a government tax, but this presumption rests solely on a late passage in the Jerusalem Talmud.[15] More likely is another suggestion to the effect that John Hyrcanus or Alexander Jannaeus increased the Temple tax, which at the time of Nehemia amounted to one-third of a shekel,[16] to the half-shekel customary later on.[17] We do not know precisely when this change from one third of a Persian silver coin to the Tyrian half-shekel took place. At all events, the difference in value must have been considerable; the Persian silver shekel weighed about 5.5 g, so a third of one was about 1.83 g of silver, while a Tyrian half-shekel had an average weight of 7.2 g of silver![18] So the introduction of the Tyrian half-shekel meant considerably more money for the Temple treasury than under the Persians. We cannot dismiss out of hand the suspicion that the Hasmoneans were responsible for the changeover to the half-shekel for the Temple tax, and that this effectively meant the introduction of a regular government tax for the entire population, Jew and non-Jew alike, or in other words, a poll tax.[19]

4.2. John Hyrcanus I (135/34—104 BCE)

John Hyrcanus, the only surviving son of Simon, was able to prevail over his brother-in-law Ptolemy, but was confronted in what was probably his first year in office, a sabbatical year, with an invasion by Antiochus VII, who lay waste to Judaea and besieged Hyrcanus in Jerusalem.[20] Antiochus cut Jerusalem off totally from the outside world and slowly starved the city out. The food supply became so short that, according to Josephus, Hyrcanus expelled all those unable to fight from the city. However, the Syrians would not allow the evacuees through the ring they had thrown around the city, so that finally Hyrcanus was forced to take them back in again for the Feast of Tabernacles, for which occasion Antiochus not only granted a truce, but "moreover sent a magnificent sacrifice" to the city.[21] Finally, Hyrcanus had to capitulate and sue for peace. Antiochus demanded the surrender of all weapons, taxes for Joppa and the cities lying outside of Judaea, hostages and the sum of five hundred silver talents, and had the battlements of the city walls destroyed. In comparison to the actions of Antiochus IV, these terms were relatively mild, but they meant the restoration of Syrian sovereignty, at least formally. Soon afterwards, John Hyrcanus also had to show military allegiance to the king when the latter embarked in 130/129 BCE on a military campaign against the Parthians.[22]

The military fiasco of this Parthian campaign and the death of Antiochus VII (in 129 BCE) weakened the Seleucid state to such a degree that this demonstration of power by the king in Judaea proved no more than a brief interlude. His successor Demetrius II, who had only shortly before been released from Parthian custody and who now embarked on his second period of rule, was immediately embroiled in internal struggles and had to fight off a pretender to the throne (Alexander Zabinas) sponsored by Ptolemy VII Physcon of Egypt. He was defeated by Alexander at Damascus and murdered a short time later (in 125 BCE). He was succeeded by his son Antiochus VIII Grypus, who managed to drive off the usurper Alexander (123/22?), but was himself ousted in 113 by his cousin and stepbrother Antiochus IX Cyzicenus, and had to share power with him as of 111 BCE.

As a result of these internal struggles for the Syrian throne, Judaea was effectively an independent state and John Hyrcanus a sovereign ruler. Immediately after the death of Antiochus VII, Hyrcanus undertook his first campaign of conquest and, step by step, extended the boundaries of his sphere of influence. He conquered Madaba in the east, Shechem and Mt. Gerizim in the north and Adora and Marissa in the south, and forced the Idumaeans to submit to circumcision.[23] He also appears to have been the first Hasmonean to employ foreign mercenaries to strengthen his military might. The fact that he acquired the money to do so by plundering the tomb of David[24] will have been viewed by many of the pious as an unhappy reminder of life under the Hellenizers, which they had hoped was now over and done with. For his second campaign of conquest, he exploited the conflict between the stepbrothers Antiochus VIII and Antiochus IX and marched on Samaria.[25] The two attempts by Antiochus IX to come to Samaria's assistance, as well as that of his generals, Callimandrus and Epicrates, were of no avail; in about 108/107 BCE, Hyrcanus conquered the city and not only destroyed it, but "left it to be swept away by the mountain-torrents, for he dug beneath it until it fell into the beds of the torrents …".[26] As he had also acquired Beth-Shean/Scythopolis only shortly before through an act of betrayal, he had now extended his territory as far as the borders of Galilee.

In foreign policy matters, John Hyrcanus continued the attempts of his predecessors to maintain good relations with Rome. At least two decrees concerning Judaea were issued by the Roman Senate during his reign.[27] These new foreign policy initiatives were probably occasioned by the two fortresses at Jaffa/Joppa and Gezer/Gazara, which had been the subject of dispute since Antiochus VII Sidetes. The precise dating of the two documents is controversial, but there are good grounds for believing that the first comes from the early part of Hyrcanus' reign (under Demetrius II, about 128–125?), while the second, which is certainly cited by Josephus at the wrong point chronologically, belongs to his final years as ruler (under Antiochus IX?). The contracting parties are the Roman Senate and the Jewish people (*dēmos*), represented by the High Priest. In both agreements, the treaty of alliance with the Romans is renewed, while in the second "Antiochus, the son of Antiochus" (= Antiochus IX?) is ordered to surrender all the fortresses and, in particular, to withdraw the garrison from Joppa.

Internally, Hyrcanus' reign created serious division. With the increasing consolidation of their power, the ruling family of Maccabees/Hasmoneans had distanced themselves ever further from the original aims of the Maccabean movement, a development which led almost inevitably to a conflict with the "pious".[28] Consequently, Hyrcanus turned to the old ruling party of the Sadducees, the wealthy priestly aristocracy, whose economic interests made them more amenable to religious compromise and who had already shown evidence of such willingness prior to the Maccabean revolt, under the Hellenizers. This internal political shift under Hyrcanus is still a vital issue in later Rabbinic literature, which mentions some anti-Pharisaic measures taken by Hyrcanus.[29]

At his death, John Hyrcanus left behind a country which, apart from the Jewish heartland, encompassed the most important cities of the coastal plain to the west, Samaria in the north, parts of Transjordan in the east and Idumaea in the south. Not for nothing, then, does Josephus extol him as an ideal ruler with "charismatic-Messianic traits",[30] to whom God had granted "three of the greatest privileges": "the rule of the nation, the office of High Priest, and the gift of prophecy".[31]

4.3. The Pharisees

The origins of the Pharisees as a clearly defined, politically effective group are obscure. Josephus, our sole source for the early period, mentions them for the first time under John Hyrcanus in a context which already implies a certain consolidation and political significance. It is likely that they emerged from the group of the "pious" (*chasidim*). This means that they took shape as a group and achieved a political profile in the period between the Maccabean struggles and John Hyrcanus.

The circumstances under which Josephus introduces the Pharisees into his history[32] are coloured by legend and somewhat mysterious. A few historical conclusions may, however, be drawn. Josephus maintains initially that the Pharisees were held in high esteem by the people and that Hyrcanus was also originally one of their disciples. However, a banquet held in their honour led to a breach with the Pharisees after one of them reproached Hyrcanus:

> "Since you have asked to be told the truth, if you wish to be righteous, give up the high-priesthood and be content with governing the people." And when Hyrcanus asked him for what reason he should give up the high–priesthood, he replied, "Because we have heard from our elders that your mother was a captive in the reign of Antiochus Epiphanes."[33]

This claim that Hyrcanus' mother had been taken captive under Antiochus IV cast doubt upon the legitimacy of Hyrcanus' birth and would therefore exclude him on principle from holding the office of High Priest. The Pharisee's reproach implies that Hyrcanus had not only usurped an office which he was not entitled to hold, but that, due to his dubious origins, he was also absolutely unfit ever to hold such office. Hyrcanus was naturally furious at this accusation and asked the Pharisees to decide on a suitable punishment for the slanderer. When, instead of the death penalty Hyrcanus expected, the Pharisees, being "naturally lenient in the matter of punishments", suggested only flagellation, Hyrcanus became so angry that he decided to

> desert the Pharisees, and to abrogate the regulations which they had established for the people, and punish those who observed them.

The historical core of this story is probably to be found in the fact that the latent opposition to the ruling Maccabean-Hasmonean dynasty first assumed concrete form under John Hyrcanus, and from then on became a force that the Hasmoneans had to reckon with. Under Hyrcanus it became evident that there was now little to distinguish the ruling family from the Hellenistic potentates, and that their government was not much different or better (i.e. truer to the principles of the Torah) than foreign rule by the Seleucids or the Hellenizers in Jerusalem who had been driven out by the Maccabees. If the Pharisees were now demanding that Hyrcanus relinquish the office of High Priest, they were at the same time calling for a return to the original ideals of the Maccabean movement. The legitimacy of the High Priest seems to have been the focal point at which the interests of all the various groups in Jerusalem converged and flared up, as it were, leading to different consequences for each of the various factions of Judaism. The Sadducees apparently found it easiest to come to terms with the ruling classes, the Essenes propagated a radical separation and withdrew to the desert, while the Pharisees were seemingly the group that attempted to put the ideal of the religious *and* political realization of the Torah into concrete political effect.

All that we know about the teachings of the early Pharisees likewise comes from Josephus, who refers on several occasions to three Jewish "schools of thought" among which, as well as the Essenes and the Sadducees, he also includes the Pharisees. In what is probably his earliest account in the *Bellum*, Josephus says of the Pharisees and the Sadducees:

> Of the two schools named first, the Pharisees are held to be the most authoritative exponents of the Law and count as the leading sect. They ascribe everything to Fate or to God: the decision whether or not to do right rests mainly with men, but in every action Fate takes some part. Every soul is imperishable, but only the souls of good men pass into other bodies, the souls of bad men being subjected to eternal punishment.

> The Sadducees, the second order, deny Fate altogether and hold that God is incapable of either committing sin or seeing it; they say that men are free to choose between good and evil, and each individual must decide which he will follow. The permanence of the soul, punishments in Hades, and rewards they deny utterly.

> Again, Pharisees are friendly to one another and seek to promote concord with the general public, but Sadducees, even towards each other, show a more disagreeable spirit, and in their relations with men like themselves they are as harsh as they might be to foreigners.

> This is all I wish to say about the Jewish schools of thought.[34]

Two things must be taken into consideration when attempting to arrive at an historical evaluation of this account by Josephus. On the one hand, Josephus is not writing for Jews, but for an educated Greek-speaking public. This is the reason for the stylization of the Jewish groups as "schools of thought" or "sects", and also perhaps the choice of themes by which he represents the groups throughout, namely, freedom of will and immortality. On the other hand, Josephus is writing at a time (namely, after the First Jewish War) when the Pharisaic tendency in the form of Rabbinic Judaism was beginning to win recognition as the only authoritative group. This probably accounts for his obvious partiality for the Pharisees (which increases in the course of his various writings).

The first point dealt with by Joseph in his account of the teachings of the three groups is freedom of the will. In this matter, the Pharisees occupy the middle ground between the Essenes and the Sadducees: whereas the Essenes teach that fate (*heimarmenē*) is all-powerful and that men can do nothing to alter it, while the Sadducees on the other hand totally deny fate and ascribe everything to the human will, the Pharisees represent the interaction of fate and human reason.[35] However much Josephus may have been influenced by the expectations of his readers, particularly in the matter of free will—the Greek reader was no doubt especially familiar with the deterministic attitude of the Essenes—the problem also has its Jewish tradition,[36] and so Josephus may well be giving a thoroughly accurate account of the essential differences between the individual groups. The "compromise formula" of the Pharisees found a direct successor in Rabbinic Judaism in the famous saying of Rabbi Akiva: "Everything is foreseen (by God), but permission (i.e. the possibility of choice) is given (to man nevertheless)".[37]

In the matter of immortality, both the Pharisees and the Essenes teach the immortality of the soul, while the Sadducees fundamentally reject any belief in immortality and assume that the soul perishes along with the body.[38] Unlike the Essenes, and apparently alone of the three groups, the Pharisees also believed in the *resurrection of the body*; how else are we to understand the phrase "but only (the souls of) good men pass into other bodies"?[39]

This point is of particular significance. The question of bodily resurrection does not as yet play a role in the Bible; it can hardly be claimed that texts such as Hos. 6:1–3, Isa. 25:8, Isa. 26:19, Isa. 53:11 ff. or Ezek. 37:1–14 refer to individual bodily resurrection. The Sadducees therefore represent a decidedly biblical point of view. Belief in resurrection only began to develop towards the end of the biblical era, and then apparently in several stages. The first stage is represented by a text such as Dan. 12:2 f. ("And many of them that sleep in the dust of the earth shall awake, some to everlasting life, and some to shame and everlasting contempt. And they that be wise shall shine as the brightness of the firmament; and they that turn many to righteousness as the stars for ever and ever.") which is clearly bound up with astral motifs and doubtless assumes resurrection only of the soul. This belief in the resurrection of the soul and reward after death was a familiar one to the Greeks and will have developed in Judaism under the influence of the Maccabean struggles (it may go back to the early Chasidim). A direct successor of this form of belief in resurrection was the Essenes' anticipation of a community of the exalted spirits of men and the angels.

The next, and crucial, step in the development of the belief in resurrection was probably taken by the Pharisees. The Pharisees, too, were still under a strong Hellenistic influence (Josephus usually speaks only of the resurrection of the soul in their case as well), but they seem to have been the first to formulate the thought of bodily resurrection, which was completely alien to the Greeks. In so doing, they took the belief in resurrection in a direction leading far beyond the Bible, and which made an enduring impression on the whole future development of Judaism.

The Pharisees were to play an important role in the history of the Hasmonean dynasty. Under Alexander Jannaeus, the Pharisees were subjected to outright persecution,[40] while under Jannaeus' successor, Salome Alexandra, they apparently rose to become the dominant party in the state.[41] Subsequently, their political influence seems to have rapidly waned. For Herod, who took calculated action against all the traditional power structures in the country, they no longer represented a serious threat. Only towards the end of his reign do they emerge as the leaders of the opposition to Herod.[42] With the end of the Herodian dynasty and Judaea's transition to the status of a Roman province, a new group arose, the party of the Zealots, who interpreted the political message of the Torah in a radical sense.[43] The Pharisees, on the other hand, seem to have concentrated largely on putting the religious aspects of the Torah into effect; in any case, they are characterized consistently in the New Testament and the Rabbinical literature as a group whose chief concern was ritual purity and adherence to dietary regulations. It is as such a "party" with a primarily religious orientation that they gradually mutate after 70 CE into Rabbinic Judaism and exert a powerful influence on the future history of Judaism.[44]

4.4. Aristobulus I (104–103 BCE)

Hyrcanus' eldest son and successor, Aristobulus I, only ruled for about one year. He was the victor of an internal power struggle against his mother, whom Hyrcanus had appointed regent, and his brothers, and was the first of the Hasmoneans to officially adopt the title of king.[45] With this turn towards the Hellenistic form of government, Aristobulus brought to its conclusion a development that had started long before and become manifest under his father, Hyrcanus. Not for nothing did Aristobulus (and his four brothers) bear a Greek name in addition to his Hebrew one (*Yehuda*), as well as being expressly designated by Josephus as *Philhellēn* ("Friend of the Greeks").[46] Whether he had his own coins minted is as much a matter of dispute as in the case of his father. In any case, none of the coins attributed to him by many researchers bears his Greek name or his royal title.

The most important foreign policy issue of his brief reign was the conquest and enforced Judaization of large parts of Ituraea in the north,[47] although precisely which region is meant by this remains an open question. Very probably, the somewhat vague reference in Josephus does not refer to the actual heartland of the Ituraeans in Lebanon, but to the northern part of Galilee, as Hyrcanus had only advanced as far as Samaria and Beth-Shean/Scythopolis, and the conquest of Galilee is otherwise unreported.

4.5. Alexander Jannaeus (103–76 BCE)

Alexander Jannaeus was the third of John Hyrcanus' sons to mount the throne. Together with his brothers, he had spent the short period of Aristobulus' reign in prison. He married his sister-in-law Salome Alexandra, Aristobulus' widow. Alexander, whose character is depicted more diversely in Jewish history than that of practically any of the other Hasmoneans, had a reign characterized by numerous wars abroad and conflicts with the Pharisees at home which escalated to the point of civil war.

As soon as he came to power, he waged war on Acco/Ptolemais and was defeated in battle at Asophon (Asaphon) by the Egyptian king, Ptolemy Lathyrus, who was ruler of Cyprus at the time and was called to their assistance by the inhabitants of Acco.[48] Alexander was saved from Ptolemy through the intervention of Cleopatra, Ptolemy's mother, who did not want her own son becoming too powerful, but this did not eliminate the danger of Egyptian supremacy. Cleopatra, to whom the Jewish territory effectively stood open, seems to have seriously considered annexing it, and was only (according to Josephus[49]) dissuaded from this plan through the intervention of her Jewish general, Ananias. So a peace treaty was agreed between Alexander and Cleopatra at Scythopolis which gave Alexander a free hand for his further undertakings. His conquests in the east included Gadara, south-east of Lake Gennesareth, and the fortress of Amathus, and in the west the coastal cities Raphia and Anthedon, as well as Gaza, a city which had long maintained its independence (96 BCE).[50] A second campaign took him again to Transjordan, where he took on the Moabites and the Gileadites, leading to the final destruction of the fortress of Amathus. He then embarked upon a war against the Nabataean king, Obedas, which proved less successful. Alexander fell into an ambush at Gadara and only just managed to escape and flee to Jerusalem.[51]

Meanwhile at home, the conflict with the "pious" that had been smoulder-ing since Hyrcanus' time reached its climax. The Pharisaic party, which had developed into an important force among the people, was no longer prepared to tolerate the "Hellenistic tyranny" of the Hasmonean princes (not for noth-ing was Alexander Jannaeus the first Hasmonean of whom we can say with certainty that he minted his own coins with his royal title on them). So Josephus reports that the people—supposedly incited by the Pharisees—pelted the king with citrus fruits when he officiated as High Priest at the festi-val of Tabernacles. Characteristically, the justification given for this action is the claim that he "was the son of a captive and was unfit to hold the office of High Priest".[52] According to Josephus, Alexander took his revenge by having his mercenaries massacre six thousand Jews.[53] The account given in the Rabbinic literature of the dispute between Jannaeus and Simeon ben Shetach,[54] despite its legendary features, points nevertheless to a fundamental conflict between the king and the Pharisees. When Alexander had to flee from the Nabataean king Obedas, open rebellion finally broke out, leading to a civil war lasting six years in which "no fewer than fifty thousand Jews" fell.[55] The Pharisees even called for assistance on Demetrius III Eukairus, the son of Antiochus VIII Grypus who, with Jewish support (!), defeated Alexander's army of mercenaries at Shechem in about 88 BCE. Alexander had to flee, but a large number of Jews went back to him after this defeat, and Demetrius withdrew. The remaining rebels were decimated and, according to Josephus,[56] eight hundred of them gruesomely executed. This reign of terror, which earned Alexander Jannaeus the title "furious young lion" in the Qumran literature,[57] caused many of his internal political opponents to leave the country for the remainder of his time in power.

Alexander took advantage of the domestic peace which had been won in so radical a manner to embark on new activities abroad. His main opponent—following the fall of the Seleucid empire and the conquest of Syria in 83 BCE by the Armenian king Tigranes—was Aretas, king of the Nabataeans, who had become very powerful, and who initially managed to defeat Alexander. This did not, however, deter Alexander Jannaeus from new campaigns in Transjordan. Within three years (approx. 83–80 BCE), he had conquered the cities of Pella, Dium and Gerasa in Galaaditis and Gaulana, Seleucia and Gamala in Gaulanitis.[58] With these last conquests, Alexander Jannaeus was able to extend the Jewish territory even further, particularly to the east. When he died three years later after a long illness (Josephus: "from heavy drinking") during the siege of the fortress of Ragaba (near to Gerasa), the continuously growing Hasmonean state had reached its maximum size to date.

4.6. Salome Alexandra (76–67 BCE)

The reign of his widow and successor Salome Alexandra was a time of peace both at home and abroad. Alexander Jannaeus is said to have instructed her on his deathbed to make peace with the Pharisees and to "not take any action, while you are on the throne, without their consent",[59] and a complete about-turn in domestic policy and reconciliation with the Pharisees are indeed the most important features of Salome's reign. She appointed her son Hyrcanus, a supporter of the Pharisees, to the office of High Priest, and also seems to have reorganized the *Gerousia*, the old representative body of the nobility and the priests, so as to favour the Pharisees. In this way, the Pharisees became the real power in the land:

> And so, while she [Alexandra] had the title of sovereign, the Pharisees had the power. For example, they recalled exiles, and freed prisoners, and, in a word, in no way differed from absolute rulers.[60]

When the Pharisees eventually set about taking their revenge on Alexander Jannaeus' closest followers, who had recommended the murder of the rebels, open resistance broke out on the part of the nobility. A delegation of Sadducees, who were followers of Salome's younger son, Aristobulus, managed to put a stop to the excesses of Pharisaic policies, thereby avoiding an armed conflict between the two rival parties for the time being. However, Alexandra could not prevent Aristobulus occupying the most important strongholds shortly before her death with the assistance of the Sadducees, so procuring for himself a good starting position for the inevitable power struggle with his brother Hyrcanus.

As regards foreign affairs, Salome's term of office passed without any outstanding incidents, except for one (unsuccessful) expedition by Aristobulus to Damascus.[61] The recurrent danger of an invasion by the Armenian king, Tigranes, was removed when Lucullus defeated Tigranes in 69 BCE and the Romans prepared to become involved in the power struggles in Palestine as well.

4.7. Aristobulus II (67–63 BCE)

As was to be expected, immediately following the death of Salome Alexandra, fratricidal war broke out between her two sons Aristobulus (II) and Hyrcanus (II). Hyrcanus was defeated in a battle near Jericho and gave up the crown and the High Priesthood in favour of Aristobulus.[62] But this did not put an end to the internal power struggle. The Idumaean Antipater, father of the future king Herod, had brought the south under his control in his role as governor of Idumaea, and now intervened on Hyrcanus' behalf in the fraternal feud at the Hasmonean court. He convinced Hyrcanus to flee to Petra to the Nabataean king, Aretas, and to request Aretas' support against his brother. Having received Hyrcanus' promise to return to him a number of the cities that Alexander Jannaeus had taken from the Nabataeans, Aretas marched against Aristobulus and defeated him in battle. Aristobulus fled to Jerusalem, where Aretas and Hyrcanus laid siege to him on the Temple Mount.

In the meantime, however, the initiative in the power struggle between the various parties in Jerusalem no longer lay solely with those directly concerned. The Romans under Pompey had advanced close to the borders of the Jewish state and skilfully exploited the internal dispute between the two brothers for their own purposes. Pompey despatched the future governor Scaurus to Judaea, where, like Antiochus IV before him, he received the rival groups who attempted to outbid each other with offers of money. He finally came out in Aristobulus' favour. Aretas and Hyrcanus had to withdraw and were then pursued and defeated in battle by Aristobulus' army.

In 64 BCE, Pompey finally set the seal on the fate of the Seleucid kingdom and set out in the spring of 63 from Antioch (?) for Damascus. There, three Jewish delegations competed simultaneously for his favour, including a group of representatives of the people as well as the spokesmen of Aristobulus and Hyrcanus. The accusation of the people's delegation[63] is particularly revealing:

> ... the nation ... asked not to be ruled by a king, saying that it was the custom of their country to obey the priests of the God who was venerated by them, but that these two, who were descended from the priests, were seeking to change their form of government in order that they might become a nation of slaves.[64]

The main bone of contention, therefore, was the monarchial system of government as introduced by Alexander Jannaeus (if not earlier). The accusation that the people were being turned into slaves shows that the Hasmonean monarchy was experienced as being no different from the tyranny of a pagan king. Behind this reproach stand not only religious (restoration of the old theocracy), but also concrete economic grounds, for the constant expansion of Jewish territory certainly entailed enormous monetary expense, which could hardly be met other than by imposing ever more taxes on the people.[65]

There can be no doubt that the sympathies of the Romans were on the side of the people (not for nothing had they concluded their treaties with the High Priests as representatives of the nation and not the Jewish kings), but

Pompey, who wanted first to march against the Nabataeans, decided officially for none of the disputing parties, but cautioned all of them to keep their peace until he had the opportunity to settle matters in Judaea. However, when Aristobulus failed to heed his injunction, Pompey altered his plans and marched on Jerusalem via Pella and Jericho. He took Aristobulus prisoner and besieged the city. Finally, the supporters of Hyrcanus opened the gates and allowed the legate Piso to occupy the city and the royal palace, while the supporters of the captive Aristobulus took refuge on the Temple Mount. In the late autumn of 63 BCE, Pompey conquered the Temple Mount from the north, thereby bringing Jerusalem fully under Roman control.[66] He made fundamental changes to the political status of Judaea:

> And he made Jerusalem tributary to the Romans, and took from
> its inhabitants the cities of Coele-Syria which they had formerly
> subdued, and placed them under his own governor; and the entire
> nation, which before had raised itself so high, he confined within
> its own borders.[67]

There then follows a long (and still incomplete) list of the Greek cities in the coastal region and in Transjordan to which Pompey granted freedom (*eleutheria*) and self-determination (*autonomia*); that is, he withdrew them from Jewish jurisdiction and placed them under the direct authority of Scaurus, the first governor of the new Roman province of Syria.

The residual Jewish state[68] had an "intermediate status" between self-government and complete integration into the Roman provincial system. The Romans had recognized that the direct incorporation of Judea into the Roman Empire was not (yet) feasible. In fact, it did not take place until after 6 CE.[69] Hyrcanus was reappointed High Priest by the Romans,[70] but was not officially subject to the governor of Syria and thus retained jurisdiction in internal affairs. On the other hand, the tribute (*stipendium*) shows that Judaea was regarded as a subject territory dependent on Rome in matters of foreign policy. The country was doubtless also divided up into tax districts and an organized system of tax collection set up. We learn nothing from the sources concerning the type and extent of the taxes, but the organization of the tax collection was sure to be the same as for all the other Roman provinces, that is, through the so-called publican societies (*societates publicanorum*) which had taken out leases on government revenue. The system of government leasing, familiar from the time of the Ptolemies and Seleucids, and then abolished under the Hasmoneans as part of the gradual process of independence from the Seleucid authorities, returned (in its specifically Roman form)[71] at the very moment that the Hasmoneans had gambled away political autonomy.

Notes

1. The appellation "Hasmonean" is synonymous in Josephus with "Maccabean".
2. I Macc. 10:36 f.
3. I Macc. 11:42–51.
4. I Macc. 15:26.
5. See p. 68 below.
6. Ant. XIII, 8:4 § 249.
7. See p. 75 below.
8. See pp. 68 f. and 74 f. below.
9. They were obviously falling back on the Seleucid and Ptolemaic system of administration, which in turn had been inherited from Alexander the Great.
10. See p. 54 above.
11. I Macc. 10:89.
12. According to Schalit, Herodes, p. 200. There is no specific report of the conquest of the Plain of Jezreel. However, since John Hyrcanus took control of Scythopolis (see p. 68 below), the Plain of Jezreel which lay just to the west will also have come into Jewish possession.
13. Cf. b Git 57 a.
14. See p. 75 f. below.
15. j MSh 5:9, fol. 56 d; j Sot 9:1, fol 24 a.
16. The demand for half a shekel already to be found in Exod. 30:13 is no doubt a post-Exilic interpolation which presupposes the increase from a third to half a shekel.
17. Schalit, Herodes, p. 269.
18. Ben-David, Jerusalem und Tyros, p. 43.
19. However, one cannot, like Schalit, regard the poll tax introduced by Jannaeus as one of the causes for the opposition of the Pharisees to the Hasmonean state apparatus (Herodes, p. 270), while at the same time supposing that, by increasing the Temple tax to half a shekel, Jannaeus was out to impress his Pharisaic opponents (Herodes, p. 269 note 421).
20. Ant. XIII, 8.2 § 236.
21. Ant. XIII, 8.2 § 242 f.
22. Ant. XIII, 8.4 §§ 250–252.
23. Ant. XIII, 9.1 §§ 255–258.
24. Ant. XIII, 8.4 § 249.
25. Ant. XIII, 10.2 f. §§ 275–281.
26. Ant. XIII, 10.3 § 281.
27. Ant. XIII, 9.2 § 260 ff.; XIV, 10.22 § 248 ff.
28. See p. 75 below.
29. Cf. m MSh 5:15; Sot 9:10.
30. Hengel, Judentum und Hellenismus, p. 560.
31. Ant. XIII, 11.7 § 299 f.; Bell. I, 2.8 § 68 f.
32. Ant. XIII, 10.5 f. §§ 288–298. A similar story is related in b Qid 66 a, but the events are relocated to the time of Alexander Jannaeus.
33. Ibid.
34. Bell. II, 8.14 §§ 162–166; cf. also Ant. XIII, 5.9 §§ 171–173; Ant. XVIII, 1.2–4 §§ 11–17.
35. The clearest statement to this effect is to be found in Ant. XVIII, 1.3 § 13

36. Cf. Eccl. 3:1–15; 9:1,3; 9:11 f.; Ecclus. 15:11–17; 16:17–23.
37. Ab 3:15.
38. See particularly Ant. XVIII, 1.4 § 16.
39. This is the only time it occurs in any of the accounts of the three "schools".
40. See p. 75 below.
41. See p. 76 below.
42. Cf. Bell. I, 33.2–4 §§ 648–655; Ant. XVII, 6.2–3 § 149 ff.
43. See p. 109 ff. below,
44. See p. 133 ff. below.
45. Ant. XIII, 11.1 § 301; Bell. I, 3.1 § 70; but not according to Strabo, Geographica XVI, 2.40: Alexander Jannaeus.
46. Ant. XIII, 11.3 § 318.
47. Ibid.
48. Ant. XIII, 12.4 § 334 f.
49. Ant. XIII, 13.2 § 354.
50. Ant. XIII, 13.3 f. § 356 ff.
51. Ant. XIII, 13.5 § 375 f.
52. Ant. XIII, 13.5 § 372 f.; Bell. I, 4.3 § 88; cf. m Suk 4:9; b Yom 26 b; j Suk 4:8, fol. 54 d.
53. Ant. XIII, 13.5 § 374.
54. BerR 91:3; j Ber 7:2, fol. 11 b; b Ber 48 a.
55. Ant. XIII, 13.5 § 376.
56. Ant. XIII, 14.2 § 379 ff.
57. 4 QpNah 1:5 f. to Nah. 2:12 f.
58. Ant. XIII, 15.3 § 393 f.; Bell. I, 4.8 § 104 f.
59. Ant. XIII, 15.5 § 403.
60. Ant. XIII, 16.2 § 409.
61. Ant. XIII, 16.3 § 418; Bell. I, 5.3 § 115 f.
62. Ant. XIV, 1.2 § 4 ff.; Bell. I, 6.1 § 120 ff.
63. According to the parallel account in Diodorus, Bibl. Hist. XL,2, this was composed of the "most outstanding (of the Jews)", that is, the Jewish aristocracy. Possibly, however, this account is influenced by the reforms under Gabinius (see p. 81 below).
64. Ant. XIV, 3.2 § 41.
65. See p. 66 f. above.
66. Ant. XIV, 4.2–4 § 61 ff.; Bell. I, 7.3 § 145 ff. and passim.
67. Ant. XIV, 4.4 § 74; Bell. I, 7.6 f. §§ 153–158.
68. Judaea, Galilee, eastern Idumaea (the district of Adoraim = Adora), Jewish Transjordan (Peraea).
69. See p. 105 below.
70. Pompey took Aristobulus and his two daughters and sons (Alexander and Antigonus: Alexander later managed to escape) with him to Rome and included them in his triumphal procession.
71. The specifically Roman aspect was the fact that only Roman citizens could become tax farmers (*publicani*) and acquire shares in the publican societies. Unlike the situation under the Seleucids, the indigenous aristocracy were excluded from the system of government leasing, although this does not mean that the native population was not involved in the collection of taxes as agents of the Roman tax farmers.

5. HEROD THE GREAT (37–4 BCE)

5.1. Herod's rise to power

5.1.1. Hyrcanus II (63–40 BCE) and the reform of Judaea

The official head of the residual Jewish state was Hyrcanus II, the elder son of Alexander Jannaeus and Salome Alexandra, in his role as High Priest (without a royal title). His younger brother Aristobulus II (together with his sons Alexander and Antigonus) did not, however, resign themselves to defeat in the struggle for power. An initial bid was made in 57 BCE by Alexander, who had escaped while being taken as a captive to Rome. The immediate cause was apparently the policy of restoration introduced by the new Roman governor Gabinius, who single-mindedly forced through the reconstruction and resettlement of the Greek cities destroyed by the Hasmoneans, and Alexander Jannaeus in particular. However, Alexander soon had to surrender in the fortress of Alexandrium, from where he was allowed free passage on condition that he surrender the Hasmonean fortresses of Hyrcania, Machaerus and Alexandrium.

Gabinius reformed the political status quo in Judaea:

> Gabinius next reinstated Hyrcanus in Jerusalem, entrusting him with the custody of the Temple, and set up a political system based on aristocracy. He divided the whole nation into five unions, one centred on Jerusalem, one on Gadara,[1] one under the protection of Amathus,[2] the fourth assigned to Jericho, and the fifth based on Sepphoris, a town in Galilee. Only too pleased to be freed from the domination of one man, the Jews were thenceforth ruled by an aristocracy.[3]

In practice, Gabinius' reforms meant the separation of the High Priesthood from the political administration, and thus a loss of power for Hyrcanus. The division of the land into five districts under the control of five separate aristocratic bodies (*synhodoi* or *synhedria*) weakened the central authority in favour of the rural aristocracy and was no doubt intended to make it easier to pursue Roman interests. While the aristocratically based constitution did not last long, the political disempowerment of the High Priest (which Hyrcanus' weak character made it easy to enforce) was to have grave consequences.

A second bid for power was made in 56 BCE by Aristobulus himself and his other son, Antigonus, who had managed to escape from Roman custody. Their venture was as unsuccessful as a further attempt by Alexander (in 55 BCE), but this rapid succession of initiatives by the Aristobulus family shows that they must have had numerous supporters in both Judaea (they managed to recruit an army in each case) and Rome (otherwise they would never have managed to escape).

With the outbreak of the civil wars in Italy (in 49 BCE), Judaea was treated more than ever as a plaything of the competing political interests in Rome. The first victims were Aristobulus and his son Alexander. Aristobulus, whom Caesar had set free in Rome in order to use him for his own purposes in Judaea, was poisoned while still in Rome by followers of Pompey, while Alexander was beheaded in Antioch on the orders of Pompey's father-in-law.

This left only the High Priest Hyrcanus and his nephew Antigonus, Aristobulus' surviving son, as contestants in the internal power struggle amongst the Jews. Hyrcanus had shown himself to be a weak personality right from the start. He was doubtless also more conservative and orthodox in his beliefs (and so closer to the Temple aristocracy) than Aristobulus, who inclined more to the Hellenistic ideal of kingship. It is one of history's ironies that it was precisely Hyrcanus who was to facilitate the rise to power of the family that, in the person of Herod, was to embody the acme of Hellenistic power structures in Palestine.

Hyrcanus' most important ally in the power struggle between himself and Aristobulus following the death of Salome Alexandra had been the Idumaean Antipater, who was married to a Nabataean and enjoyed good relations with the Nabataean king Aretas III. Antipater was *stratēgos* (military commander) of Idumaea, a district south of Jerusalem which had first been conquered and forcibly judaized under John Hyrcanus. Antipater continued to stand by Hyrcanus as events unfolded, although this was not so much because he was a faithful adherent of the latter's political line, but rather in order to use him as a means to achieve power in Palestine himself.

After the death of Pompey (in 48 BCE), Hyrcanus and his "henchman" Antipater had no alternative but to attempt to win the approval of Caesar. When Caesar came to Syria in 47 BCE, the two rival parties—Hyrcanus/Antipater and Antigonus—competed for his favour (just as in former times: in 64 BCE with Pompey's governor Scaurus, in 63 BCE with

Pompey himself). Caesar decided in favour of the Hyrcanus/Antipater team (probably by way of reward for the military support Antipater had given him in Alexandria)[4] and revised the measures implemented by Pompey and Gabinius. The political system in Judaea was now reformed for the third time in less than twenty years. In a series of decrees which come down to us through Josephus,[5] Caesar decided as follows:

1. Hyrcanus was appointed High Priest and ruler (*ethnarchēs*) of the people. Both offices were expressly conferred as hereditary titles. Associated with this was permission to collect the tithe and to live in accordance with "ancestral customs" (*kata ta patria ethē*). This latter did not imply the granting of self-government in the full sense, but applied to the right of jurisdiction in internal Jewish disputes.

2. Hyrcanus was awarded the honorary title "Ally and Friend of the Roman People". This title was also hereditary.

3. Hyrcanus was given permission to rebuild the walls of Jerusalem that had been demolished by Pompey. The city of Joppa was returned to him with its harbour, as well as the royal estates in the Plain of Jezreel and additional unspecified properties belonging to the kings of Syria and Phoenicia. This was of great importance economically, for with the important port of Joppa and the fertile Plain of Jezreel, Hyrcanus regained possession of a rich source of revenue. He was granted important privileges for the Jews of the Diaspora, especially those in Alexandria and Asia Minor.

4. The special position held by Antipater alongside Hyrcanus was confirmed. Antipater received Roman citizenship and the title "*epitropos* (= procurator) of Judaea". The associated official duties were not defined, but Antipater no doubt possessed the real military and political power.

5. The territory of Judaea was exempted from the obligation to furnish auxiliary troops and to provide quarters for the Roman army.

6. An annual tribute was payable for the city of Joppa and the right to levy customs duties there. An exception was made for the seventh year "wherein they neither plow nor take fruit from the trees". The tribute comprised a land tax (*tributum soli*) and a proportion of land and harbour taxes. The amount of this tribute is precisely specified: it came to 20,675 *modii*[6] of grain.[7]

7. And finally, an annual tribute was also to be levied for the territory of Judaea, likewise excluding the seventh year. The amount of this tribute was probably one quarter of the field crops.[8] Hyrcanus was officially responsible for delivery of the tribute (in the city of Sidon), but here too, real power probably lay in the hands of Antipater.

We can see from these various provisions that Caesar did not grant Judaea full autonomy. The tribute, externally a sign of subjection to a foreign power and internally an oppressive burden for the people, remained in force.

Nevertheless, Caesar's concessions were still considerable, and it has been rightly emphasized that, from the point of view of constitutional law, Judaea was *en route* to a status comparable to that of the "free cities exempt from taxation" (*civitates liberae et immunes*).

Antipater, who exercised the real power in the state, installed his two sons, Phasael and Herod, as military commanders (*stratēgoi*) of Jerusalem and Galilee. Herod gave an immediate sample of his talents as a ruler by capturing and executing a bandit chief or rebel leader (it is hard to distinguish between the two, which fact is characteristic of the social banditry of the time)[9] by the name of Ezekias/Hiskia in Galilee.[10] This immediately earned him the disapproval of the Jewish aristocracy, who saw it as an infringement (and rightly so, in terms of formal law) of the sole authority of the Synhedrion in Jerusalem to impose the death penalty. Moreover, Galilee was the stronghold of the Hasmoneans, and the Jerusalem aristocracy will have recognized the threat to the Hasmonean dynasty posed by this energetic family of Idumaean upstarts. Hyrcanus had to summon him before the Synhedrion in Jerusalem, where he only avoided being sentenced to death through the intervention of the Syrian governor, who then appointed him *stratēgos* of Coele-Syria and perhaps also Samaria shortly after his return to Galilee.[11] This was an indication of the shape of things to come: the upstart Herod began to assert himself against the established might of the Temple aristocracy with massive support from the Romans, who knew very well what talents were available here for exploitation for their own political purposes.

The intensifying power struggle in Rome had a direct influence on the fate of Palestine. Caesar was assassinated in 44 BCE, and C. Cassius, one of his assassins, went to Syria in order to establish a power base in the conflict with Mark Antony. Herod, together with his brother Phasael (their father Antipater had been murdered in 43 BCE), once more sided with the Romans, and gave energetic support to Cassius in extorting enormous taxes from Judaea:

> ... descending upon the cities, he [= Cassius] collected arms and soldiers from them, and imposed heavy tribute upon them. Worst of all was his treatment of Judaea, from which he extracted seven hundred talents of silver. But Antipater, seeing that affairs were in fearful disorder, apportioned the exacting of money and gave each of his sons a part to collect, and gave orders that some of it was to be raised by Malichus, who was hostile toward him, and the rest by others. And Herod, being the first to raise the sum set for him from Galilee, became especially friendly with Cassius. For he thought it prudent to court the Romans and secure their goodwill at the expense of others. But the officials of the other cities, every last man of them, were sold as slaves, and at that

time Cassius reduced to servitude four cities, of which the most important were Gophna and Emmaus, the others being Lydda and Thamna.[12]

This account is of particular interest for the system of tax collection under Antipater. Antipater was evidently operating here as a sort of "general tax farmer" in the same way as the Tobiad Joseph under the Ptolemies. He assigns the right to collect taxes to those close to him or independent subordinates, who can thereby ingratiate themselves with the occupying power (which Herod was particularly successful at doing). But unlike the system under both the Ptolemies and the Seleucids, the tax farmers are not held liable for the guaranteed tax revenue—the tribute of seven hundred silver talents is exorbitant in comparison with the tribute in the Seleucid period—but the municipal authorities, together with the total population of the cities. The four cities mentioned were all capitals of toparchies in Judaea; if, out of a total of eleven toparchies in Judaea,[13] four were unable to pay the required tribute and their population was sold into slavery, this shows the extent of the tax burden placed on the country under Cassius (and gives some indication of the means used by Herod to "get results").

Cassius' reign was not to last long. When Brutus and Cassius were defeated by Antony and Octavian in 42 BCE, the opposing parties in Judaea had to compete once again for the favour of the new rulers, and once again Herod (and Phasael) managed to outdo the Jewish aristocracy, especially as they still enjoyed the advocacy of Hyrcanus. Both were appointed tetrarchs of the Jewish territory under the nominal "sovereignty" of Hyrcanus as ethnarch.

In 40 BCE, there was a massive invasion by the Parthians—the Parthians were the constant opponents of Rome on the eastern border of the empire—who rapidly succeeded in overrunning the entire Near East. For Antigonus, Hyrcanus' and Herod's rival, the Parthians were opportune allies, and he succeeded in coming to power in Jerusalem with their help (against payment of a tribute of one thousand talents and five hundred women).[14] Hyrcanus and Phasael were taken prisoner, while Herod succeeded in fleeing to Rome after bringing his family to safety in the fortress of Masada. Phasael committed suicide, and Hyrcanus' ears were cut off to disqualify him from ever becoming High Priest again.

5.1.2. Mattathias Antigonus (40–37 BCE)

The brief interlude of his reign was to be the final attempt by the old Hasmonean aristocracy to attain power in Judaea. Like his Hasmonean predecessors, Antigonus had coins minted with the royal title. However, his rule could only be maintained while the Parthians were able to hold out against the Romans in the Near East, and this was never possible for long. Herod was officially appointed king of Judaea by the Roman Senate (in 40 BCE) and immediately set about reconquering Judaea (while the Romans fought against the Parthians).

The struggle for power between the two rivals, Antigonus and Herod, was not simply that of two competing pretenders to the throne, but was also a struggle between the representatives of two different world-views and the political systems based on these. Antigonus regarded himself as the sole legitimate king, with a customary right (*ethos*) to this kingdom on account of his membership of the Hasmonean family; in his eyes, Herod was, as an Idumaean, a mere "commoner" (*idiotēs*) and a "half-Jew" (*hēmiioudaios*) to boot, and thus totally unfit to be king.[15] This politico-religious difference also had a social dimension: Herod evidently recruited his supporters chiefly from the rich land-owning classes,[16] while the Hasmoneans relied for their support mainly on the rural population, who were unable to meet their tax demands.[17] This social opposition also expressed itself territorially, as Antigonus' supporters came from Judaea and the greater part of Galilee, while Herod's followers were, naturally enough, to be found primarily amongst the non-indigenous inhabitants of Idumaea and Samaria. The resistance to Herod was thus initially concentrated in Hasmonean Galilee. A typical example would be the bands of "brigands" rooted out by Herod from the caves of Arbela (west of Lake Gennesareth).[18]

Following Herod's conquest of Galilee, a decisive battle was fought near Bethel by Herod and one of Antigonus' generals, resulting in a victory for Herod. Antigonus' sphere of influence was thereby reduced to the immediate vicinity of Jerusalem, and Herod was able to embark upon the siege of Jerusalem in the spring of 37 BCE. During the siege, he made a brief visit to Samaria in order to marry Mariamme, Hyrcanus' grand-daughter (and thus a Hasmonean), no doubt not out of love, but for dynastic reasons: Herod was attempting to legitimate his claim on the royal title.

After the marriage, he turned his attentions once more to the siege of Jerusalem, now with the support of the governor of Syria (Sosius). The city fell after forty days. Antigonus was taken prisoner and beheaded in Antioch at Herod's instigation (according to all the contemporary sources, this was the first time that the Romans had imposed the death penalty on a king). Herod had great difficulty in ridding himself once more of his Roman allies and, above all, in preventing the plundering of Jerusalem, which could not be in his interests (he succeeded only by dispensing large gifts of money).[19] With Antigonus' execution, Hasmonean rule in Judaea had finally collapsed, and power had fallen into the hands of a usurper.

5.2. Government and economy under Herod

The Jewish state under Herod was a *kingdom* under Rome's auspices and was identical in every respect to other such client kingdoms under Roman sovereignty. Herod received the title of king, but only as a counter-move to Antigonus' appointment by the Parthians. His official status was that of a *rex socius et amicus populi Romani*, that is, a king who was the "ally and friend of the Roman people", similar to many other client kings. The legal basis for his kingship was his nomination by the Senate on Antony's recommendation (in 40 BCE), followed by confirmation by Octavian/Augustus after the battle of Actium (31 BCE). Unlike the Hasmoneans, there was no official treaty of alliance. His kingship was granted him only *ad personam* and for his lifetime, whereas Caesar had conferred the office of ethnarch on Hyrcanus as a hereditary title. According to Josephus,[20] Augustus had indeed granted him the right to nominate his successor, but he reserved the right to make the final decision himself, as events after Herod's death were to show. Herod's limited minting rights (he was allowed to mint only copper coins) were also in no way different from those of other client kings of Rome. Apart from the tribute, the most important aspect of his political dependency on Rome was the fact that he was not allowed to have an independent foreign policy: that is, he could not sign treaties with foreign rulers or conduct wars without the consent of Rome.

On the other hand, the Romans gave him a totally free hand in internal affairs, and in this respect Herod could rule with unlimited authority. But it was not so much the power of the ruler over the people (Hyrcanus and Antipater were also largely independent as regards domestic policy), but rather the legal status of the people which had undergone a radical transformation with the accession of Herod to the throne. In appointing Herod king, the Romans put an end to the alliance between the Roman and the Jewish peoples which had obtained since the first treaty of friendship between Judas Maccabeus and the Roman Senate as the representatives of their respective nations. The Jewish people was no longer recognized as a distinct political entity by the Romans or by Herod, the representative of Roman state power; it ceased to be "a negotiating party in their own right *vis-à-vis* the Roman people".[21] This new power relation affected all areas of public life, manifesting itself most clearly in a complex control apparatus for purposes of state security (secret police and informer network) and in the oath of loyalty which Herod demanded of all his subjects.[22]

The *armed forces* certainly constituted one of the main pillars of Herod's system of government. As had already been the case under the Hasmoneans, Jews served in his army alongside foreign mercenaries, but there were also non-Jewish mercenaries from the territories under his control (who were apparently given preference). Herod seems to have intentionally settled the non-Jewish mercenaries in enclosed city centres[23] to act as a counterbalance to the Jewish population, who were not very well-disposed towards him. He possibly also preferred to recruit the civil service bureaucracy from these circles.

Herod also adopted the structures of *public administration* from his Hasmonean predecessors, which had themselves been based on the forms of organization put in place by the Seleucids and the Ptolemies. The Jewish part of the kingdom was divided into toparchies, of which Josephus specifies eleven for Judaea proper: Jerusalem, Gophna, Acrabata, Thamna, Lydda, Emmaus, Pella (= Beth Netofah?), Idumaea (= west Idumaea with the capital, Marisa), En-Gedi (= east Idumaea), Herodium and Jericho.[24] Galilee was probably divided into five toparchies and the Jewish Transjordan into three, giving a total of nineteen toparchies under Herod.

Although we possess practically no information regarding the organization of the bureaucracy, there was probably a toparch (*toparchēs*) at the head of the toparchy, as well as comarchs at the head of the individual villages, which formed the smallest administrative units. Their administrative staff included local and village clerks (*topogrammateis* and *kōmogrammateis*), who would have played an important role in the compilation of tax rolls. Above the toparch was a royal official (*stratēgos*), who was directly responsible to the king for supervision of the civil and military administration.

By way of contrast, the administrative structure of the non-Jewish part of Herod's kingdom seems to have been oriented largely towards the organizational form inherited from the Hellenistic *poleis* with their associated estates (*chōra* = *territorium*). The non-Jewish territories were therefore probably divided according to their respective municipalities, and the official designation of the administrative unit (as distinct from the Jewish toparchy) was probably the *meris*. The most important of these municipal districts would have been Gaza, Anthedon, Joppa, Caesarea, Sebaste, Gadara and Hippus; nothing, however, is known about the administrative structure of the large regions in the north-east of the kingdom (Auranitis, Trachonitis, Batanaea and Gaulanitis). At the head of the municipal districts would have stood a meridarch (*meridarchēs*), to whom, as in the toparchies, was attached a governor answerable only to the king (perhaps with the title of *archōn*). There can be no doubt that the entire organization of the administration in both the Jewish and non-Jewish parts of the kingdom was tailored to the person of the king, who effectively controlled the bureaucratic apparatus and concentrated all the important decision-making powers in his hands.

The degree to which the exercise of power was oriented to the person of the king can be seen particularly clearly in the *judicial system*. With Herod's appointment as king, the constitutional basis of the state was changed so that the traditional "laws of the fathers" no longer formed the basis of the legal system, but the laws of the Roman empire: the Torah was replaced by Roman law. As a consequence, the powers of legal supervision formerly exercized by the "autonomous" Jewish body, the Synhedrion, now passed to Herod. To be sure, Herod did not dare to dissolve the Synhedrion, but its influence was totally undermined (he had most of its members executed upon coming to power). Wherever he could, that is, wherever it would not cause open revolt, Herod intervened in the administration of justice and attempted to enforce Roman or Hellenistic legal norms. Josephus reports one such example of Herod's legal practice, which can surely stand for many similar cases:

> In his administration of the state the king in an earnest effort to put a stop to the successive acts of injustice committed both in the city and in the country made a law in no way resembling earlier ones, and he enforced it himself. It provided that housebreakers should be sold (into slavery) and be deported from the kingdom—a punishment that not only weighed heavily upon those who suffered it but also involved a violation of the laws of the country[25] [laws of their fathers].

The case in question is that of a debtor (house-breaker) who, according to biblical law, could at most be sold only to a Jewish master, which meant he would only serve as a slave for a limited period of time.[26] Inasmuch as Herod here decrees that slaves should be sold abroad, he puts himself in direct opposition to the law of the Torah. The "arrogance of a tyrant" which Josephus sees at work here is hardly mere political despotism, but possibly a deliberate attempt to get rid of internal political opponents.

For special legal cases, that is, those involving the security of the state, Herod also set up his own courts. Such were probably those courts consisting of "friends and relatives of the king" which find frequent mention in Josephus, apparently constituted on the model of the Roman "family courts" and over which Herod personally presided as *pater familias*, as it were.

Herod was also totally autonomous in the *fiscal administration* of his kingdom. The country was essentially the property of the emperor, who had given it to Herod to hold in usufruct. The private property of Herod in the narrow sense was immense. Apart from a huge fortune in cash, which he evidently used for profitable business transactions and which he needed for numerous and generous gifts, he also presided over his family's estates in Idumaea. The most important part of his assets, however, was the property he had seized from the Hasmoneans and his political opponents. As legal successor to the Hasmoneans, he owned the fertile former royal estates, which meant that Herod was undoubtedly the biggest landowner in the realm.

The sources provide little information regarding the state's tax revenues. We know that, like his predecessors, Herod had to pay a *tribute* to Rome. The exact amount is uncertain, but it would have been considerable and was, perhaps, already linked in Herod's time to a general obligation to register, that is, to a *census*. It was raised through a variety of taxes, part of the proceeds from these being paid over to Rome. The individual taxes were as follows:

1. *Poll tax*: This was customary under the Seleucids, was abolished by the first Hasmoneans, and then probably reintroduced under Jannaeus. It was probably based on the inhabitants' movable property, which was assessed and one percentage of its value paid over.[27]

2. *Land tax*: The land tax was raised in two ways: as a tax on real estate (*tributum soli*), usually paid in cash, and as a tax on earnings, a proportional tax on produce which was paid in kind. The exact amount is not known. It may have been a quarter of the crops as under Caesar, or a third as under the Seleucids (although this is unlikely). We do not know whether a distinction was made between the royal farmers and the "free" peasantry, but it is doubtful whether there was a free peasantry under Herod, as the king controlled the greater part of the land.

3. The lucrative *salt tax* was likewise already levied by the Seleucids, abolished by the Hasmoneans and very probably reintroduced by Herod.

4. The same applies for the *wreath tax* (*aurum coronarium*), which had evolved over time from a voluntary donation into an obligatory tax.

5. The same applies for the *turnover tax* for traders and businessmen.

6. A *house tax* was possibly introduced by Herod.

7. One of the most important sources of revenue lay in the *customs duties*, which were levied by all the rulers, including the Hasmoneans, and which took the form of mainland and transit duties as well as harbour charges. As the municipal region was divided into a number of customs districts at each of whose "borders" duties were imposed, the internal customs duties were particularly lucrative for the state and correspondingly burdensome for commerce. Moreover, the duties were often very high: a tariff rate of 25% on goods value was apparently not uncommon.

Like the taxes, the customs duties were initially leased to Roman tax farmers (*publicani*), and probably since Gabinius were collected directly by the state and its representatives. Herod seems to have reintroduced the system of local and indigenous tax and duty farmers (*telōnai*), a familiar feature of

Ptolemaic and Seleucid government which we encounter in its heyday in the New Testament, and which earned the "publicans"[28] the loathing of the people.

In addition to the customs duties, tolls and groundage were no doubt charged for the use of roads and ports.

Upon taking office, Herod would certainly have been confronted with a desperate *economic situation*. As a predominantly agrarian country, Palestine was reliant on a flourishing agricultural economy to support the (growing) population. The policy of conquest carried out by the Hasmoneans had led to a substantial increase in the amount of land under cultivation, but this development had suffered a reversal through the cession of territory under Pompey and the re-Hellenization of the cities under Gabinius, resulting in the impoverishment of large sections of the rural population. Herod no doubt recognized that an effective taxation policy depended on the economic productivity of the population. He therefore used the various additional territories he had been granted for purposes of increased productivity. In particular, he seems to have settled peasants who had lost their land in the large Transjordanian territories in the eastern part of his kingdom. A good example of such development of fallow areas is the establishment of the city of Phasaelis in the lower Jordan valley,[29] whose estates eventually became the most fertile in the whole of Palestine. So it would be unfair to accuse Herod of unbridled exploitation of the people, as, through his large-scale development projects, he certainly did a considerable amount to increase agricultural production and thereby the prosperity of the population. There are therefore good grounds for believing "that at the end of the Herodian era the economic situation of the people was sounder than at the beginning".[30]

5.3. A summary of the events of Herod's reign

Upon his appointment as king in 37 BCE, Herod's initial concern was to consolidate his power. His most significant domestic opponents were the Hasmonean family and the traditional power structures connected with the Hasmoneans, above all the office of High Priest and the aristocracy; abroad, his main enemy was Cleopatra, the queen of Egypt, who had a close relationship with Herod's patron, Mark Antony.

Herod's first offensive was aimed at the rich aristocratic families that had supported Antigonus. Immediately after taking Jerusalem, he "killed forty-five of the leading men of Antigonus' party" and confiscated their property.[31] At the same time, the aristocratic members of the Synhedrion were apparently executed, thereby practically eliminating the most important institution of the aristocracy.[32] However, according to Josephus, the Pharisees were spared, as they had advised capitulation during the seige of Jerusalem.[33] As the Pharisees were popular with the people, Herod may also have hoped to use them to win the people over.

The most important power base of the Hasmoneans was undoubtedly the High Priesthood, which always stood in a strained relationship to the office of king. As Herod received his legitimation solely by virtue of the kingship conferred upon him by Rome, and as a "foreigner" could never have become High Priest, it was only logical that he should devalue the office of High Priest. Consequently, soon after coming to power, he appointed as High Priest a certain Ananel from an unknown priestly family from Babylon (or possibly Egypt?). In so doing, he passed over the rightful claim of the Hasmonean Aristobulus, the younger brother of his wife, Mariamme. Indeed, as members of the priestly class of Joiarib, and thus non-Zadokites, the Hasmoneans also had no entitlement to the office of High Priest if strict traditional criteria were applied, but the office had been in the Hasmonean family since Jonathan the Maccabee, that is, for about a hundred and twenty years, and they may well have acquired as much legitimacy in the eyes of the "pious" as had formerly been accorded solely to the Zadokites (and certainly more than a High Priest who owed his appointment solely to Herod's patronage). When Alexandra, Aristobulus' mother, protested against this open affront to the Hasmonean family—whether she even, as Josephus claims,[34] conspired with Cleopatra and Antony in Egypt must remain an open question—Herod realized that he had acted too quickly and stood in danger of causing unrest amongst the people, whereupon he removed Ananel from office and appointed Aristobulus High Priest. He, too, was not to last long in office. During the first Feast of Tabernacles at which he officiated as High Priest (probably in 36 BCE), the people seem to have shown their sympathy for the legitimate offspring of the Hasmoneans all too openly, despite the fact that, according to Josephus, "it would have been more advisable, out of regard for Herod, to have shown greater restraint in expressing their gratitude for the benefits which they had received".[35] Herod realized that Aristobulus could develop into a serious rival for power, and had him murdered immediately after the Feast of Tabernacles:

> When the festival was over and they were being entertained at Jericho as the guest of Alexandra, he [= Herod] showed great friendliness to the youth and led him on to a safe place, and he was ready to join in his play and to act like a young man in order to please him. But as the place was naturally very hot, they soon went out in a group for a stroll, and stood beside the swimming-pools, of which there were several large ones around the palace,

and cooled themselves off from the excessive heat of noon. At first they watched some of the servants and friends (of Herod) as they swam, and then, at Herod's urging, the youth was induced (to join them). But with darkness coming on while he swam, some of the friends, who had been given orders to do so, kept pressing him down and holding him under water as if in sport, and they did not let up until they had quite suffocated him. In this manner was Aristobulus done away with when he was at most eighteen years old and had held the high priesthood for a year. This office Ananel again obtained for himself.[36]

Aristobulus' murder put an end to the succession to the office of High Priest within one privileged family. By ensuring that the office was no longer hereditary and for life, Herod (like the Seleucid kings) turned it into an instrument of his domestic policy and reduced the High Priest to a mere religious official "dependent on the whim and will of the king".[37] He took the High Priest's robes into his personal safe-keeping, thereby setting a fateful precedent which the Romans were to exploit after his death to justify their right of disposition over the High Priest's vestments.[38]

The most important outside threat to his rule was Cleopatra, the queen of Egypt. As successor to the Ptolemies, she made a legal claim on Palestine and wanted to reinstate the old Ptolemaic rule over "Syria and Phoenicia". Through her liaison with Mark Antony, she was able to achieve at least partial success: Herod had to cede Gaza to her and, most importantly, Jericho, a territory which was especially lucrative due to its palm and balsam plantations (34 BCE), and then lease them back from her for a no doubt considerable sum.[39] Josephus reports that she even attempted to seduce Herod during a visit to Judaea so that she could denounce him subsequently to Mark Antony.[40] It is difficult to determine whether this is merely an attempt to add to the well-known legend created around Cleopatra. What seems certain, however, is that Cleopatra was by no means satisfied with the cession of Gaza and Jericho and hoped to succeed Herod if he were to fall from grace with Antony. When war broke out between Antony and Octavian in 32 BCE, she ensured (for this reason) that Herod could not come to the assistance of his master (and thus put the latter in his debt in the event of Antony's victory), but instead had to wage war on the Nabataeans, who owed Cleopatra rent.

This intrigue of Cleopatra proved to be Herod's salvation. The war against the Nabataeans saved him from going into battle on the losing side, and made it easier for him to go over to Octavian following the latter's victory over Antony on the 2nd of September, 31 BCE, at the battle of Actium. Before going to Rhodes to meet Octavian, he took the precaution of having the aged Hyrcanus killed, thereby eliminating the last remaining Hasmonean who might have posed a threat to him as a possible rival for Octavian's favour. In Rhodes, he managed to convince Octavian of his unconditional loyalty to Rome (to which end his victory over the Nabataeans certainly also contributed), and the latter confirmed his appointment as king of Judaea in the spring of 30 BCE.[41] When Herod met Octavian again following the suicide of Antony and Cleopatra in August 30 BCE in Alexandria, Octavian granted extensive additions to Jewish territory. He returned Gaza and Jericho, that is, both the territories that Antony had given to Cleopatra, and in addition gave Herod the cities of Anthedon, Joppa and Straton's Tower on the coastal plain—with Gaza and Joppa, he possessed the two most important ports in Palestine, and he himself was soon to develop Straton's Tower, now renamed Caesarea, into one of the largest ports in the Mediterranean—as well as Samaria and the cities of Gadara and Hippus in Transjordan, which Pompey had himself severed from the Hasmonean empire.[42]

Following the meeting with Octavian, Herod added the name of his own wife, Mariamme, to the long list of murdered Hasmoneans. The circumstances surrounding her execution remain obscure. Before departing for the meeting with Augustus, Herod had left Mariamme in the care of a certain Soemus, with (according to Joseph) instructions to kill her if he did not return safely from Augustus. Mariamme, who had found this out, did not show any particular enthusiasm for this extreme love upon his return, especially as it was now the second time this was said to have occurred; and indeed, Josephus recounts a similar story when Herod was summoned to Antony following the murder of Aristobulus and was likewise unsure whether he would come safely out of the affair.[43] Herod's sister and mother, for whom the proud Hasmonean had long been a thorn in their side, fanned the flames of suspicion by spreading rumours that Mariamme was guilty of marital infidelity and had also attempted to have Herod murdered. Herod had Soemus executed immediately (as he had betrayed his "secret instructions" to Mariamme), and had his wife put on trial and then likewise executed (in 29 BCE).[44]

Precisely this duplication of events (and the fact that the second story does not appear in the parallel account in the *Bellum*) has led many historians to cast doubt on the historical veracity of the second story. This would then leave no apparent reason for Mariamme's execution. However, Mariamme seems to have been the victim of Herod's almost pathological distrust of the Hasmonean family, which did not stop even at his own wife, despite the fact that, according to Josephus, he genuinely loved her. At any event, after her death he indulged in wild excesses which made him seriously ill. His mother-in-law, Alexandra, tried to avail herself of this opportunity to make provisions for the event of his non-recovery. However, Herod did recover and immediately (in 28 BCE) ordered the execution of Alexandra, who had indeed been the *spiritus rector* of most of the intrigues against him.

After executing the most important members of the Hasmonean aristocracy, Herod had plenty of scope to consolidate his power internally. The following years—from about 25 to 13 BCE—represent the heyday of Herod's reign. He embarked on an extravagant building programme, which—together with development of the communications network—undoubtedly also boosted the country's economy. In Jerusalem, he built the Antonia fortress at the north-west corner of the Temple, named in honour of Mark Antony, as well as a theatre, an amphitheatre, a new royal palace and, last but not least, the Temple itself, one of the most magnificent buildings of the ancient world. The building work in Jerusalem gave rise to a class of skilled workers who were faced with unemployment following the completion of the Temple under Agrippa II, so that Agrippa had the city paved with marble as a job creation scheme.[45] Herod also founded or rebuilt numerous cities, fortresses and palaces, including the cities of Samaria/Sebaste (in honour of Augustus), Straton's Tower/Caesarea with its great harbour, which was of outstanding economic significance (and which also had a temple of Augustus), Antipatris in honour of his father, Phasaelis in honour of his brother, Anthedon/Agrippium in honour of Agrippa, Gaba in west Galilee (like Sebaste, a city of military veterans); the fortresses and palaces of Alexandrium, Machaerus, Hyrcania, Masada, Herodium (south of Jerusalem, built in his own honour and later to be his burial place), Jericho (rebuilding of the former palace of the Hasmoneans at Wadi Qelt). And finally, he also proved to be a generous patron of Hellenistic culture, erecting numerous buildings in Greek cities outside his kingdom (including temples), building aqueducts, dedicating woods and parks, paving public areas with marble, donating religious offerings and even financing the Olympic games.[46]

Herod maintained excellent relations with his overlord, that is, with Octavian/Augustus in particular. He visited Augustus on a number of occasions and sent his sons Alexander and Aristobulus to Rome to be educated. He was friendly with the general Agrippa, son-in-law and friend of Augustus. Agrippa even visited him in Jerusalem (in 15 BCE) and offered up a sacrifice in the Temple. Augustus rewarded the faithful vassal of Rome with an additional large gift, the incorporation into Herod's kingdom of the large Transjordanian territories of Trachonitis, Batanaea and Auranitis. His good relations with Rome even allowed him to intervene on a number of occasions on behalf of the Jews in the Diaspora (that is, outside his own jurisdiction).

The last years of Herod's reign (from about 13 to 4 BCE) are characterized above all by struggles over the succession within his own family. His attempt to marry into the Hasmonean aristocracy backfired on him as the offspring of the various branches of his family could not get on with each other either (particularly the "Hasmonean" and the "Idumaean" branches). Herod had ten wives in all, by whom he had numerous sons. The most important are:

— his first wife, Doris, son Antipater: both of them were banished;
— his second wife, Mariamme (Hyrcanus' granddaughter), sons Alexander and Aristobulus (a third son died in Rome);
— his third wife, Mariamme (daughter of a priest from Alexandria, whom he made High Priest), son Herod;
— his fourth wife, Malthace (a Samaritan), sons Archelaus and Antipas;
— his fifth wife, Cleopatra (from Jerusalem), son Philip.

In 18 or 17 BCE, Herod went in person to Rome where Alexander and Aristobulus, the sons of the Hasmonean Mariamme, were being educated and brought them home to live at the court in Jerusalem in preparation for the succession. All did not go well, however, especially as Herod's sister, Salome, was doing her best to stir up the old rivalry between the Hasmoneans and the Idumaeans and was so intent on regarding them both as would-be avengers of their mother, Mariamme, that Herod began to believe it himself and his sons to behave accordingly. Consequently, he restored his eldest son, Antipater, to favour in order to provide a counterbalance against them. Antipater in turn did everything he could to undermine domestic harmony between Herod and Alexander and Aristobulus, until Herod finally accused them both of high treason before Augustus. The two parties were initially reconciled (on Augustus' advice), but this was to be followed by a lengthy succession of mutual recriminations and brief reconciliations, until finally both sons were executed (probably in 7 BCE) following an official trial (in Samaria/Sebaste, where Herod had married their mother, Mariamme).[47]

The eldest son, Antipater, now believed the question of the succession had been resolved in his favour, but was unable to bide his time until the seventy-year-old Herod died. He conspired with Herod's brother Pheroras and was imprisoned. But Herod's days were also numbered. He became seriously ill and vainly sought a cure in the warm springs at Callirrhoe east of the Jordan. Nevertheless, he was still active enough five days before his death to have Antipater executed immediately upon receiving permission from Rome.[48] He himself died probably just before the Feast of Passover in 4 BCE and was buried in the fortress of Herodium near Bethlehem, which he had built himself.[49]

5.4. Assessment

A balanced assessment of such a dynamic and complex personality as Herod would be an almost impossible undertaking, so I shall single out just a few of the most important factors which must be taken into consideration.

First of all, there is the irrefutable fact that, in the eyes of his Jewish subjects, he was a usurper who had destroyed the legitimate dynasty of the Hasmoneans in order to grab power for himself. This is certainly true, but just as certainly does not represent the whole picture. If one considers how greatly the last Hasmoneans were hated by the "pious", how their Hellenistic kingdom was regarded as a perversion of all the old ideals (including those of the Maccabees), then any comparison with the Hasmoneans cannot avoid a certain irony. The Hasmoneans, at least towards the end, were hardly less influenced by the ideal of Hellenistic kingship than Herod.

However, there can be no doubt that Herod took this ideal to its peak of development in Palestine. Although a Jew (but to his enemies a recently converted proselyte), he was by nature and inclination a Hellenist, comparable to the Hellenists under Antiochus IV Epiphanes and the Tobiad family who provoked the Maccabean revolt (and it is one of the ironies of history that the rebels themselves ultimately came to embody that against which they had revolted). Evidence of these Hellenistic tendencies can be found in the buildings and temples he donated to Greek cities. According to Josephus, he also erected a theatre and an amphitheatre in Jerusalem, which in themselves would have been provocation enough in the eyes of the "pious" (although no archaeological evidence of these has been produced so far). He surrounded himself at court with Greeks and men steeped in Greek culture. The most famous of these was Nicolaus of Damascus, author of a history of the world which has only come down to us through Josephus, who made extensive use of it in his own works.

The most important traditional pillars of the Jewish religion and the Jewish state, the Synhedrion and the office of High Priest, were exploited by him purely for his own purposes. The role of the Synhedrion was cut back to such an extent that its continued existence was hardly more than nominal, and he appointed and dismissed the High Priests at his own discretion. His preferred candidates came mostly from the Diaspora, clearly a tactic aimed at curtailing the political influence of the old aristocratic Sadducee families.

In all his enthusiasm for Greek culture and civilization, he was nevertheless careful not to overstep certain bounds of the Jewish religion. He was, for instance, anxious to ensure that he did not overly offend the party of the Pharisees, who enjoyed widespread support amongst the populace. It is also a striking fact that no human images were featured on his coins. Similarly, he largely avoided affixing images to public buildings in Jerusalem; the eagle on the Temple facade mentioned by Josephus was rightly regarded as sacrilegious by the Pharisees. And when Syllaeus the Nabataean wished to marry his sister Salome, Herod is said to have demanded that he first convert to Judaism, thus effectively preventing the marriage taking place.

In economic matters, too, he seems to have done a lot for the country's development. To be sure, he was unremitting in his imposition of taxes (he would otherwise hardly have been in a position to finance his extensive undertakings and generous donations), but he also endeavoured to improve and develop the country's agriculture. This policy of land reclamation was furthered by his founding of a number of cities, although power politics was also an important factor here (the settlement of mercenaries, the dissemination of Hellenistic culture).

All in all, enforced "Hellenization" is probably the most outstanding characteristic of his reign. This may be judged negatively or positively according to one's point of view. What is certain is that his reign provided his people with a period of relative peace, and that he was able to manage the difficult and complex relationship with his Roman overlord in such a way as to preserve at least a modicum of national Jewish identity (and probably as much as could be salvaged under the circumstances). This is far too little for those who want everything, of course, but later events would show where the politics of an unconditional "all or nothing" would lead. What cannot be denied is that Herod's reign was the last significant period of limited Jewish autonomy—until the founding of the State of Israel.

Notes

1. The identity of this city is disputed. Some read "Gazara", that is, Gezer in north–west Judaea, others "Adora" (in Idumaea).
2. East of the Jordan.
3. Bell. I, 8.5 § 169 f.; cf. Ant. XIV, 5.4 § 90 f.
4. Ant. XIV, 8.1 § 127 f.
5. Ant. XIV, 8.5 §§ 143–148; Ant. XIV, 10.2–7 §§ 190–212.
6. A *modius* amounted to about 8.7 l, so that the annual tribute for Joppa was approx. 179,872.50 l of grain.
7. The tribute for Joppa is based on a specific reading of the disputed §§ 202 and 206 in Josephus: cf. the detailed discussion in Schalit, Herodes, pp. 777–781.
8. This passage (§ 203) is also disputed. I follow Schalit, Herodes, p. 780, in interpreting the phrase *tō deuterō etei* as "in the following year", i.e. in the year after the sabbatical year exempted from the tribute. However, unlike Schalit, I see no

reason to conclude from this that the tribute in the year subsequent to the sabbatical year was higher than usual (namely, a quarter of the crops) and that one can infer from this that the "normal" tribute was about one fifth (Schalit, Herodes, p. 780 and p. 149). The tribute payable in the post–sabbatical year is the "normal" tribute, and this was considerable (even if less than under the Seleucids).

9. See p. 109 below.
10. Ant. XIV, 9.2 § 159.
11. Ant. XIV, 9.3–5 § 163 ff.
12. Ant. XIV, 11.2 §§ 272–275.
13. See p. 88 below.
14. Ant. XIV, 13.3 § 331.
15. Ant. XIV, 15.2 § 403.
16. Ant. XIV, 13.3 § 345; XIV, 15.10 § 450.
17. Ant. XIV, 15.5 §§ 420–430.
18. Ant. XIV, 15.5 §§ 421–430. Of note here are not only the military tactics, which we shall encounter frequently, but also the typological narration of the episode by Josephus: Herod's magnanimous behaviour, self-sacrifice and fanaticism of the Jews (the wife of the elderly "brigand" with her seven sons is an inversion of the mother and her seven sons who resisted Antiochus IV Epiphanes!), equation of "brigands" with patriots, etc.
19. Ant. XIV, 16.1–4 § 468 ff.
20. Ant. XV, 10.1 § 343; Bell. I, 23.3 § 454 and *passim*.
21. Schalit, Herodes, p. 225.
22. Ant. XV, 10.4 §§ 368–371.
23. Cf. the redevelopment of Samaria/Sebaste, Ant. XV, 8.5 § 296 f.
24. Bell. III, 3.8 §§ 54–56; cf. Pliny, Nat. Hist. V, 14.70.
25. Ant. XVI, 1.1 §§ 1–5.
26. Cf. Deut. 15:12.
27. Cf. Appianus, Syr. 50.
28. The "publicans" in the New Testament are therefore tax and duty farmers who were liable with their assets for the fixed revenues from taxes and customs duties, and could credit any surplus as profit. See also p. 107 below.
29. Ant. XVI, 5.2 § 145.
30. Schalit, Herodes, p. 328.
31. Ant. XV, 1.2 §§ 5–7; Bell. 129, 18.4 § 358.
32. Ant. XIV, 9.4 § 175.
33. Ant. XV, 1.1 § 3.
34. Ant. XV, 2.6 §§ 25–30; Bell. I, 22.3 § 439.
35. Ant. XV, 3.3 § 52.
36. Ant. XV, 3.3 §§ 53–56.
37. Schalit, Herodes, p. 312.
38. Ant. XV, 11.4 § 403 f.
39. Ant. XV, 4.2 § 96.
40. Ant. XV, 4.2 §§ 97–99.
41. Ant. XV, 6.6–7 § 187 ff.
42. Ant. XV, 7.3 § 217; Bell. I, 20.3 § 396.
43. Ant. XV, 3.5–9 § 62 ff.
44. Ant. XV, 7.1–6 § 202 ff.

45. Ant. XX, 9.7 §§ 219–222.
46. Bell. I, 21.11 f. §§ 422–428; Ant. XVI, 5.3 §§ 146–149
47. Ant. XVI, 11.7 §§ 392–394.
48. Ant. XVII, 7.1 §§ 182–187.
49. Ant. XVII, 8.1 § 191; 8.3 § 196 ff.

6. FROM HEROD TO THE FIRST JEWISH WAR

6.1. The settlement of the succession

In his last will and testament, Herod had decreed that Archelaus, the eldest son of his fourth wife Malthace (the Samaritan), was to inherit the title of king, while his brother Antipas, Malthace's younger son, was to become tetrarch of Galilee and Peraea, and Philip, the son of his fifth wife, Cleopatra the Jerusalemite, would be tetrarch of Gaulanitis, Trachonitis, Batanaea and Paneas. As was only to be expected, upon his death the brothers quarrelled over the inheritance and argued their claims before Augustus in Rome. At the same time, a number of disturbances and revolts broke out in Palestine, which were brutally suppressed by the governor of Syria, Varus. These signal the beginning of a long period of unrest which led almost inevitably to the great war with Rome. The centre of unrest was in the north, in Galilee and Peraea. In Galilee, a certain Judas (the son of Ezekias, with whom Herod had already had dealings) organized a band of guerillas who terrorized the whole of Galilee;[1] in Peraea, one of Herod's former slaves by the name of Simon proclaimed himself king;[2] and finally, the same was also reported by Josephus of a former shepherd by the name of Athronges who, together with his four brothers, terrorized all of Judaea.[3] What all these movements had in common was the obvious fact that they did not emanate from the cities but from the rural population, and that their various leaders laid claim to the title of king. So we may infer that the troublemakers who Josephus contemptuously dismisses as "bands of brigands" were in fact radical social-Messianic groups with strong support amongst the rural populace:

> And so Judaea was filled with brigandage. Anyone might make himself king as the head of a band of rebels whom he fell in with, and then would press on to the destruction of the community, causing trouble to few Romans and then only to a small degree but bringing the greatest slaughter upon their own people.[4]

Meanwhile, Augustus hesitated for some time before settling the dispute over the succession. He allowed all the parties concerned to present their cases (including a delegation from the people who requested Augustus to deliver them from the whole Herodian clan and place the country under the direct control of Rome),[5] but ultimately decided to substantially endorse Herod's will:[6]

> *Archelaus* received Judaea, Samaria and Idumaea (the cities of Gaza, Gadara and Hippus were added to the province of Syria) and the title of ethnarch, not king;

> *Antipas* received Galilee and Peraea and the title of tetrarch;

> *Philip* received Batanaea, Trachonitis, Auranitis, Gaulanitis and perhaps also Ituraea,[7] as well as the title of tetrarch.

I shall now deal with each of the individual regions separately according to the territorial division of Palestine under the three heirs.

6.2. Philip (4 BCE–33/34 CE)

The regions that Philip received constituted anything but a Jewish heartland. They were all latterday additions to the Jewish territories and had a mixed population in which Syrians and Greeks were predominant. There is nothing much to report about Philip's reign. He was evidently the most peaceable of Herod's sons, and Josephus can find nothing negative to say about him. Like Herod, he loved building and redeveloped two cities, Paneas = Caesarea (Philippi) and Bethsaida (north of Lake Gennesareth) = Julias (in honour of Augustus' daughter). He was absolutely loyal to the Romans and reigned, apparently with the approval of his subjects, in full exercise of his powers as a Hellenistic potentate. That he could do so without any resistance was probably due to the fact that the "heathens" formed the majority of the population in his territory, so that it attracted little interest from the "pious" Jews. He was able to mint coins, for example, bearing images of Augustus and Tiberius without encountering any objection.

After his death, his territory was added to the Roman province of Syria, but soon (in 37 CE under Caligula) was allotted once more to a Herodian (Agrippa).

6.3. Herod Antipas (4 BCE–39 CE)

Herod Antipas—the Herod of the New Testament—had received Galilee and Peraea (that is, without the cities of the Decapolis). Of all the sons, he remained truest to type in respect of his father's negative qualities (cunning, ambitious, a lover of luxury); the New Testament[8] calls him a "fox". He rebuilt Sepphoris and founded Tiberias (named after the emperor Tiberius) as his capital. The fact that he chose the city solely on grounds of his own personal prefence (proximity to the warm springs of Hammath) without consideration of the fact that it was situated on an ancient burial ground did not exactly endear him to his orthodox Jewish subjects. He had to colonize the city by force, which resulted in a very mixed population of pagans and Jews. Tiberias was built entirely on the Hellenistic model: a stadium, a splendid palace (decorated with animal images), a city council (*boulē*) with a council of elders, but also a magnificent synagogue. Like Herod before him, he did not dare to enter into open conflict with traditional Judaism and so, for instance, avoided the use of images on his coins.

Antipas' undoing was his wife Herodias, the daughter of Aristobulus (who had been executed in 7 BCE) and the wife of his half-brother Herod (one of the second Mariamme's sons). In order to marry her, he divorced his first wife. As she was the daughter of Aretas, the king of the Nabataeans and a long-standing enemy of the eastern borders of the empire, this led to complications in foreign relations and finally resulted in war in 36 CE, which ended in total defeat for Antipas.

Internally, he was also faced with mounting opposition from a largely orthodox population. The appearance of John the Baptist in Peraea is symptomatic. Josephus[9] explains the enmity between the two as being due above all to Antipas' fear of John's political influence on the people, while according to the New Testament,[10] John was said to have denounced Antipas' unlawful marriage to Herodias. Both factors probably played a part, but the danger of political unrest would certainly have been the most important consideration. At any rate, Antipas had John imprisoned in the fortress of Machaerus and executed. Josephus and the New Testament do not agree on this either: according to Josephus, John appears to have been executed immediately, while according to the New Testament, Antipas was initially hesitant and only sentenced him to death following an intrigue by Herodias.[11]

It was likewise during Antipas' reign that Jesus first appeared in Galilee (whom Antipas, stricken by a bad conscience, initially thought was John risen from the dead).[12] According to Luke's Gospel, Antipas was in Jerusalem for the Passover festival when Jesus was taken prisoner and condemned to death.

As Jesus came from Galilee, Pilate (the Roman procurator) handed him over to Antipas for sentencing. Antipas, however, sent him back to Pilate and left it to him to pronounce the death sentence.[13]

The emergence of John the Baptist and Jesus must certainly be seen in the context of the social and political upheavals at the beginning of the first century CE. Whether and to what extent early Christianity can be understood as a Zealot movement similar to other social-Messianic movements[14] is a matter of dispute. They certainly have much in common, such as the emphasis on social factors in Jesus' sermons, the disdain for familial ties, the demand for unconditional self-sacrifice and even martyrdom, the pronounced mood of apocalyptic expectation in the earliest sections of the Gospels, as well as the strained relations with the Roman authorities clearly evident in many passages. On the other hand, the ready recourse to violence and political assassination that characterizes the (later) Zealots is certainly not a feature of the New Testament, just as the radical New Testament ethics of love is hardly to be reconciled with the ideology of the Zealots. It should also be borne in mind that, the further away we get from the beginnings of Christianity, the more its actively political aspects recede into the background, so that this tendency in the New Testament must also be taken into consideration in any assessment of the historical events. At any rate, whatever its relationship to the Zealots, early Christianity was a part of *Jewish* history and thus just one tendency among the many and varied religio-political groups which went to make up Judaism at the beginning of the Christian era. There is no historical foundation for any claim that this early Christianity had a special role to play, unless one were to interpret its beginnings in the light of future developments for purposes of dogmatic theology. Such a procedure would certainly be problematic on theological grounds alone, and would in no way reflect the historical reality.

To return to Antipas: his ambitious wife had not only brought him into conflict with the king of the Nabataeans, but was also responsible for putting an end to his political career. When Caligula came to power in 37 CE, he conferred Philip's tetrarchy and the title of king upon Agrippa, son of Aristobulus (who had been executed in 7 BCE) and thus Herodias' brother. Herodias urged her husband to petition Caligula for a royal title for himself as well. As a consequence, Caligula deposed him (for allegedly stockpiling weapons) and banished him to Lugdunum in Gaul (39 CE). His tetrarchy—that is, Galilee and Peraea—was awarded to Agrippa.[15]

6.4. Archelaus (4 BCE–6 CE)

The elder son of Malthace the Samaritan had been awarded the heartland of the Herodian empire, namely Judaea, Samaria and Idumaea (with the major cities of Jerusalem, Samaria/Sebaste, Caesarea and Jaffa/Joppa). He was the worst of Herod's sons and imposed a brutal reign of terror. His regime proved to be so unbearable that a Jewish delegation was able to persuade Augustus to have him removed from office. After just under ten years in power, he was banished to Vienne in Gaul.[16] This termination of Archelaus' government brought with it an important change in the status of his territory; Judaea was placed under direct Roman rule and turned into a Roman province. This led to a rapid deterioration in the political and economic situation.

6.5. Judaea under Roman rule (6–41 CE)

6.5.1. Legal status of the province

The provincial system in the Roman empire was divided into three categories.[17] A basic distinction was made between imperial and senatorial provinces, that is, provinces under senatorial control and those controlled directly by the emperor. The former were usually safe territories, while the latter required the permanent military presence of the emperor due to external and internal political difficulties. Both types of province had a governor of senatorial rank, either a former consul (usually allocated to the larger ones) or a former praetor; the most important imperial province with a *legatus Augusti pro praetore* from the group of former consuls was Syria. There was also a third category of province, likewise under direct imperial control, to which governors of equestrian rank were assigned; such governors were given the title of *praefectus* or (from Claudius onwards) *procurator*. This third category was relatively rare and reserved for provinces with strong indigenous cultures or whose inhabitants were regarded as barbarians (these were not necessarily mutually exclusive from the Roman point of view). The most famous example was Egypt, which had a special status and, despite its size and significance, was only ever ruled by an equestrian with the title of *praefectus Aegypti*. Judaea also came into this category after 6 CE, with the governor of Syria apparently exercising some degree of ultimate authority over the new province. There is certainly evidence of a number of interventions by the Syrian governor in Judaea, although it can by no means be inferred from this that Judaea formed part of Syria for administrative purposes.

The residence of the Roman procurator was Caesarea. The procurator headed the administration, exercised the highest juridical authority and had command over the troops stationed in the country.[18] As a rule (Egypt was an exception), provinces governed by a procurator or prefect had only auxiliary troops (*auxilia*) at their disposal, not a resident legion, and this was the case in Judaea. Unlike the legions, the auxiliary troops (with the exception of the officers) were recruited from the indigenous population who did not have Roman rights of citizenship, although the Jewish inhabitants of Judaea were exempted from military service. Apart from Caesarea, there are records of garrisons in Jerusalem (at least during the main festivals to prevent disturbances), Samaria/Sebaste, Cyprus near Jericho, Machaerus, the Plain of Jezreel and Ascalon.

One of the the procurator's most important administrative functions was the collection of taxes. The Romans would essentially have taken over Herod's taxation system, with little alteration to the type and amount of taxes already being levied. The basis for tax assessment was the national census, which was conducted immediately following the conversion of Judaea into a procuratorial province under the Syrian governor Quirinus (and thus apparently simultaneously with a census in Syria) in 6 or 7 CE;[19] this is the same census mentioned in Luke 2:2 and wrongly attributed to the reign of Herod the Great.

The two most important taxes under direct Roman rule were, as before, the land tax (*tributum soli*) and the poll tax (*tributum capitis*). The *tributum soli* was paid partly in kind (a proportion of the crop yield) and partly in money; the *tributum capitis* consisted of a property tax varied according to the individual's personal assets[20] and a "poll tax" in the narrower sense, that is, a tax levied on every individual citizen regardless of personal wealth. We do not know precisely who was liable to pay this tax, although we do know that, at a somewhat later date in Syria, men had to pay the poll tax from the age of fourteen to sixty-five, and women from twelve to sixty-five.[21] The "penny" (= a silver *denarius*) mentioned in the New Testament[22] possibly gives some indication of the amount set for the poll tax. Tacitus mentions that the provinces of Syria and Judaea petitioned the emperor Tiberius for a reduction in taxes,[23] which shows that they were felt as a heavy burden.

It is particularly difficult to determine how the taxes and the customs duties (both belonged closely together) were collected. The sources do not provide a uniform picture in this regard. In the New Testament we hear of the "publican" Levi ben Alphaeus in Capernaum,[24] and also a rich "chief among the publicans" (*architelōnēs*) in Jericho by the name of Zacchaeus;[25] Josephus mentions a rich "tax-collector" called John in 66 CE in Caesarea,[26] but at the same time states that, likewise in 66 CE, the magistrates (*archontes*) and councillors (*bouleutai*) of Jerusalem collected the outstanding sums in order to delay the threatened outbreak of war.[27] It has been inferred from this that the direct taxes were no longer collected by tax farmers (*telōnai, publicani*) but by the municipal authorities, whereas the customs duties continued to be leased out to *publicani* (Roman or local tax farmers).

However, the overall picture is probably more complex. Close attention must be paid to geographical variation when considering the various sources.

The "chief of the publicans" in Jericho and the "tax-collector" in Caesarea no doubt carried out their activities in the territory of the Roman province of Judaea; both will have been responsible solely for the custom tolls, the former on the border between Judaea and Peraea (the latter formed part of Herod Antipas' domain), the latter in Judaea's major shipping ports. The direct taxes, on the other hand, were evidently collected by the councillors in Jerusalem in their capacity as members of the municipal authority; that is, the distinction between the system of collection for direct taxes and that for the customs duties holds good for Judaea.[28] The case of Levi the "publican" in Mark 2:14 and the parallel passages in the other Gospels is somewhat different. Capernaum belonged to the territory of Herod Antipas, where there was no reason to adopt the Roman system of taxation. The "publicans" in Galilee were therefore mostly tax farmers, and as such no doubt the direct successors of the old Hellenistic system of leasing by the state, which Herod had evidently reintroduced.[29]

In addition to the revenue from taxes and customs duties, the returns from Judaea's bountiful royal estates were now also flowing into the coffers of the Roman state. This was particularly the case for the famous balsam plantations in the vicinity of Jericho and En Gedi, whose systematic exploitation was remarked upon by Pliny.[30]

The legal authority of the procurator extended in principle to every aspect of the administration of justice. In practice, however, ordinary civil and criminal law remained in the hands of the local Jewish authorities, who thereby enjoyed a limited internal autonomy. The procurators retained the right to impose the death penalty for political offences, and they did so extensively, as we can see from cases occurring under Pontius Pilate (Jesus), Cuspius Fadus (Theudas) and Tiberius Alexander (Simon and James), as well as the excesses of the last procurators. Overall, then, the Jewish people in Judaea retained a considerable measure of political and religious autonomy (in theory, at any rate, although less in practice according to the degree of corruption of the procurator). Josephus compares the transition from Archelaus to direct Roman government to a change-over from monarchic to aristocratic rule.[31] Judaea was—internally at least—once again a community ruled by aristocrats, in which the Synhedrion under the presidency of the High Priest (and thus the Temple aristocracy in particular) evidently exerted considerable influence once more. To be sure, in the initial phase of the Roman province of Judaea, the Romans reserved the right to appoint and depose the High Priest as they pleased. Only in the second phase (44–66 CE) was this right transferred to the client kings Herod of Chalcis and Agrippa II. Jewish religious customs were respected, and the Jews were exempted from emperor-worship (except under Caligula).[32]

6.5.2. The procurators

This comparatively tolerant system could only function as well as those responsible, that is, the procurators, allowed it to. Little is known about the first procurators other than their names and the approximate durations of their reigns:

1. Coponius (6–9 CE);
2. Marcus Ambibulus (9–12 CE);
3. Annius Rufus (12–15 CE);
4. Valerius Gratus (15–26 CE);
5. Pontius Pilate (26–36 CE);
6. Marcellus (36–37 CE);
7. Marullus (37–41 CE).[33]

Many amongst the Jewish population may well initially have regarded Roman rule as a liberation from the yoke of the detested Herodians, while others recognized the potential dangers right from the start and fought against the Romans, seeing them as brutal oppressors who were leading the Jewish people irrevocably into slavery.[34] This latter group was to gain increasing support as time went on, and the excesses of the procuratorial governors became more and more flagrant (especially from Pontius Pilate onward). As with the Seleucids and Herod, the aristocratic upper classes found it easiest to establish good long-term relations with their Roman rulers, especially as their privileges remained relatively intact and their economic interests were also largely unaffected.

The procurator we know most about (and not only because of the trial of Jesus) is Pontius Pilate. Pilate appears to have been particularly insensitive to Jewish concerns. For instance, he deliberately provoked the Jews by doing precisely what his predecessors had always avoided and ordering the Roman troops to bring their standards (which bore the image of the emperor) into Jerusalem;[35] he subsequently financed the construction of an aqueduct to Jerusalem—in itself, a very useful project—with money taken from the Temple treasury,[36] which also would not exactly have endeared him to orthodox Jews. His similarly brutal actions against the Samaritans[37] ultimately proved his downfall and led to his dismissal.

The strained relations between the Roman authorities and the Jewish people reached a new low under Caligula (37–41 CE). Under him (and possibly at his instigation) there occurred one of the worst anti-Jewish pogroms in Alexandria (38 CE; in 40 CE, Jewish and Greek delegations were despatched to Caligula, as described in Philo's *Legatio ad Gaium*). His order (39/40) to erect his statue in the Jerusalem Temple could only be circumvented by the skilful delaying tactics of the Syrian governor Petronius and the intervention of Agrippa I, who (rightly) feared a major uprising. Caligula revoked his decree, but ordered the refractory governor to commit suicide and now planned to have the statue sent secretly to Jerusalem. Only his own assassination (in January 41) prevented this act of madness from being carried out and saved the governor of Syria from suicide.

Caligula's successor, Claudius, immediately initiated a change of policy towards the Jews. He entrusted Agrippa (who had already been awarded the tetrarchy of Philip and the title of king in 37 CE, and the tetrarchy of Antipas in 39 CE) with Judaea and Samaria, the largest part of Archelaus' former territory. This meant that Agrippa now presided over a kingdom of about the same size as that of his grandfather Herod. At the same time, the rank of consul was conferred on him.

6.5.3. The Zealots

Josephus associates the conversion of Judaea into a Roman province with the emergence of the Zealots as a politically active "party":

> The territory of Archelaus was brought under direct Roman rule, and a man of equestrian rank at Rome, Coponius, was sent as procurator with authority from Caesar to inflict the death penalty. In his time a Galilaean named Judas tried to stir the natives to revolt, saying that they would be cowards if they submitted to paying taxes to the Romans, and after serving God alone accepted human masters. This man was a sophist (*sophistēs*) with a sect of his own (*idias haireseōs*), and was quite unlike the others.[38]

According to Ant. XVIII, 1.1, § 4, the Judas of Galilee referred to here as the founder of the Zealots came from Gamala in Gaulanitis, but seems to have been regarded as a Galilaean as the centre of his activities lay in Galilee.[39] He was the son of the "bandit chief" Ezekias/Hiskia against whom Herod had fought during his first political post as *stratēgos* of Galilee,[40] and had himself already emerged as organizer of the revolt in Galilee immediately following the death of Herod.[41] The origins of the Zealot movement therefore go back a long way, yet their connection with the beginning of the legal incorporation of Judaea into the Roman provincial system is no mere coincidence.

The term most frequently used by Josephus for members of the various groups known collectively as "Zealots" is *lēstai* (Lat. *latrones*, Heb. *listim*)— "bandits, brigands". This term designates all the armed opponents of Roman state power, regardless of whether they were "mere" criminals or resistance groups with primarily patriotic and political motives. As both were inextricably interlinked in Roman eyes on account of their common social roots, the Romans treated all resistance groups as bandits who—unlike the regular troops of enemy countries—stood outside of any law. So when Josephus employs the term "brigand", he is adopting the discriminatory Roman usage and ignoring the social and religious elements of the movement.

The term *sikaroi*—"Sicarii"[42] seems likewise to originate with the Roman opponents of the resistance fighters. Josephus uses it mainly to characterize the Masada group of activists, that is, the followers of Menahem who fled to Masada after his murder.[43] On the other hand, the term *zēlōtai* (Heb. *qana'im*)—"zealots" is no doubt the resistance fighters' own honourable self-designation, a deliberate reference to biblical precedent.[44] Josephus uses the term mainly for the group around Eleazar b. Simon,[45] but there is justification for believing that the term was already employed for the resistance fighters prior to the Jewish War and is thus an appropriate designation for the movements sparked off by Judas.[46]

The credo of the Zealots, that is, their political and religious ideals, is summarized by Josephus as follows:[47]

> As for the fourth of the philosophies [of the Jews],[48] Judas the Galilaean set himself up as leader of it. This school agrees in all other respects with the opinions of the Pharisees, except that they have a passion for liberty that is almost unconquerable, since they are convinced that God alone is their leader and master. They think little of submitting to death in unusual forms and permitting vengeance to fall on kinsmen and friends if only they may avoid calling any man master. Inasmuch as the people have seen the steadfastness of their resolution amid such circumstances, I may forgo any further account. For I have no fear that anything reported of them will be considered incredible. The danger is, rather, that report may minimize the indifference with which they accept the grinding misery of pain.

Initial stress is placed upon the closeness of the Zealots to the large "party" of the Pharisees. This is further emphasized by the remark that, besides Judas, a Pharisee by the name of *Zadok* was co-founder of the "fourth school of philosophy".[49] It may therefore be supposed that the Zealot movement was an offshoot of the Pharisees and may be regarded as their "left wing", as it were.

Essentially, the "doctrine" of the Zealots is characterized by the concept of freedom and the exclusive sovereignty of God. Both belong closely together and constitute the recurring theme in every account of the Zealot movement.

The Zealots' pursuit of freedom found its clearest expression on the coins issued during the Jewish War, whose inscriptions *cherut tsion* ("Freedom of Zion") and *lig'ullat tsion* ("for the Redemption of Zion") give voice to the expectation of political liberty and eschatological redemption. Every form of temporal power—and certainly that of an emperor who claimed divinity for himself—contradicts the sovereignty of God and must therefore be opposed. The Zealots' radical concept of God and freedom is thus the immediate cause of their political activism, and their movement is only comprehensible when seen in its radical-Messianic and social context. This is also the only explanation for Josephus' repeated allegation that most of the Zealot leaders laid claim to the royal title, as well as the unusual degree of self-sacrifice and fanaticism of the Zealots, which does not seem to fit in with the picture of "ordinary" bandits and brigands which Josephus tries to paint for his Roman public.[50] We know nothing about the Zealots' interpretation of the Torah, but there can be no doubt that they wished to restore the original unity between the Torah's religious and political aspects and objected to any distinction between a "merely religious" as opposed to a political fulfilment of the Torah as a flouting of the divine will. It is possibly precisely here that the crucial difference between Zealots and Pharisees lay, insofar as the latter began increasingly to adapt to the political actuality and were prepared to restrict themselves to the "religious aspect" of the Torah.

One direct expression of the Zealots' concept of freedom was their rejection of the census and the Roman system of taxation. This is the clearest example of the social implications of the Zealot movement. Tax and tribute were the omnipresent symbol of heathen rule and would lead directly to slavery (if they could no longer be raised). It is therefore no accident that Simon bar Gioras, one of the later Zealot leaders, put freedom for slaves on his political agenda,[51] and that one of the initial actions of the rebels at the beginning of the war was to destroy the archives containing the money-lenders' bonds.[52] As the payment of taxes and tribute were by no means a consequence of the conversion of Judaea into a Roman province, but were a constant throughout Jewish history, having been levied both under Roman rule and under the Seleucids and Ptolemies, it is unclear why the Zealot movement became such a powerful political force at this particular point in time. It has been conjectured that the previous exemption from the tribute during the sabbatical year[53] was rescinded under direct Roman rule, but there is no mention of this in the sources. The tax burden may suffice as a cause, as it certainly did not become any lighter under direct Roman rule than under Herod and was no doubt more direct, that is, without the benefit of a "Jewish" king tolerated by Rome to act as an intermediary. A further possibility is perhaps indicated by Josephus' comment that Archelaus' estate was sold at the same time the *census* was taken.[54] This would have been a reference to the royal estates in Judaea and in the Plain of Jezreel, which thereby came into the possession of non-Jews. This means that the former "royal farmers" were deprived of their land, or else had to eke out an existence as tenants of foreign landowners. It is conceivable that, in addition to the smallholders in Galilee, Judas recruited his followers from such dispossessed and tenant farmers.

We know nothing about the eventual fate of the founder of the Zealots. Only the New Testament mentions in passing that Judas perished and his followers were dispersed,[55] but it remains unclear when and how this happened. What is certain is that the movement he initiated carried on after his death, and that his family played a central part in it. There are therefore good grounds for regarding this as a kind of dynastic leadership, not dissimilar to that of the Maccabees. Two of Judas' sons, Simon and James, were crucified as rebel leaders by the procurator Tiberius Alexander between 45 and 48 CE,[56] his younger son, Menahem, played an important role in the Jewish War,[57] while his grandson Eleazar was commander of Masada, the last fortress to put up resistance.[58]

A family tree may help to clarify their relationship:

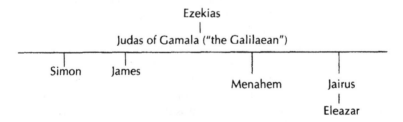

6.6. Agrippa I (37–44 CE)

Agrippa's brief reign over Herod's entire kingdom (41–44 CE) receives nothing but favourable assessments in the sources. Like the Hasmonean Salome Alexandra before him, he seems to have initiated a change in internal policy and given preference to the Pharisees. At all events, both Josephus and the rabbinic literature are unanimous in their praise of his singular "piety".[59] On the other hand, this clearly did not make him popular with his pagan, and especially his Christian subjects; he is blamed for the execution of James, and Peter only escaped through a miracle.[60]

His turn towards traditional Jewish piety and politics was evidently also aimed at strengthening national elements, and so carried with it the risk of conflict with Rome. His attempt to build a new wall to fortify the north of

Jerusalem (the so-called North Wall) was brought to a halt by the governor of
Syria, as was a conference with five other Roman vassal kings whom he had
invited to Tiberias.[61]

Admittedly, the research is unsure as to what ultimately fuelled his religious devotion, whether it really sprang from an inner need or was rather the
result of political calculation. At any rate, it seems to have been restricted
largely to his own domain, and it certainly did not prevent him, like his
grandfather Herod before him, from giving lavish support to Greek culture
outside of Palestine through monetary donations and the construction of magnificent buildings.[62] He also sponsored games in Caearea in honour of the
emperor and even erected statues of his daughters there.[63] Only those of his
coins minted in Jerusalem bore no image, whereas others bore his image and
that of the emperor.

His reign was too brief to enable a definitive assessment of his policies.
He died suddenly in Caesarea in 44 CE of unknown causes. The two
accounts of his death, in Josephus and the New Testament,[64] agree that it
took place in Caesarea after he had appeared before the people in royal robes
to be greeted by the shout: "May you be propitious to us! If we have hitherto
feared you as a man, yet henceforth we agree that you are more than mortal
in your being!" (Josephus), or "It is the voice of a god, and not of a man!"
(NT). In the New Testament, an "angel of the Lord" immediately kills him
for this blasphemy, while according to Josephus, he sees an owl which he
recognizes as a portent of doom presaging his imminent death (which then
occurs five days later). The similar depiction of his death in both sources—in
the New Testament he is eaten by worms, in Josephus he suffers from ago-
nizing abdominal pains—can only go to reinforce the suspicion that he was
poisoned and that, rather than the angel or the owl, responsibility lies with
the Romans, who were concerned at his political ambitions and the high
esteem he enjoyed amongst his people.

6.7. Agrippa II (50?–92/93 CE)

Agrippa's son, likewise called Agrippa, was seventeen years old when his
father died. He was not appointed successor by Claudius, but remained in
Rome. Palestine, that is, the entire former territory of Agrippa within its
Herodian borders, was once more turned into a Roman province administered
by a procurator under the overall supervision of the governor of Syria.

In 50 CE, Agrippa II was given the kingdom of Herod of Chalcis in the
Lebanon together with control of the Temple and the right to appoint the High
Priest. In 53, he was also given Philip's former tetrarchy, that is, Batanaea,

Trachonitis, Auranitis and Gaulanitis, and in 61, parts of Galilee and Peraea. Agrippa II also attempted to keep up appearances before the Jews while otherwise living as a Hellenistic potentate; all his coins bear the images of the reigning emperors. He is mentioned in the New Testament in connection with Paul's trial and heard his defence.[65] He supported the Romans during the revolution, and after the war Vespasian granted him large new territories in the north, where there were no Jewish inhabitants. He appears to have ruled over his remaining Jewish territories until 85 or 86 and probably died in 92/93 CE without heirs; his kingdom was incorporated into the province of Syria.

His private life caused a scandal on account of his liaison with his sister Berenice, who in turn began an affair with Titus during the war. It seems that Titus wanted to marry her, but was forced to abandon the idea when he became emperor for internal political reasons.

6.8. The Roman procurators (44–66 CE)

Following the death of Agrippa I, the greater part of Palestine came once more under direct Roman control (44 CE). This last period before the outbreak of war is characterized by a progressive deterioration in the internal political situation, so that war became almost inevitable. The (seven) procurators were almost all incompetent, concerned only to exploit the province financially and, it would sometimes seem, to injure intentionally the national and religious feelings of the Jews. During this period, the "bands of brigands" began to reappear, that is, the Zealot movement, who were eventually to lead the people into open revolt against Rome.

The first two procurators, Cuspius Fadus and Tiberius Julius Alexander, were still comparatively moderate. Under *Cuspius Fadus* (44–46 CE) there was the first instance of an uprising with messianic-apocalyptic overtones, whose political implications the procurator recognized and feared. A certain Theudas persuaded "a huge mass of people" to follow him to the Jordan to witness the wondrous spectacle of him parting the waters so that they could go across in safety, just like Moses had done with the Red Sea. On Cuspius Fadus' orders, the crowd was violently dispersed and Theudas captured and beheaded.[66]

His successor *Tiberius Alexander* (46–48 CE) came from a famous Jewish family in Alexandria (he was the nephew of the Jewish philosopher Philo of Alexandria), but had abandoned Judaism and made his career in Roman service. Under his administration there was a great famine in Palestine,[67] which was a catastrophe for the impoverished rural population and no doubt led to increased support for the Zealots. Tiberius managed to capture the

Zealot leaders Simon and James (the sons of Judas the Galilaean) and had them crucified.[68]

Tiberius Alexander was succeeded by *Ventidius Cumanus* (48–52 CE), under whom there was a marked increase in violent confrontations, some incidents being provoked by the Romans and others by the Jews. The first incident which provoked public outrage was triggered off during the Feast of Passover by a Roman soldier belonging to the cohort stationed in Jerusalem for the festival, who "pulled up his garment and bent over indecently, turning his backside towards the Jews" gathered in the Temple. When the people then began to pelt the soldiers with stones, the procurator called in his army, thereby causing the Jews to stampede in panic and leading, according to Josephus, to thirty thousand people being crushed to death.[69]

The next incident was provoked by "bandits" (almost certainly Zealots) who robbed an imperial slave called Stephanus. As punishment, Ventidius Cumanus odered the looting of the surrounding villages, during which a soldier tore up and burnt a Torah scroll. The procurator, fearing open revolt, had the soldier put to death.[70]

The most serious incident occurred when a Galilaean Jew was killed by Samaritans while on his way to Jerusalem for the Feast of Tabernacles. When Cumanus, who had been bribed by the Samaritans, refused to have the perpetrator punished, bands of Zealots led by a certain Eleazar b. Dinaeus and Alexander took their own revenge by laying waste Samaritan villages and murdering the inhabitants. Cumanus was able to quell the revolt quickly, but was subsequently deposed and sent into exile by Claudius.[71] This incident also swelled the ranks of the Zealots:

> … but many turned to banditry as there was no one to stop them,
> and all over the country plundering went on and the bolder spirits
> rose in revolt.[72]

The next procurator was *Felix* (52–60 CE), a freedman of the imperial family (the conferring of the procuratorship on a freedman was unusual, and was the result of the increased influence exerted by freedmen at the court of Claudius). Felix played a major role in the decline of Roman rule in Palestine and (unintentionally) helped increase Zealot influence. He had some success in putting down Zealot activity in the open countryside, and also managed to capture the Zealot leader Eleazar b. Dinaeus, whom he sent to Rome,[73] but the Zealots then developed a new tactic: they mingled with the crowds and attacked their victims with short daggers hidden in their clothing, and so were able to kill them without being detected. This special type of Zealot is referred to in the sources as *sikarioi* (Lat. *sicarii*, from *sica*—a short, curved dagger). Thus the struggle was taken increasingly into the cities, and especially

Jerusalem. One of their victims was the High Priest Jonathan, whom they murdered at Felix's instigation, which goes to show that Felix had no qualms about using Rome's enemies for his own purposes. As the Zealots hated the priestly nobility, whom they regarded as exploiters of the people and friends of the Romans, almost as much as the Romans themselves, they too had no difficulty with such a collaboration, even with the procurator.[74]

This period was also characterized by the appearance on the scene of numerous enthusiastic prophets and demagogues who made all sorts of promises to the people and led them into the desert in order to show them apocalyptic wonders. This, too, was a result of the tense atmosphere, and at the same time helped raise the temperature still further. The most notorious instance was the appearance of an "Egyptian", who is also mentioned in the New Testament,[75] and against whom—and his considerable band of followers—Felix launched an armed attack.[76]

Felix's private life also aroused the anger of the Jewish people. He had married Drusilla, daughter of Agrippa I, who divorced her first husband on his account.[77] This marriage of a Jewess to a pagan—the Herodians had at least insisted in similar cases that the pagan husband be circumcised (which thwarted a great many marriages)—and, moreover, to the Roman procurator, was an outrageous crime in the eyes of the "pious".

The situation became more and more chaotic towards the end of Felix's period in office. The procurator found himself increasingly unable to take effective action against the Zealots. The leading families amongst the priestly and urban nobility employed small armies of bodyguards for their protection, who then fought amongst themselves and terrorized the population. The priestly nobility enriched itself at the expense of the lower clergy by stealing their tithes, so that they too were driven into the arms of the Zealots.[78] A dispute between the Jewish and the "Syrian" (= Hellenistic) inhabitants of Caesarea over equality of citizenship finally led to Felix being relieved of his office by Nero.[79]

His successor, *Porcius Festus*, only ruled for a brief period (60–62 CE). At the beginning of his period in office, Nero decided the dispute between the Hellenistic and the Jewish inhabitants of Caesarea in favour of the "heathens", thereby relegating the Jews to virtual second-class citizens.[80] According to Josephus, the dispute continued to smoulder, and the discrimination against the Jews was one of the contributing factors leading to the outbreak of war a few years later.

Under Festus, a dispute also broke out between the priests and King Agrippa II. This concerned a wall that the priests had erected in the Temple to block the view from the royal palace, which overlooked the Temple. This angered Agrippa, as it prevented him from carrying out his inspection duties in his preferred manner, namely, by surveying the activities in the Temple courtyard from above.[81] Nero decided in the priests' favour, although Agrippa later took his revenge by opposing the will of the priests and granting privileges to the Levites which went against the "ancestral laws".[82] This episode demonstrates that bitter enmity existed not only between the priestly nobility and the Zealots, but also between the priestly nobility and the Herodians. When the revolt eventually broke out, the priestly nobility (or certain factions amongst them) preferred to make common cause with the Zealots rather than the Herodians, whom they put virtually on a par with the Romans (especially Agrippa II).

The next procurator was *Albinus* (62–64 CE). Before he took office, the High Priest at the time, Ananus II (b. Ananus), took advantage of the power vacuum in Jerusalem and, acting as a representative of the Sadducee "party", used his position in the Synhedrion to impose the death penalty on a number of his opponents, one of whom was James, the brother of Jesus and leader of the Christians in Jerusalem.[83] As Ananus was here clearly exceeding his authority—the right to impose capital punishment lay in the hands of the procurator—Albinus had him deposed by Agrippa shortly after his arrival.

Otherwise Albinus, after taking some initial measures against the *sicarii*, seems soon to have given up the fight against the Zealots, who increasingly gained the upper hand throughout the country. He restricted himself chiefly to taking bribes from every side, including even the Zealots (he set up regular exchanges of prisoners for money or prisoners of the opposing party).[84] Upon being recalled, he emptied the prisons by executing the major criminals and releasing the rest, apparently with the intention of speeding up the now inevitable course of events. "Thus the prison was cleared of inmates and the land was infested with brigands", as Josephus comments on his departure.[85]

The last of the procurators, *Gessius Florus* (64–66 CE), was the worst of all, according to Josephus; compared with him, the reign of his predecessor had been peaceful and successful.[86] Florus tried to extort the maximum possible amount of taxes from the province, which was now descending into total chaos. When he plundered the Temple treasury, probably in an attempt to make up the ever-worsening deficit in tax revenues resulting from the desperate economic situation, open revolt broke out in Jerusalem.

Notes

1. Ant. XVII, 10.5 § 271 f.; Bell. II, 4.1 § 56.
2. Ant. XVII, 10.6 § 273 f.; Bell, II, 4.2 §§ 57–59.
3. Ant. XVII, 10.7 §§ 278–284; Bell. II, 4.3 §§ 60–65.
4. Ant. XVII, 10.8 § 285.

5. The following reproach against Herod's regime is typical: "... he had not ceased to adorn neighbouring cities that were inhabited by foreigners although this led to the ruin [through taxation] and disappearance of cities located in his own kingdom" (Ant. XVII, 11.2 § 306).
6. Ant. XVII, 11.4 § 317 ff.; Bell. II, 6.3 §§ 93–100.
7. According to Luke 3:1.
8. Luke 13:32.
9. Ant. XVIII, 5.2 §§ 117–119.
10. Matt. 14:3 f.; Mark 6:17 f.; Luke 3:19 f.
11. Matt. 14:6–11; Mark 6:21–28; Luke 9:9.
12. Matt. 14:1 f.; Mark 6:14–16; Luke 9:7–9.
13. Luke 23:7–12.
14. See p. 109 ff. below.
15. Ant. XVIII, 7.2 § 252; Bell. II, 9.6 § 183.
16. Ant. XVII, 13.2–3 § 342 ff.; Bell. II, 7.3 §§ 111–113.
17. Strabo, Geographica XVII, 3.25.
18. The right to mint coins was also conferred on the procurator. The mint was apparently located in Caesarea. Only bronze coins were minted, and these were of official imperial currency.
19. Ant. XVIII, 1.1 § 1 f.
20. Appianus, Syr. 50: 1% of the property valuation (in Syria).
21. Ulpian, Digesta L, 15.3.
22. Mark 12:13–17; Matt. 22:15–22; Luke 20:20–6.
23. Tacitus, Annals II.42: "The provinces of Syria and Judaea, exhausted by the burden, requested a reduction in the tribute."
24. Mark 2:14; Matt. 9:9—here he is called Matthew; Luke 5:27.
25. Luke 19:1 ff.
26. Bell. II, 14.4 § 287.
27. Bell. II, 17.1 § 404 f.
28. Although even here the possibility cannot be ruled out that tax farmers were also employed to collect taxes in addition to the municipal authorities. Possibly both systems, the one allocating responsibility to the municipal authorities and the other leasing taxes out to tax farmers, existed side by side for a period.
29. See p. 91 above.
30. Pliny, Nat. Hist. XII, 113.
31. Ant. XX, 10.5 § 251.
32. See p. 108 below.
33. It is sometimes argued that the last two names in fact refer to one and the same person.
34. See p. 109 ff. below.
35. Bell. II, 9.2–3 §§ 169–174; Ant. XVIII, 3.1 §§ 55–59.
36. Bell. II, 9.4 §§ 175–177; Ant. XVIII, 3.2 §§ 60–62.
37. Ant. XVIII, 4.1 § 87.
38. Bell. II, 8.1 § 117 f.; cf. Ant. XVIII, 1.1 §§ 1–10.
39. Cf. also Acts 5:37.
40. See p. 84 above.
41. See p. 101 above.
42. Derived from the Latin *sica*—"dagger" and used to describe their modus operandi; see p. 115 below.

43. See p. 122 below.
44. Pinchas the Zealot; cf. Num. 25:6–13.
45. See p. 127 below.
46. The "Galilaeans" mentioned by Justin (Dial. c. Tryph. 80.2), Hegesippus (Eusebius, HE IV, 22.7) and Epictetus (Arrian, Diss. IV, 7.6) are no doubt also references to the Zealots; the term refers to Galilee as the centre of the movement.
47. Ant. XVIII, 1.6 § 23 f.
48. In addition to those of the Pharisees, the Sadducees and the Essenes; see p. 71 f. above.
49. Ant. XVIII, 1.1 §§ 4, 9.
50. Not for nothing is "folly" an important category under which Josephus subsumes the Zealot movement; cf. Ant. XVIII, 1.6 § 25, for instance.
51. See p. 126 below.
52. See p. 121 f. below.
53. See p. 83 above.
54. Ant. XVII, 13.5 § 355.
55. Acts 5:37.
56. See p. 115 below.
57. See p. 122 below.
58. See p. 128 f. below.
59. Ant. XIX, 7.3 § 331; m Sot 7:8.
60. Acts 12:1–19.
61. Ant. XIX, 8.1 §§ 338–342.
62. Ant. XIX, 7.5 §§ 335–337.
63. Ant. XIX, 9.1 § 357.
64. Ant. XIX, 8.2 §§ 343–352; Acts 12:19–23.
65. Acts 25:13 ff.
66. Ant. XX, 5.1 §§ 97–99; cf. also Acts 5:36.
67. Ant. XX, 5.2 § 101; III, 15.3 § 320; Acts 11:28.
68. Ant. XX, 5.2 § 102.
69. Bell. II, 12.1 §§ 223–227; Ant. XX, 5.3 §§ 105–111.
70. Bell. II, 12.2 §§ 228–231; Ant. XX, 5.4 §§ 113–117.
71. Bell. II, 12.3–7 §§ 232–246; Ant. XX. 6.1–3 §§ 118–136.
72. Bell. II, 12.5 § 238.
73. Ant. XX, 8.5 § 161.
74. Ant. XX, 8.5 §§ 161–163; Bell. II, 13.3 §§ 254–257.
75. Acts 21:38.
76. Bell. II, 13.5 §§ 261–263; Ant. XX, 8.6 §§ 169–172.
77. Ant. XX, 7.2 §§ 141–143.
78. Ant. XX, 8.8 § 180 f.
79. Bell. II, 13.7 §§ 266–270; Ant. XX, 8.7 §§ 173–177.
80. Ant. XX, 8.9 § 183 f.; Bell. II, 14.4 § 284.
81. Ant. XX, 8.11 §§ 190–195.
82. Ant. XX, 9.6 §§ 216–218.
83. Ant. XX, 9.1 §§ 197–200.
84. Bell. II, 14.1 §§ 272–276.
85. Ant. XX, 9.5 § 215.
86. Bell. II, 14.2 § 277.

7. THE FIRST JEWISH WAR (66–74 CE)

7.1. The beginnings

The procurator Gessius Florus' plundering of the Temple treasury marks the
point at which subversive activity by individual groups turned into open popular revolt. Josephus also specifies the date this took place: the 16th of
Artemisius (April/May) 66 CE.[1] Florus was forced to withdraw to Caesarea,
leaving only a single Roman cohort behind in Jerusalem. The Zealots captured Masada (under the leadership of Menahem, son of Judas the
Galilaean),[2] while in Jerusalem the Temple Captain (*segan*) Eleazar, son of
Ananias the High Priest, ordered the suspension of the daily sacrifice for the
emperor. This was the decisive act of the rebellion and constituted an official
breach in relations between the Jerusalem religious community and their
Roman overlords:

> At the same time in the Temple courts Eleazar, son of Ananias the
> High Priest and a very confident young man, who was Temple
> Captain, persuaded the ministers of the Temple to accept no gift
> or offering from a foreigner. This it was that made war with
> Rome inevitable; for they abolished the sacrifices offered for
> Rome and Caesar himself ...[3]

A power struggle now broke out in Jerusalem between the remaining members of the peace party (the High Priests, the Pharisees and the Herodians)
and the Zealots, who now had the support of Eleazar the Temple Captain (the
reasons for this are unclear and are much debated in the research). The peace
party asked King Agrippa II for military support, but this proved largely inef-
fective. After bitter fighting, Agrippa's troops had to retreat to Herod's
palace, and the rebels set fire to the palace of Ananias the High Priest and that
of Agrippa and Berenice. They also burned down the public archives, for reasons given by Josephus as follows:

121

... then they took their fire to the Record Office, eager to destroy
the money-lenders' bonds and so make impossible the recovery
of debts, in order to secure the support of an army of debtors and
enable the poor to rise with impunity against the rich.[4]

Here is clear evidence of the social motivation behind the uprising, one of
whose objectives was certainly the redistribution of landed property, so much
of which lay in the hands of a privileged elite.

Shortly afterwards, the Antonia fortress and Herod's palace were also captured by the rebels. The Zealot party had meanwhile been reinforced by
Menahem, who, in the words of Josephus, entered Jerusalem "like a king".[5]
This remark carries with it the implication of Messianic claims and demonstrates the way in which religious, social and military factors were all inter-
mingled in the rebellion. Menahem took charge of the siege of Herod's
palace. Agrippa's troops surrendered and were allowed to withdraw
unharmed, while the Roman troops sought refuge in the fortified towers of
Hippicus, Phasael and Mariamme. The main representative of the peace
party, the High Priest Ananias, was murdered by the rebels, and the Roman
troops, who had surrendered in return for a promise of safe conduct, were
massacred.[6]

The murder of the High Priest Ananias caused a serious split in the Zealot
movement. The Temple Captain Eleazar, son of the High Priest, whose decision to terminate the daily sacrifice for the emperor had helped the Zealots to
their initial success, now distanced himself from Menahem—the long-
standing rift between priesthood and laity may also have played a role here—
and led a conspiracy against him. When Menahem entered the Temple "in
pomp to worship, decked with kingly robes", he was attacked and murdered
by Eleazar and his supporters.[7] Those of Menahem's followers who managed
to escape fled to Masada, where they were to play no further role until the
end of the war.

Meanwhile, Cestius Gallus, the governor of Syria, made a belated attempt
to put down the rebellion. Together with his 12th legion, he was ambushed by
the Jews near Beth-Horon and suffered a crushing defeat (October/
November, 66 CE).[8] To be sure, the military success of the Jews should not
be overrated—the Syrian troops were renowned for their lack of discipline—
but this victory was nevertheless of great significance for future developments. Even the remaining opponents of the war were carried away by the
general exhilaration at this initial triumph (which was not to be repeated),
while the radicals no doubt regarded this victory as heralding the final war of
extermination against the despised Romans. By now, minting would already
have begun of the first coins dated according to the years of the revolt.

The rebels now began (for the first time since the outbreak of the revolt) to organize the war systematically. Remarkably, leadership (still) lay in the hands of the predominantly moderate upper classes, that is, the High Priests and the Pharisees, rather than with the ultra-radical Zealots. Commanders were despatched to all the individual regions (toparchies) of the province to carry out the military organization of the rebellion.

We know most about the commander of Galilee. This was Joseph ben Mattitiahu, a member of the priestly nobility better known to us as Josephus Flavius, who was later to write a detailed eye-witness account of events. The fact that he was a member of the aristocracy who had just returned from Rome naturally made him highly suspect in the eyes of the radical Zealots. Consequently, he met with immediate opposition in Galilee from the partisan leader, John of Gischala, who doubted that he was truly an enemy of Rome and suspected that his real objective was a negotiated peace with the Romans rather than the ultimate eschatological showdown (with justification, as it turned out). Josephus subsequently had several narrow escapes from attempts on his life by John of Gischala.[9]

7.2. The war in Galilee (67 CE)

As the Romans were forced for geographical reasons to attack from the north, the difficult task of fighting the first, and potentially decisive, battle against the Romans fell to Josephus. After the defeat of Cestius Gallus, Nero commissioned the experienced general Vespasian to suppress the revolt. He began his campaign in the spring of 67 together with his son Titus. They had at their disposal three complete legions (the 5th, 10th and 15th), twenty-three cohorts, six divisions of cavalry and an assortment of other auxiliaries provided by friendly kings, a total of some sixty thousand men.[10] Even before the commencement of actual hostilities, Sepphoris, one of the most important cities of Galilee, declared its loyalty to Rome and asked for a Roman garrison.[11]

Sepphoris remained the only city to declare open allegiance to the Romans right from the start. However, the example of the city of Tiberias, whose factional disputes Josephus describes in detail,[12] also shows the extent to which the more prosperous inhabitants of the cities—and especially the members of the Hellenistically organized city council (boulē)—were pro-Roman in their leanings, while the resistance was concentrated in the poorer sections of the urban and rural population. When Josephus ordered the "council and principal men" of Tiberias to demolish the Tiberian palace of Herod Antipas, which was decorated with images of animals, the city fathers procrastinated and finally assented with reluctance, but they were anticipated in the task by Jesus

b. Sapphias, "the ringleader ... of the party of the sailors and destitute class", who set the palace on fire.[13] This same Jesus b. Sapphias, who was then *archōn* of Tiberias, set himself up as spokesman for the revolutionary party and Josephus' opponents, who cast doubt on his revolutionary commitment:

> The principal instigator of the mob was Jesus, son of Sapphias, at that time chief magistrate of Tiberias, a knave with an instinct for introducing disorder into grave matters, and unrivalled in fomenting sedition and revolution. With a copy of the laws of Moses in his hands, he now stepped forward and said: "If you cannot, for your own sakes, citizens, detest Josephus, fix your eyes on your ancestral laws, which your commander-in-chief intended to betray, and for their sakes hate the crime and punish the audacious criminal."[14]

The revolutionary party in Galilee was therefore characterized by a combination of social, religious (the emphasis on the "ancestral laws" is typical) and also, perhaps, democratic factors (opposition to the dominance of wealthy citizens on the *boulē*). The difference in social background was one of the main reasons for the distrust in which these radical groups held Josephus.

The first military confrontation between the Roman and the Jewish troops was supposed to take place near Garis (close to Sepphoris), but did not actually occur, as most of Josephus' men ran away from the approaching Roman troops.[15] Josephus retreated to the fortress of Jotapata, where he was besieged and defeated by Vespasian (June/July 67). Josephus provides an extremely interesting account of his own fate following the fall of Jotapata, in which he attributes his survival to divine providence[16] and his prophecy that Vespasian would become emperor.[17] In reality, Josephus is here skilfully fabricating his own legend in order to justify his "defection" to the enemy camp of the Romans.

Shortly after the fall of Jotapata, Tiberias surrendered without a fight;[18] Tarichea was captured,[19] followed by the important fortress of Gamala in Gaulanitis[20] and Mount Tabor.[21] Finally, Gischala also surrendered—the radical Zealot leader John of Gischala managed to flee to Jerusalem—, and so, by the end of 67 CE, the whole of Galilee was once more under Roman control.[22]

7.3. The years 68 and 69 CE

The following two years, 68 and 69, are characterized by civil war in Jerusalem and Vespasian's conquest of the remainder of the country.

In Jerusalem, the extreme wing of the Zealots seized power, led by John of Gischala, who had fled there from Galilee. The Zealots immediately took action against the pro-Roman and moderate factions of the ruling classes, imprisoning and murdering their leading representatives.[23] They also pushed aside the ruling high-priestly families and chose a High Priest by lot:

> Through their atrocities ran a vein of ironic pretence more exasperating than the actions themselves. For to test the submissiveness of the people and prove their own strength, they attempted to appoint the high priests by lot, though ... the succession was by birth. The excuse given for this arrangement was ancient custom; they said that from time immemorial the high priesthood had been conferred by lot. In reality this was a reversal of the regular practice and a device for consolidating their power by arbitrary appointments. Assembling one of the clans from which high priests were chosen, a clan called Eniachin, they drew lots for a high priest. The luck of the draw furnished the clearest proof of the depths to which they had sunk. The office fell to one Phanias [= Pinchas], son of Samuel, of the village of Aphtha, a man not only not descended from high priests but too boorish to have any clear notion of what the high priesthood might be. Anyway they dragged him willy-nilly from his holding and disguised him from head to foot like an actor on the stage, robing him in the sacred vestments and teaching him his cues. To the perpetrators this shocking sacrilege was the occasion for ribald mirth, but the other priests, watching from a distance this mockery of their law, burst into tears, cut to the heart by this travesty of the sacred rites.[24]

What Josephus here so indignantly dismisses as a "mockery" was far from being simply a parody of a time-honoured institution, but was rather an attempt to revive the office of High Priest. The ruling high-priestly families since the time of Herod were, as non-Zadokites, no more qualified for the High Priesthood than any other class of priest and, moreover, were politically compromised. So, if the Zealots arranged for the appointment of a High Priest from another family, their aim was clearly to override the privileged aristocratic priestly families and possibly even to reinstate the Zadokites as the sole high-priestly dynasty.[25] In choosing the High Priest by lot, they were very probably intentionally introducing a democratic element into the appointment which, while not laid down by tradition, was hardly less legitimate than the sharing of the office amongst a few privileged families.

The attempt of the moderate forces around the Pharisee Simon b. Gamaliel and the High Priests Ananus b. Ananus and Jesus b. Gamala to regain the initiative and expel the Zealots proved of no avail. John of Gischala was able to smuggle the Idumaeans into the city and to establish a reign of terror with their support.[26] The moderate party was totally destroyed, the High Priests Ananus b. Ananus and Jesus b. Gamala were murdered, and, following the withdrawal of the Idumaeans, John of Gischala became the unopposed supreme ruler of Jerusalem.[27]

Vespasian meanwhile captured Peraea and (with Antipatris, Lydda, Jamnia, Emmaus, Samaria, Neapolis and Jericho) the most important cities in the vicinity of the Jewish heartland. Following Nero's death on 9 June 68, he then suspended all further activities until May/June 69 CE due to the uncertain situation in Rome.

This suspension of hostilities was hardly turned to advantage by the rebels. While John of Gischala continued his reign of terror in Jerusalem, another extremist Zealot leader, Simon bar Gioras—as his name indicates, he was the son of a proselyte—, terrorized the countryside and brought Idumaea under his control. In March/April 69, he was admitted into Jerusalem by its citizens and the Idumaeans in order to liberate the city from John's tyrannical regime.[28] However, this only sparked off a new civil war between the supporters of John, who occupied the Temple Mount, and those of Simon, who took control of the upper city.

Simon bar Gioras also combined social activities with Messianic ambitions. His supporters consisted for the most part of freed slaves and smallholders,[29] which is further indication of the extent to which the outbreak of the rebellion was the result of Roman repression combined with the catastrophic economic situation of the majority of the population (and also highlights the major role played by social factors in the emergence of Messianic movements).

Simon's activities led Vespasian to intervene in events once more, this time in May/June 69. He conquered the greater part of the Jewish heartland (Gophna, Acrabata, Bethel, Ephraim and Hebron), and so, with the exception of Jerusalem and the fortresses of Herodium, Masada and Machaerus, brought the whole province once more under his control. The civil war in Rome led to a further interruption in hostilities. On July 1st 69, Vespasian was proclaimed emperor by the Egyptian legions, and within a short while was recognized as emperor throughout the entire eastern part of the empire. He spent the period until spring 70 in Alexandria awaiting further developments in Rome, and entrusted his son Titus with the continuance of the war against the Jews.

At the same time as Titus was preparing to besiege Jerusalem, the Zealot movement had suffered a further split. In addition to the factions led by John (on the Temple Mount) and Simon (in the upper and parts of the lower city), a

new "party" under the priest Eleazar b. Simon set itself up in the inner forecourt of the Temple, probably recruiting mainly from the lower priesthood.
All three groups fought viciously against each other and were even said to
have set fire to supplies stored in Jerusalem so as to prevent them falling into
the hands of their rivals.[30]

7.4. The conquest of Jerusalem 70 CE

The siege of Jerusalem began a few days before Passover in 70 CE. As well
as the 5th, 10th and 15th legions, Titus also had the 12th legion at his disposal, the same legion whose defeat under Cestius Gallus had sparked off the
war. During the Passover festival, John of Gischala's men murdered Eleazar,
the leader of the third party of Zealots who had entrenched themselves in the
Temple forecourt, after he had opened the Temple to the people for the festival.[31] The two remaining Zealot leaders, John of Gischala and Simon bar
Giora, only ceased hostilities and joined forces to defend the city when the
Romans began to construct ramparts for the siege.

   The Romans started their offensive at the weakest point of the fortifications, the so-called third wall, construction of which was begun under
Agrippa I and only completed shortly before the siege (to the west, north of
the present Jaffa Gate). They succeeded in breaking through towards the end
of May,[32] and shortly afterwards also broke through the more important second wall.[33] This left only the Temple and lower city and the separately fortified upper city. The first ramparts to be built were undermined by the rebels
and collapsed. Titus then built a wall encircling all the remaining part of the
city so as to starve out the population more effectively. This time, the Romans
concentrated on the fortress of Antonia, which was captured at the end of
July.[34] Shortly afterwards, on the 6th of August, the daily sacrifice in the
Temple was suspended, and on the 9th/10th of Av (= the end of August)
70 CE, the Temple was captured and burnt down:

> As the legions charged in, neither persuasion nor threat could
> check their impetuosity: passion alone was in command. Crowded
> together round the entrances many were trampled by their friends,
> many fell among the still hot and smoking ruins of the colonnades
> and died as miserably as the defeated. As they neared the
> Sanctuary they pretended not even to hear Caesar's commands
> and urged the men in front to throw in more firebrands. The parti-
> sans were no longer in a position to help; everywhere was slaugh-
> ter and flight. Most of the victims were peaceful citizens, weak

and unarmed, butchered wherever they were caught. Round the
Altar the heap of corpses grew higher and higher, while down the
Sanctuary steps poured a river of blood and the bodies of those
killed at the top slithered to the bottom.[35]

The extent of Titus' own participation is the subject of much dispute in the
research. Josephus repeatedly asserts that Titus intended to prevent the
destruction of the Temple,[36] but these claims can only increase our suspi-
cions as they obviously reflect the viewpoint of a favourite of the Flavian
imperial family.

All that remained now was the upper city, which was strongly fortified and
separated from the Temple by a deep valley. Ramparts were erected to the
north-west (near Herod's palace) and the north-east, and in early September
the upper city also fell to the Romans.[37] All the inhabitants were killed or
sent to forced labour, while a select few were retained for the triumphal procession. The city was totally destroyed, and John of Gischala and Simon bar
Gioras were taken to Rome for the triumphal procession. Only the three towers of Herod's palace (Hippicus, Phasael and Mariamme) and a section of the
(west) wall were left standing. According to Josephus and the rabbinic literature, these were to serve as a memorial to the city's strong defences and
Titus' victory, as well as providing protection for the Roman garrison
installed in Jerusalem.[38]

7.5. The end of the war

With the fall of Jerusalem, the war was essentially over; all that remained
were the fortresses of Herodium, Machaerus and Masada. Titus returned to
Rome and, in 71 CE, celebrated the triumph with his father Vespasian and his
brother Domitian, following which Simon bar Gioras was executed and John
of Gischala thrown into prison. This difference in treatment of the two Zealot
leaders implies that the Romans regarded Simon bar Gioras as the more dangerous opponent (perhaps because he was more socially active and more radical). The triumphal procession is depicted on the Arch of Titus. Amongst the
objects on display were the Table of the Shewbread and the Seven-Branched
Lampstand; the latter, exactly as portrayed on the Arch of Titus, was later to
become the official emblem in the coat of arms of the State of Israel.

Titus assigned the task of capturing the last three fortresses to the governor
of Judaea, Lucilius Bassus.[39] Herodium and Machaerus soon surrendered;
Masada, under the leadership of the Zealot Eleazar b. Jairus (the grandson of
Judas the Galilaean), put up considerable resistance and was only captured in

April 74 CE[40] by Flavius Silva, the new governor, after the remaining occupants had committed suicide:

> ... and when ten of them had been chosen by lot to be the executioners of the rest, every man flung himself down beside his wife and children where they lay, put his arms round them, and exposed his throat to those who must perform the painful office. These unflinchingly slaughtered them all, then agreed on the same rule for each other, so that the one who drew the lot should kill the nine and last of all himself ... and the one man left till last first surveyed the serried ranks of the dead, in case amidst all the slaughter anyone was still left in need of his hand; then finding that all had been dispatched, he set the palace blazing fiercely, and summoning all his strength drove his sword right through his body and fell dead by the side of his family ... The victims numbered nine hundred and sixty, women and children included. The tragedy was enacted on 15th of Xanthicos.[41]

Yigael Yadin believes that the discovery of an ostracon bearing the inscription *Ben Ya'ir* provides archaeological evidence of this dramatic casting of lots,[42] but other interpretations are also possible. The theological[43] or nationalistic glorification of this suicide ought to take into account the tendentious nature of Josephus' report, as well as noting the structural similarities to his account of the conquest of Jotapata,[44] even if in this case—as Josephus himself was involved—the outcome was quite different.

Notes

1. Bell. II, 14.6 § 293; II, 15.2 § 315.
2. Bell. II, 17.2 § 408; II, 17.8 § 433.
3. Bell. II, 17.2 § 409 f.
4. Bell. II, 17.6 § 427.
5. Bell. II, 17.8 § 434.
6. Bell. II, 17.8 f. § 440 f.
7. Bell. II, 17.9 §§ 442–448.
8. Bell. II, 19.2 §§ 517–522.
9. Bell. II, 21 § 585 ff.
10. Bell. III, 4.2 §§ 64–69.
11. Bell. III, 3.4 §§ 30–34.
12. Vita 9 §§ 32–39.
13. Vita 12 § 66.
14. Vita 27 § 134 f.
15. Bell. III, 6.3 § 129 f.

16. Bell. III, 8.7 § 391.
17. Bell. III, 8.9 §§ 400–402.
18. Bell. III, 9.8 §§ 453–461.
19. Bell. III, 10.1-5 §§ 462–502.
20. Bell. IV, 1.2-10 §§ 9–83.
21. Bell. IV, 1.8 §§ 54–61.
22. Bell. IV, 2.2-5 §§ 92–120.
23. Bell. IV, 3.4-5 §§ 138–146.
24. Bell. IV, 3.7-8 §§ 152–157.
25. According to J. Jeremias, Jerusalem zur Zeit Jesu (3rd ed.), Göttingen, 1962, p. 217 f. (=II. B., p. 53 f.) [Bibliography], the priestly clan Eniachin were descendants of the Zadokites.
26. Bell. IV, 4.5-7 §§ 283–300; IV, 5.1 § 305 ff.
27. Bell. IV, 6.1 §§ 353–357.
28. Bell. IV, 9.11 f. §§ 573–577.
29. Bell. IV, 9.3 § 508.
30. Bell. V, 1.4 §§ 22–26; Tacitus, Hist. V, 12; ARNB ch. 7, p. 20 and *passim*.
31. Bell. V, 3.1 §§ 98–105.
32. Bell. V, 7.2 § 302.
33. Bell. V, 7.3 f. §§ 303–331.
34. Bell. VI, 1.7 f. §§ 68–92.
35. Bell. VI, 4.6 §§ 257–259.
36. Bell. VI, 4.3 § 241; VI, 4.5 § 251 f.; VI, 4.6 §§ 254 ff., 261, 266.
37. Bell. VI, 8.5 § 407 f.
38. Bell. VI, 9.1 § 413; VII, 1.1 § 1 f.; EchaRB p. 69.
39. Bell. VII, 6.1–4 §§ 163–209.
40. This date (as opposed to the traditional dating of 73 CE) is based on the fact that Flavius Silva did not become governor of Judaea until 73 and therefore can only have captured Masada in April 74 (the month of April is specified in Josephus' account: the 15th of Xanthicos corresponds to the month of Nisan = March/ April in the Jewish calendar).
41. Bell. VII, 9.1 §§ 395–401.
42. Masada, p. 201.
43. Michel-Bauernfeind, Der jüdische Krieg II/2, p. 280, note 185: "This was, then, a kind of ritual slaughter whereby the victim's throat was cut in accordance with the traditional Jewish code of practice. Confirmation of the liturgical basis for the incident is provided by the emphasis placed upon the selection of a group of ten men to carry out the sacrifice ... If this interpretation of the text is correct, then the events in Masada can no longer be regarded as having anything to do with a suicide."
44. See p. 124 above.

8. BETWEEN THE WARS: FROM 74 TO 132 CE

8.1. The consequences of the war

The consequences of the first great war of the Jews against Rome were extremely far-reaching and their significance for the future history of Judaism can hardly be over-estimated. The immediate political consequences were drastic. As has already been mentioned, before the war Judaea was a Roman province of the third category, that is, under the administration of a procurator of equestrian rank and under the overall control of the governor of Syria. After the war it became an independent Roman province with the official name of *Judaea* and under the administration of a governor of praetorian rank,[1] and was therefore moved up into the second category (it was only later, in about 120 CE, that Judaea became a consular province, that is, with a governor of consular rank). This new status of the province also implies that a standing legion was stationed in Judaea, namely, the *legio X Fretensis*, which had also taken part in the war. The headquarters of the 10th legion was the totally destroyed Jerusalem; the governor resided with parts of the 10th legion in Caesarea (Maritima), which Vespasian had converted into a Roman colony.[2]

The consequences of the war were also devastating for the people of Judaea. Entire communities had been totally destroyed and depopulated. Josephus and Tacitus report massive casualties amongst the population;[3] the modern research puts the figure at up to one-third of the Jewish population of Palestine. Naturally, this also had catastrophic economic consequences; the rural population, which had already suffered exploitation enough before the war, was now impoverished even further. The land (it is uncertain whether this implies landed property *in toto*[4] or only the so-called royal estates, which were anyway extensive enough) became the property of the emperor, that is, Vespasian, who sold it or leased it out on his own authority and for his own financial benefit (Vespasian established a large military colony for veterans of the war in the vicinity of Emmaus, near Jerusalem).[5] Most, if not all, Jewish farmers thus became *coloni* (tenant farmers), who were allowed to work the

131

land in return for payment of rent and whose position was midway between that of slaves and freemen. The grave economic consequences of the new property relations is demonstrated by the *sikarikon* law mentioned in the Mishnah,[6] which was concerned to secure Jewish property as far as was possible and, above all, to facilitate the repurchase of land which had been lost during or following the revolt.[7] Even Josephus' estates near Jerusalem were occupied by Roman troops and thus as good as expropriated. As compensation, Titus presented him with estates in the Plain of Jezreel (that is, royal estates), and Vespasian later granted him "a considerable tract of land in Judaea".[8]

Internally, the first war also resulted in a major upheaval in Jewish religious life. Judaism had been centered for centuries around the Temple cult as the focal point of religious life, but it now had to reorientate itself totally and adjust to a life not only without a state, but also without a Temple. To be sure, the significance of the Temple cult for the Jewish religion should not be overestimated; it had already been on the decline under the last of the Hasmoneans and especially under Herod. The criticism of the Temple from certain quarters (as can be found in some of the Qumran manuscripts or in the New Testament, for example) had certainly also had its effect. Nevertheless, the destruction of the Temple, especially as its finality became increasingly apparent, demanded a fundamental rethink, a radical new beginning. Certainly, it was by no means clear right from the outset that the destruction of the Temple would be definitive—after all, the destruction of the first Temple (in 586 BCE) was followed by the erection of a second—, yet we have no indication that any attempts at reconstruction were made.[9] Neither do we hear of anyone laying claim to the office of High Priest (an absolute necessity for the orderly "functioning" of the Temple cult); the High Priesthood disappeared for good with the destruction of the second Temple. An external sign of the quality of finality which the destruction of the Temple soon assumed in the consciousness of the people was the fact that the Temple tax now had to be paid in the form of the *fiscus Judaicus* to the temple of Jupiter Capitolinus in Rome.[10] This represented less a financial burden—the Temple tax was two drachmas—than an unprecedented and dispiriting humiliation for the pious orthodoxy (the *chasidim*).

As well as the Temple, a second very important state and religious institution was also affected: the Synhedrion. The Synhedrion had the status of guarantor of Jewish political independence. It was headed by the High Priest and, despite the growing influence of the Pharisees, was undoubtedly dominated largely by the aristocratic and economically influential Sadducee families. With the destruction of Jerusalem and the Temple, the administrative authority of the Synhedrion and the Sadducee "party" also disappeared.

8.2. The rabbis

Essentially, all that remained of the so-called "religious parties" prior to 70 CE was the one group which had survived the fiasco of the war relatively unscathed and was the only body capable of coming to a long-term arrangement with the Romans: the moderate wing of the Pharisees, who went down in history as "rabbis" and who was to be the major formative influence on Judaism over the following centuries.

The title *Rabbi* originally meant "my teacher" or "my master", but soon came to stand solely for "teacher" or "master" without the possessive pronoun "my". The Babylonian scholars—as distinct from their Palestinian colleagues—bore the title *Rab* (that is, "teacher" or "master" without the possessive pronoun "my"), while the leaders of rabbinic Judaism after 70 CE were to receive the special honorary title *Rabban* ("our teacher" or "our master"). The general term designating the status of the scholars is *chachamim*—"sages" or *talmide chachamim*—"pupils of sages" or "pupils of scholars".

There is no documentary evidence for the existence of the title *Rabbi* (and its various equivalents) until after 70 CE, which indicates the emergence in Judaism of a new order which had not previously existed in this form. The roots of this new class were the Pharisees on the one hand and, on the other, an old group (or more precisely, a profession) with quite distinct origins from those of the Pharisees—the *soferim*, or scribes. It should not, however, be assumed that the scribal and the Pharisaic traditions led entirely separate existences prior to their confluence in the new "caste" of rabbis. On the contrary, both traditions would already have entered into various forms of affiliation prior to 70 CE, so that there were Pharisees who were also scribes and scribes who were also Pharisees.

The *soferim*, who probably existed as a distinct "class" before the Pharisees, were often to be found in high administrative positions and must therefore have been politically influential. It was they who formulated the ideal of "Torah-centrism", that is, the principle that the Torah should serve as the centre of religious life, and was to be studied, interpreted and applied to all aspects of daily existence.

The later Pharisees, in the form in which they existed in the period preceding the destruction of the Temple, propagated a cult-centred religiosity which, like the cult of the priests in the Temple, was focussed on the Temple. The crucial difference to the priestly ideal consisted in the fact that they did not merely confine their religious practices to the Temple, but tried to extend the sanctity of the Temple to all other areas of daily life; that is, they attempted to turn the whole of Israel into priests and the private house or, more precisely, the private table, into a model of the Temple. This meant that the Temple itself and the Temple cult were ultimately no longer necessary and could be dispensed with. Anyone who adhered to the purity and dietary laws developed by them made his house and his table into a temple and helped spread the sanctity formerly proper to the Temple throughout the whole of Israel.

It seems that the ideals of both these groups, the late Pharisees and the *soferim*, were taken up by the new group of rabbis after 70 CE and were an important formative influence on them. The sanctity of the Temple was extended to all areas of daily life, but this sanctity was no longer tied to the Temple and mediated via the cult, but transmitted through the study and application of the Torah. In place of the Temple, the Torah was now the exclusive focal point; only the teachings and appropriate application of the Torah would make Israel into a holy nation. The "middlemen" and guarantors of this "new" holiness were no longer the priests, but the rabbis.

The classic document of the rabbis' newly acquired self-confidence is the initial chapter of the *Pirke Abot* ("Sayings of the Fathers"), in which the rabbis provide the legitimation for themselves and their teachings:

> Moses received the Torah at Sinai and transmitted it to Joshua,
> Joshua to the elders, and the elders to the Prophets, and the
> Prophets to the men of the Great Synagogue.[11]

From the men of the Great Synagogue, the succession passes seamlessly via Simon the Just, Antigonus of Socho and the five pairs (*zugot*) of scholars to Hillel and Shammai, and then via Gamaliel I and Simon b. Gamaliel I to its culmination in R. Jehudah ha-Nasi, the editor of the Mishnah,[12] who represents the highpoint of rabbinic Judaism. The rabbis thus regard themselves as the only true successors to Moses, the prophets and the Pharisees, and the Torah transmitted—i.e. definitively interpreted—by them is the Torah of Moses.

The rabbi in the Talmudic era was no mere functionary, but the embodiment of the attempt to lead one's life in accordance with the ideals of the Torah, that is, a specific way of life. The crown of the Torah was not to be used for purposes of self-aggrandizement or as a spade to dig with, that is, as a means to earn a living.[13] This was, of course, an ideal that was hard to live up to, at least in economically difficult times. The rabbis therefore had no choice but to take up a trade or profession, and we know of many rabbis who worked on the land or as artisans (as smiths, tanners, carpenters, laundrymen, tailors, cobblers, as well as scribes). Unlike later developments since the Middle Ages and in the modern era in particular, the rabbis did not hold official posts in the synagogue.

How, then, did one become a rabbi? Originally, by adopting the ideals of the rabbinic movement (in particular, by keeping the purity and dietary laws).

However, soon after 70 CE, a further criterion for the acquisition of the status
of rabbi came into effect: affiliation to a recognized rabbi, that is, a teacher-
pupil relationship, often lasting for many years and characterized by a specific way of life (cohabitation of teacher and pupil, joint study, often also
"waiting on" the rabbi, etc.). "Appoint for thyself a teacher (*rav*) and acquire
for thyself a companion (*chaver*)" as it says in the *Pirke Abot*, or: "Let the
honour of thy disciple be as dear to thee as the honour of thy colleague, and
the honour of thy colleague as the reverence for thy teacher, and the reverence for thy teacher as the fear of Heaven".[14] The official conclusion of the
teacher-pupil relationship was marked by the ordination (*minnuy* or *semi-
chah*) of the pupil by the teacher, which authorized him to become an independent teacher and to make rulings in halachic matters, as well as to carry
out judicial functions.

However significant the position and authority of the rabbis may have been
on account of their competence in matters of religious law and their own
claims to authority, one must nevertheless be careful not to overestimate the
rabbis' role and its influence on the people. We should not forget that our
knowledge of the rabbinic era is based almost exclusively on the writings of
these same rabbis, and so must of necessity be one-sided. Even the writings
of the rabbis themselves (the rabbinic literature) contain suggestions of disputes between the people and the rabbis and criticisms of their claims to leadership and of their vanity and arrogance, and even hints of mockery—all
indications that the ideal picture painted by the rabbis themselves never actually existed to the degree they would have wished.

8.3. Johanan ben Zakkai

The rabbi most closely associated with the reform of Judaism after the catastrophe of 70 CE is Johanan b. Zakkai. There is little reliable information
about him. According to tradition, he was one of the foremost Pharisees from
the period of the destruction of the Temple, but this claim was no doubt made
retrospectively and is historically improbable. It is more likely that he was a
representative of the class of scribes in rabbinical Judaism. What is fairly certain is that he was responsible for a number of legal innovations aimed at
facilitating the continuation of religious life following the destruction of the
Temple, and which are known as the *taqqanot* (ordinances enacted by virtue
of rabbinic authority which do not have a biblical basis) of Jabneh. A collection of such *taqqanot* issued by Johanan b. Zakkai is included in the
Mishnah:[15]

If the festive day of the [two-day] New Year fell on a Sabbath, they used to blow the *shofar* in the Temple[16] but not in the country: after the destruction of the Temple, Rabban Johanan b. Zakkai ordained that it should be blown in every place where there was a court.

R. Eliezer said: Rabban Johanan b. Zakkai laid down this rule for Jabneh only. They said to him: It applies equally to Jabneh and to any place where there is a court. ...

Originally the *lulab*[17] was taken[18] in the Sanctuary during seven days and in the country only one day.[19] When the Temple was destroyed Rabban Johanan b. Zakkai ordained that the *lulab* should be taken in the country seven days, in remembrance of the Sanctuary. [He] also [ordained] that during the whole of the Day of Waving,[20] the new corn should be forbidden.

Originally they used to accept testimony with regard to the new moon during the whole of the day.[21] On one occasion the witnesses were late in arriving, and the levites went wrong in the daily hymn.[22] It was therefore ordained that testimony should be accepted only until the afternoon sacrifice,[23] and that if witnesses came after the afternoon sacrifice that day should be kept as holy and also the next day. After the destruction of the Temple Rabban Johanan b. Zakkai ordained that testimony with regard to the new moon should be received during the whole of the day. ...

No final conclusions can be drawn from this small sample regarding the type of innovations introduced by Johanan b. Zakkai, but we can nevertheless make out a clear tendency. None of the ordinances concerns the laws of purity and impurity so characteristic of the Pharisees (in the New Testament and the rabbinic literature). The agricultural laws, which likewise play a great role for the Pharisees, are only represented by one regulation: the new corn may not—as in the Temple—be eaten on the second day of the Passover festival (= the 16th of Nisan); Johanan b. Zakkai here reserves this right strictly for the Temple. The clear intention of all the other *taqqanot*, on the other hand, is to amend the existing regulations in such a way that they can be complied with even without the existence of the Temple: if the New Year festival falls on a sabbath, the *shofar* may be blown anywhere there is a court (and not only in the Temple in Jerusalem); the *lulab* may also be carried outside of Jerusalem on all seven days of the Feast of Tabernacles; evidence of the new moon may once again be accepted throughout the entire day and not only until the early afternoon. At the same time, R. Eliezer's later addition already shows the tendency to ascribe a special role to Jabneh and regard it as a replacement for Jerusalem and the Temple.

8.4. Jabneh

The reconstitution of Judaism as rabbinic Judaism is closely linked to the figure of Johanan b. Zakkai and the city of Jabneh/Jamnia. The small town of Jabneh lies on the coastal plain and was probably owned directly by the emperor. How Johanan b. Zakkai and his followers came to settle in Jabneh is related in a famous story in the rabbinic literature:

> When Vespasian came to destroy Jerusalem, he said to them [= the inhabitants of Jerusalem]: Wretches! Why do you want to destroy this city and see the Temple burn? All I ask of you is that you send me a bow or an arrow [= as a sign of surrender] and I shall leave you be! They answered: Just as we marched out against your two predecessors and killed them, so shall we march against you and kill you!

> When R. Johanan b. Zakkai heard [this], he called together the inhabitants of Jerusalem and spoke to them: My children, why do you destroy this city and [why] do you want to burn down the Temple? What does he ask of you? He asks nothing of you except a bow or an arrow and he will leave you be! They replied: Just as we marched out against the two before him and killed them, so shall we march against him and kill him!

> Vespasian had men encamped by the walls of Jerusalem, and they wrote down every word that they heard on arrows and dispatched [them] beyond the wall to show that R. Johanan b. Zakkai was a friend of the emperor.

> When R. Johanan b. Zakkai had talked to them thus for one, two, then three days and they [still] did not accept [what he said], he called for his pupils R. Eliezer and R. Joshua. He said to them: My sons, take me away from here! Make me a coffin and I will sleep in it! R. Eliezer held his head, R. Joshua held his feet, and they carried him forth until, at sunset, they arrived at the gates of Jerusalem.

> There, the gate-keepers said to them: Who is that? They answered them: It is a dead man. Don't you know that a dead man may not

remain overnight in Jerusalem? Then they [= the gate-keepers] replied: If it is a dead man, then take him out!

They took him out and conveyed him until they came to Vespasian. [There] they opened the coffin, and he stood before him. [Vespasian] said to him: Are you R. Johanan b. Zakkai? Tell me what you want from me! He answered him: I ask of you only Jabneh, that I may go there to teach my pupils, and set up [a house of] prayer, and observe all the commandments. [Vespasian] said to him: Go and do anything you want!

Then [Johanan b. Zakkai] said to [Vespasian]: May I tell you something? He answered: Speak! Then [Johanan b. Zakkai] said to him: You will soon be called upon to rule!—How do you know this? He answered him: It has been passed down to us that the Temple will not fall into the hands of a common man, but only into the hands of a king, for it is written: And he shall cut down the thickets of the forest with iron, and Lebanon[24] shall fall by a mighty one (Isa. 10:34).

It is said that before one, two or three days had passed, two envoys came to him from his city [= Rome] [and informed him] that the emperor was dead and that he had been appointed ruler.[25]

This story, which comes down to us in several different versions, may be regarded as a founding myth of rabbinic Judaism. Superficially, it displays a remarkable similarity to the story of Josephus after the fall of Jotapata and is no doubt influenced by this story. Like Josephus, Johanan b. Zakkai is a friend of the Romans who prefers to go over to them rather than (like the Zealots) allow everything to be razed to the ground; like Josephus, Johanan b. Zakkai prophesies to Vespasian his imminent appointment as emperor. The point of each stories is, however, totally different. Josephus saves his own life in order to spend his remaining years far away from Judaea as a favourite of the heathen ruler; Johanan b. Zakkai saves his life in order to resurrect Judaism in Jabneh in the form of rabbinic Judaism.[26] In this case, then, the request for Jabneh is the central message of the story. This is formulated even more clearly in the other versions of the story, in statements such as: "Give me Jabneh and its Wise Men, and the dynasty of Rabban Gamaliel ..."[27] or even simply: "I ask of you Jabneh, that I may study Torah there ... and observe all the remaining commandments".[28] The sole objective of rabbinic Judaism was to observe the Torah in as appropriate and comprehensive a fashion as was possible after 70 CE, and this aim was guaranteed by the patriarchs as the legitimate leaders of this rabbinic Judaism. The Torah may well have been all that remained to the Jews after the destruction of Jerusalem and the Temple, but it was the single most important thing in Judaism, its essence and its real strength, which ultimately even proved to be stronger than Rome.

Jabneh's importance after 70 CE as the geographical and spiritual centre of rabbinic Judaism was so great that one may justifiably refer to the period from the destruction of the Temple to the Bar Kochba uprising as the "Jabneh period". It was here that, under Johanan b. Zakkai and Gamaliel II, the son of Simon/Shimon b. Gamaliel I (the leader of the Pharisees before 70 and during the war),[29] the foundation of rabbinic Judaism was laid, and the material which was later to make up the Mishnah was first formulated and sifted through.[30] This is why the period of Jabneh is often referred to as the formative period of rabbinic Judaism.

Jabneh is associated in Christian theology with two events in particular, both of which were of special significance for the early development of Christianity during this period: the establishment of the canon and the so-called "heretics' blessing".

The canon of books constituting the Hebrew Bible is supposed to have been formally established in Jabneh. This was done in response to the rise of Christianity, in order to clearly differentiate the two religions and counter Christianity's claims on sacred writings.

Recent research has shown that Christian theology greatly exaggerates in this matter. The sources in the rabbinic literature[31] indicate merely that the canonicity of certain Biblical books was discussed—such as Ecclesiastes, the Song of Songs and Ecclesiasticus, but also Daniel and Esther—but that the canon had by no means already been established in the early Jabneh period (that is, towards the end of the first century CE). Discussions concerning the canonicity of specific biblical books certainly continued until the period following the Bar Kochba revolt, the so-called Usha period. This means that Christianity could not have played the role in the formation of the Jewish canon that many Christian theologians would like to claim for it. From the rabbinic point of view, Christianity doubtless had no significance whatsoever during the Jabneh period and certainly did not constitute a reason for fixing the canon.

A similar case is made for the introduction of the so-called *birkat ha-minim*[32] in the prayer of "Eighteen Benedictions".[33] Here too, many Christian theologians hold that the cursing of the *minim* ("heretics") in the twelfth benediction in this prayer is aimed expressly and exclusively at the Christians and likewise has the demarcation of the "synagogue" from the "church" in mind.

This thesis contains an element of truth, insofar as the emphatic cursing of the *minim*[34] was incorporated in the prayer of Eighteen Benedictions under Gamaliel II—although probably not as a totally new benediction, but through the reworking and extension of an already existing one—, but there is no evidence to show that it originally and primarily referred to the Christians in the strict sense of the word. Closer examination of the individual versions shows that the *birkat ha-minim* applies in the first instance to two specific groups, namely, Jewish heretics of various provenance and orientation, and the Roman authorities. It goes without saying that Christians might subsequently also be numbered amongst the heretics (they were doubtless originally regarded as a Jewish sect), but any such later development cannot be viewed in immediate conjunction with the introduction of the *birkat ha-minim*.

We do not know precisely how long Johanan b. Zakkai was active in Jabneh; the rabbinic reports concerning his "retirement" to Beror Chail (a small town south-east of Ascalon) are unclear and tendentious. What is certain is that his "flight" to the Romans stirred up a lot of resentment and made him the subject of much controversy. At any rate, the above-mentioned Gamaliel II seems to have taken his place sometime between 80 and 90 CE. Under him, the work carried out at Jabneh increasingly took on political dimensions and seems to have gained steadily in influence, even coming to the attention of the Romans. The tradition according to which Gamaliel II travelled to Syria to obtain authority from a "hegemon" (m Ed 7:7; b San 11a) is frequently interpreted as an allusion to his official recognition as a Jewish representative by the Romans. As, however, there is no mention of what this authority was for, one must take care not to overinterpret this tradition. It is very doubtful whether the office of "patriarch" (or *nasi*, in the technical sense of the term) already existed in this early period—for the rabbinic tradition, of course, not only was Gamaliel II a patriarch, but Johanan b. Zakkai as well: he also bears the honorary title of *Rabban*,[35]— but as time went on an incipient Jewish autonomy in Jabneh was tacitly tolerated by the Romans and eventually officially recognized. A reported journey to Rome by Gamaliel may well be historically true, even though it was certainly not the "state visit" that many researchers claim.

We do not know the date of Gamaliel II's death. We may safely assume that he did not live until the Bar Kochba revolt but died much earlier, probably sometime between 100 and 120 CE. There is also general agreement that his son, Shimon b. Gamaliel II, did not take up the succession directly, but that other schools were dominant in the period from about 120 CE until the beginning of the Bar Kochba revolt, above all those of the two outstanding rabbis of their day: Rabbi Akiba (in Bene Baraq near present-day Tel Aviv) and Rabbi Ishmael (in southern Judaea).

8.5. The revolt under Trajan (115–117 CE)[36]

Following the catastrophe of the first great war against Rome, it remained peaceful in Palestine and the Jewish Diaspora for a relatively long period of time. The desire of the people and its leaders for Messianic adventures had largely vanished or had else been repressed. However, the great uprising in the Diaspora in the first half of the second century was to show that Messianism still remained an active political force to be reckoned with.

The revolt broke out under Trajan and was a consequence—at least indirectly—of his campaign against the Parthians in the east of the empire. During his absence in Mesopotamia (115 CE), and evidently taking deliberate advantage of the fact that his military forces were concentrated there, the Jews in Egypt and Cyrenaica rose up, to be followed a short while later by the Jews of Cyprus and eventually Mesopotamia as well. According to the sources, the revolt was directed in each case against the "heathen" (Graeco-Roman) neighbours of the Jews in the areas concerned. Dio in particular gives account of massacres and unbelievable atrocities perpetrated by the Jews against the heathen population.[37] In the Cyrenaica, the Jews were led by Lucuas (according to Eusebius)[38] or Andreas (according to Dio),[39] in Cyprus, by Artemion.[40] Trajan considered the revolt so serious that he sent one of his foremost generals, Marcius Turbo, to the Cyrenaica to put it down (which he was only able to do after protracted fighting). In Cyprus, the bloodbath unleashed by the Jews against their heathen neighbours was so bad that, after the quelling of the revolt, no Jew was allowed to set foot on the island again (according to Dio, even the survivors of shipwrecks were immediately put to death).[41]

Especially dangerous for Trajan was the involvement of the Mesopotamian Jews in the uprising on the politically sensitive eastern frontier of the empire and in a region, which he had only just taken from the Parthians. Here, Trajan appointed the Moorish general Lusius Quietus to crush the rebellion. He carried out his task so thoroughly that he was subsequently rewarded by Trajan with the governorship of the province of Judaea.

There is some dispute in the research as to whether Palestine, or parts of Palestine, was also involved in the revolt. The case for such involvement rests on a brief comment by Pseudo-Spartianus (the supposed biographer of Hadrian in the *Historia Augusta*), who mentions Libya and Palestine together,[42] as well as a *pulmus shel qitus* ("War of Qitus")[43] which crops up at various points in the rabbinic literature, although it is not even clear precisely who this "Qitus" refers to (Lusius Quietus or Quintus Marcius Turbo?), let alone whether the war in question took place in Palestine. Similarly, the legendary tale of the martyrdom of the two brothers, Lulianus/ Julianus and

Pappus, under Trajan in Laodicaea (in northern Syria!)[44] contributes little towards the solution of the problem. All these scattered references are of little historical value, and contemporary researchers tend to assume that the Jews of Palestine played no part in the war. The situation in Palestine was certainly very different from that in the Diaspora, and it would appear that the revolt under Trajan was essentially a revolt of the Diaspora which arose as a result of the conditions specific to the Graeco-Roman Diaspora Jewry (cultural assimilation with concurrent intensification of—fatal—contradictions, economic rivalry, etc.).

The fact that the revolt in the Diaspora did not spread to Judaea may well have something to do with a further change in the status of the Roman province of Judaea. There is increasing evidence that, at about the same time as the revolts in the Diaspora, Judaea was converted from a praetorian province (the status it had held since 74 CE)[45] to a consular one. This "promotion" to the highest category of the Roman provincial system implied—in addition to a governor of consular rank—that two legions were now permanently stationed in the province instead of just one as previously. For Judaea, this meant that, in addition to the 10th legion installed in Judaea after the first war, a further legion was now transferred to the province (possibly the *legio II Traiana*). It would therefore appear that, in converting Judaea into a consular province and thereby doubling the number of troops stationed permanently in Judaea, the Romans were making a deliberate (and successful) attempt to prevent the revolt spreading to Palestine.

Notes

1. We have only incomplete information regarding the names and terms of office of the governors between the two wars.
2. Under the name *Colonia Prima Flavia Augusta Caesarensis*; cf. Pliny, Nat. Hist. V, 14 § 69.
3. Bell. VI, 9.3 § 420: 100,000 people. This figure is certainly a gross exaggeration.
4. This is the usual interpretation of Bell. VII, 6.6 § 216 f. However, the precise meaning is unclear.
5. Bell. VII, 6.6 § 217.
6. m Git 5.6.
7. It is unclear why the law is so called. Some authorities believe it derives from the Sicarii (see p. 115 above), others from the *lex de sicariis et veneficis*, which forbade castration (see p. 146 below). It is accordingly unclear whether the law refers to the consequences of the First Jewish War or the Bar Kochba revolt.
8. Vita 76 §§ 422–425.
9. The various references to a continuation of the sacrificial cult despite the destruction of the Temple (cf. Clemens 41.2–3; m Pes 7.2; m Ed 8.6) are all unreliable.
10. Bell. VII, 6.6 § 218.

11. m Ab 1.1. Translations of quotations from the Mishnah and the Babylonian Talmud are based on the edition The Babylonian Talmud, ed. Rabbi Dr. I. Epstein (The Soncino Press, London, 1935–1952).
12. See p. 164 ff. below.
13. m Ab 4.5.
14. m Ab 1.8; 4.12.
15. m RHSh 4.1–4.
16. As required on the occasion of the New Year festival. This requirement, however, conflicts with the Sabbath commandment.
17. *Pars pro toto* for the four species of plants used on the Feast of Tabernacles, consisting of a palm branch (*lulab*), twigs of willow and myrtle, and an *etrog* (citron).
18. I.e. carried during the procession in the Temple.
19. During the procession in the synagogue.
20. The day (the 16th of Nisan = the second day of the Passover festival) on which the *comer* (sheaf of barley) was "swung" in the Temple, and the new barley was eaten.
21. I.e. during the whole of the last day of the last month of the year (Elul).
22. They did not know whether they should sing the hymn for an ordinary day or for a festival day.
23. The *minchah* service in the early afternoon.
24. Traditional code-word for the Temple.
25. ARNA ch. 4, p. 22 f.
26. The construction put upon the stories should not be confused or equated with the actual *historical* reality.
27. b Git 56 b.
28. ARNB ch. 6, p. 19.
29. See p. 125 above.
30. See p. 164 ff. below.
31. Especially m Yad 3.5.
32. "Heretics' blessing", euphemism for "cursing of the heretics".
33. Apart from the *Shema* ("Hear, O Israel"), the main component of the daily synagogue service. It is recited three times a day.
34. In some versions of the *birkat ha-minim* the *notsrim* ("Christians") as well.
35. See p. 133 above.
36. Although the focal point of the revolt clearly lay in the Diaspora, it is briefly dealt with here, as the participation of the Palestinian Jews in the revolt is a subject of much discussion in the research.
37. Dio Cassius, HR LXVIII, 32.1–3.
38. HE IV, 2.4.
39. HR LXVIII, 32.1.
40. Dio Cassius, HR LXVIII, 32.2.
41. Ibid. LXVIII, 32.3.
42. HA, Vita Hadr. 5.2: "In Libya and also in Palestine the rebels overreached themselves".
43. m Sot 9.14 and *passim*.
44. Sifra *emor, pereq* 9.5; b Taan 18b; j Taan 2.13, fol. 66a; j Meg 1.6, fol. 70c.
45. See p. 131 above.

9. THE BAR KOCHBA REVOLT

The most important historical event in the era of rabbinic Judaism was the so-called Bar Kochba revolt. This second Jewish uprising against Rome is only comparable in its significance and its far-reaching consequences with the first uprising of 70 CE, although there is one essential difference to this initial revolt: the source material on which we must rely in order to reconstruct the events is incomparably inferior to that for the earlier Jewish war, not least because we lack a historian of the stature of a Flavius Josephus, to whom we are indebted for the greater part of our knowledge of the first revolt. We are therefore forced to rely on a few, mostly legendary accounts in the rabbinic literature and a handful of comments by the Graeco-Roman authors, although these have recently been supplemented by the finds from the Judaean Desert, which represent a not inconsiderable addition to our knowledge of the period.

9.1. The causes of the revolt

The origin of the Bar Kochba revolt remains a crucial and hotly disputed issue to this day. The question as to what led to the revolt is an important one since the relatively peaceful internal development of Judaism in the period following the first revolt until the outbreak of the second (probably in 132 CE) provides us with no obvious grounds for a renewed outbreak of war against Rome. The revolt in the Diaspora[1] does not come into consideration as a cause for this new and very bloody war, especially since Trajan's successor Hadrian (117–138 CE) inaugurated a revision of the Roman policy of expansion with a new emphasis on pacification, a policy which certainly took in the eastern provinces of the empire.

The sources give us three different reasons to choose from. Pseudo-Spartianus, for instance, reports in the *Historia Augusta*:

> In their impetuosity the Jews also began a war, as they had been
> forbidden to mutilate their genitals.[2]

So, according to Pseudo-Spartianus, the Jews started the revolt because they
had been forbidden to practice circumcision. The historian Dio Cassius, on
the other hand, states in his *Roman History*[3] that the reason for the war was
Hadrian's intention to refound the city of Jerusalem as a Roman colony to be
called Aelia Capitolina and containing a new, pagan temple.[4] Finally, according to a rabbinic source,[5] the war came about following a promise by Hadrian
to the Jews that he would rebuild the Jewish Temple, which he then retracted
due to the insinuations of a malevolent Samaritan. Of these three reasons, the
last-named is quite rightly regarded by most researchers as the least probable,
particularly in view of the numerous legendary features of the rabbinic
account (the malevolent Samaritan, for instance, is a familiar figure in the
Jewish literature). The problem therefore comes down to the prohibition on
circumcision and the founding of Aelia Capitolina as the possible reasons for
the war, and most researchers are inclined to take both factors into account.

As regards circumcision, we know that the emperors Domitian and Nerva
had already forbidden castration at the end of the first century,[6] that Hadrian
had intensified this ban on castration (by threatening offenders with the death
penalty),[7] and that finally Antoninus Pius, Hadrian's successor, had expressly
permitted the Jews to have their sons circumcised (but not proselytes).[8] So
although there is no evidence of a ban on circumcision by Hadrian (except for
the comment in Pseudo-Spartianus, to which we may attach little reliability),
we may infer such a prohibition from his successor's granting of permission
to carry out circumcision and thus see this as the cause of the war. The rabbinic sources do indeed maintain that Hadrian issued numerous anti-Jewish
decrees after the Bar Kochba revolt, including a ban on circumcision, but the
problem is whether such a ban was likely to have been in existence prior to
the war and so could be taken as its cause.

We must first ask why Hadrian should suddenly have forbidden circumcision specifically for the Jews. The advocates of this theory point to the phil-
hellenic and "enlightened" attitude of the emperor, for whom circumcision
was simply a barbaric custom which ought to be abolished. It is possible that
Hadrian was indeed of this opinion; at the same time, however, as the political pragmatist that he certainly also was, he ought to have been well aware
that such a prohibition would almost inevitably provoke a revolt on the part
of the Jews, and this does not sit well with Hadrian's systematic pursuit of
policies promoting peace. If these fundamental considerations already make
it unlikely enough that Hadrian would suddenly decide to issue a decree prohibiting circumcision, there is also a positive indication in the rabbinic litera-

ture that a specific ban on circumcision does not come under consideration as a reason for the war. Various texts in the rabbinic literature discuss the question as to whether someone who had submitted himself to epispasm, that is, had an operation to restore his foreskin artificially (we are familiar with this practice from the period of religious persecution under Antiochus IV Epiphanes),[9] would have to be recircumcised if he wished to be accepted back into the Jewish community. Many rabbis were evidently of the opinion that a repeated circumcision was to be avoided as this could be dangerous for the person concerned. Others, however, insisted on a fresh circumcision, justifying their opinion as follows:

> Many allowed themselves to be circumcised anew in the days of
> Ben Koziba [= Bar Kochba], had sons and did not die.[10]

This incidental remark can only be interpreted as implying that, before the Bar Kochba uprising, there were many Jews who had had an operation to restore their foreskin, and these—as was the case in the second century BCE under Antiochus IV—must have been Hellenized or Romanized "enlightened" Jews who rejected circumcision as a barbaric practice and wanted to adapt themselves to their "heathen" environment. These assimilated Jews either had themselves recircumcised out of enthusiasm at the initial success of the revolt and as an expression of renewed nationalist fervour, or else (and this is also a possibility) were forced to do so by Bar Kochba. Unfortunately, we have no further information on this matter.

Whatever the case may be, such an interpretation of the rabbinic text throws a new light on the situation in Palestine on the eve of the second Jewish war. It was not a malevolent or, at best, unsuspecting Hadrian who provoked a senseless war with his ban on circumcision, but the Jews of Palestine were themselves by no means so unanimously orthodox and anti-Roman as most of the rabbinic sources and the later historiography would have us believe. So the foundation of Aelia Capitolina would appear very likely as a possible cause of the war. Hadrian assumed the role of *restitutor* throughout the entire Roman empire and especially in the border provinces, and founded or restored a number of major cities. As regards Judaea, we know that he founded pagan temples in Tiberias and even in Sepphoris, but we have no record of any resistance by the native Jewish population. Why should he not also revive Jerusalem as a Hellenistic-Roman city, especially if a not insignificant part of the Jewish population fell in with these plans and wishes? The uprising would then not be the revolt of Judaism as such against the evil and reviled Roman overlords, but the rebellion of a quite specific—and initially, perhaps, relatively small—group of the "pious" (*chasidim*) against not only the Romans, but also against an influential group within Judaism itself. The closest parallel would be the Maccabean revolt, where an initially relatively insignificant group of orthodox Chasidim came out in opposition not only to foreign rule by the Seleucids, but also to the powerful Hellenistic party which had developed in their own nation.

9.2. Bar Kochba

The sources give various different versions of the name of the leader of the revolt. Only the finds from the Judaean Desert have given us certainty as to how the various forms of the name are to be interpreted.

The coins issued by the rebels bear only his first name, Shimon/Simon, often together with the title *Nasi*.[11] However, the rabbinic literature, the Christian sources and the letters and documents from the Judaean desert also provide a surname. This surname is given in the rabbinic literature as Ben or Bar Koziba,[12] in the Christian sources as *Chochebas* or *Barchochebas*, and in the Hebrew/Aramaic letters and documents from the Judaean Desert as Bar or Ben Kosiba[13] (and in a Greek papyrus *Chôsiba*). In the light of these finds, there can be no further doubt that Ben/Bar Kosiba was the authentic surname of Bar Kochba, and the forms Ben/Bar Koziba and Bar Kochba are to be understood as tendentious interpretations of this original name, Bar Kochba in a positive sense ("Son of the Star"), Bar Koziba in a negative one ("Son of the Lie = Liar").

On the other hand, it still remains uncertain what the surname Ben/Bar Kosiba means. There are two basic possibilities here: either we derive his surname from his father's name (as a patronymic), or regard it as indicating his place of origin. A final decision cannot be made on the basis of the currently available source material, but on purely linguistic grounds a patronymic would seem more likely, as designations of origin are usually expressed in a different fashion, at least in the rabbinic literature.

We have no reliable information regarding Bar Kochba's family. The rabbinic comment that he was the nephew of R. Eleazar ha-Modai is very probably a literary topos without historical foundation; all attempts to construct a Davidian genealogy on the basis of this supposed kinship are therefore untenable. Whatever his origins and his family background, the leader of the second great revolt against Rome emerges just as suddenly from the mists of history as he was later—after the failure of the revolt—to disappear once more into them.

We can learn more, however, if we enquire into the titles given to the leader of the revolt. These titles supply us with information regarding the connotations associated with the revolt and map out, as it were, the frame of reference within which the revolt took place.

9.2.1. Messiah

To be sure, neither the coins nor the letters and documents from the Judaean Desert employ the title of king or Messiah. There can, however, be no doubt that the Bar Kochba revolt and its leader had Messianic implications. Evidence of this can be found in both the rabbinic literature and the Christian sources.

The most important passage in the Rabbinic literature is to be found in the Jerusalem Talmud:

> R. Shimon ben Jochai said, R. Akiba my teacher used to explain the passage, "A star shall go forth from Jacob" (Num. 24:17) thus: "Koziba goes forth from Jacob." Again, when R. Akiba saw Bar Koziba, he cried out, "This is King Messiah."
>
> Thereupon R. Johanan b. Torta said to him: "Akiba, grass will grow out of your cheek-bones and the Son of David will still not have come."[14]

With this Messianic interpretation of Num. 24:17, Akiba harks back to an old exegetical tradition. Already in the Septuagint, the verse is translated: "A star shall come forth out of Jacob, a man shall rise out of Israel." Without doubt, this absolute use of the term "man" (*anthrōpos*) is a reference to a Messianic figure. We find a similar translation in the Aramaic Targum: "When the king shall rise up out of Jacob and mighty shall be the Messiah out of Israel."[15]

This verse also plays a special role in the texts of the Qumran community and writings associated with them. The Testament of Judah, for instance, refers to the royal Messiah from the House of David as follows: "And after this there shall arise for you a *Star* from Jacob in peace: and a *man* shall arise from my posterity like the Sun of righteousness ... Then he will illumine the sceptre of my *kingdom* ..."[16] And in the Damascus Rule: "The *star* is the Interpreter of the Law who shall come to Damascus; as it is written, ... (Num. 24:17). The sceptre is the *Prince* of the whole congregation, and when he comes *he shall smite all the children of Seth*."[17]

These examples suffice to show that the Messianic interpretation of Num. 24:17 was relatively common amongst the Jews, and although it may have been particularly favoured by the Qumran community, it certainly was not exclusive to them. So if this verse was used to support the claim that Bar

Kochba was the Messiah, it by no means implies the special affinity to the Qumran community that many researchers propose.

Of the available Christian sources for the revolt, Eusebius and Justin in particular point to its Messianic character. Eusebius writes:

> At that time a certain Bar Chochebas by name, which means 'star', was the general of the Jews, who among other characteristics was a cut-throat and a bandit, but who relied on his name, as if dealing with slaves, and boasted that he was a star that had come down from heaven to shed light upon them in their misery.[18]

So Eusebius is aware of the meaning of Bar Kochba's surname and its Messianic implications. The "coming down" from Heaven and the "shedding of light" contain an element of 'suddenness', which may be interpreted as a surprising and sudden redemption. However, the negative undertone predominates in his account. Bar Kochba was in reality "a cut-throat and a bandit (lēstrikos)"; his supporters were the socially disadvantaged, who followed him in slavish dependency and were led astray by his Messianic claims. We are evidently dealing here with the same estimation of a Messianic movement as consisting of nothing but lawless bandits and robbers, the result of unfavourable social circumstances, that characterized Josephus' assessment of the first Jewish war.

The other Christian witness, Justin, is one of the few contemporary commentators who mentions the Bar Kochba revolt. He writes:

> In the recent Jewish war, Bar Kochba [Barchochebas], the leader of the Jewish uprising, ordered that only the Christians should be subjected to dreadful torments, unless they renounced and blasphemed Jesus Christ.[19]

We have no other information concerning Bar Kochba's relations with the Christians. As the Bar Kochba letters indicate that Bar Kochba took ruthless action against his opponents, it is certainly conceivable that he also fought against the Christians, who (naturally) refused to support him. There may have been a number of reasons for the Christians' rejection of Bar Kochba, but the most obvious would have been the fact that here Messiah stood against Messiah, and that the Christians were unable to follow Bar Kochba due to the obviously Messianic nature of his movement. The historical crux of this persecution of the Christians may, however, lie less—as Justin seems to suggest —in religious differences than in the inseparability of Messianic and political ambitions.

Many researchers also see the symbols employed on the coins issued by the rebels (particularly the star and the grapes) as an indication of the

Messianic nature of the revolt. While the star is problematic and the subject of much dispute, this does seem conceivable in the case of the grapes, as grapes featured often in the literature as an important symbol for the fruitfulness of the land of Israel in the Messianic era.

9.2.2. Nasi

Unlike the title of Messiah, which can only be inferred and was certainly never employed as a title in the proper sense of the word, the designation *Nasi* ("prince" or "princely leader") was without doubt Bar Kochba's official title. It occurs both in the documents and letters from the Judaean Desert and on the coins.

What is the precise significance of the title of *Nasi*? We are familiar with the term *Nasi* as the designation for the tribal leaders of the people of Israel during their wanderings in the desert, but this will hardly have been the dominant connotation in Bar Kochba's use of this title, and may not even have been implied at all. We come closer to the meaning of the term with Ezekiel's usage, who clearly employs it in an eschatological-Messianic context. In Ez. 37:24 ff., the eschatological David is referred to as king and *Nasi* simultaneously and apparently synonymously: that is, *Nasi* may here be the designation for the eschatological king. Whether the title of *Nasi* was also employed by the Maccabees is disputed, but it clearly plays a major role in the Qumran community. In the so-called Blessings of Qumran, the *Nasi* is addressed as follows:

> May the Lord raise you up to everlasting heights, and as a fortified tower upon a high wall!
>
> [May you smite the peoples] with the might of your hand and ravage the earth with your sceptre; may you bring death to the ungodly with the breath of your lips! ...
>
> May He make your horns of iron and your hooves of bronze; may you toss like a young bull [and trample the peoples] like the mire of the streets!
>
> For God has established you as the sceptre. The rulers ... [and all the kings of the] nations shall serve you.[20]

It cannot be established with any certainty whether and to what extent this eschatological-Messianic interpretation of the title of *Nasi* in a number of the Qumran texts affected the way Bar Kochba and his followers saw themselves.

Nevertheless, the time difference between the last offshoots of the Qumran community in the first century CE and the Bar Kochba revolt in the first half of the second century CE is not so great that this can be entirely discounted. One thing both movements would have had in common was the fight against Rome, for it is almost certain that the term "Kittim" in the Qumran texts stemming from the final phase of the Qumran community is a reference to the Romans. So even though it cannot be proved, it is nevertheless conceivable that the title of *Nasi* would have had similar Messianic and apocalyptic connotations for Bar Kochba to those it had for the Essenes, even if there was no direct and unequivocal influence on the former by the latter. The construction put upon the office of *Nasi* in Qumran did not appear out of thin air, but was probably influenced in turn by the apocalyptic *Nasi* of Ezekiel.[21]

It was in his capacity as *Nasi* that Bar Kochba led the war against Rome, with the aim of freeing Judaea from Roman rule. "Redemption" (*ge'ullah*) and "freedom" (*cherut*) are, therefore, the key terms which are constantly to be found on the coins and documents from the period of the revolt. Both terms indicate the complexity of the expectations bound up with the revolt, which cannot be reduced to one single factor, but can only be duly assessed in their interweaving of religious with political and social motivations. Typical of Bar Kochba's claim to authority is the standard preamble to the leasehold agreements from Wadi Murabba'at:

> On the so-and-so-many of the year 1 (2, 3, 4) of the Redemption
> of Israel by Shimon bar Kosiba, the *Nasi* of Israel ...

As the *Nasi* of Israel, Bar Kochba is the leader of the revolt and consequently also responsible for the political, religious and social restitution of Israel. This further implies that Bar Kochba lays claim to ownership of the land. The territory liberated from the Romans becomes the official property of the *Nasi* as representative of the new Israel, that is, he asserts the same claim to the "royal lands" as the Hasmonean kings. This can likewise be seen clearly from the leasehold agreements:

> On the 20th Shevat in the year two
> of the Redemption of Israel by Shimon
> ben Kosiba, the *Nasi* of Israel.
> In the camp situated in Herodium
> Eleazar ben ha-Shiloni said
> to Hillel ben Garis: I, of my own free will,
> have leased from you some land
> that I have taken on lease in Ir Nachash;
> I have leased it from Shimon, the *Nasi*
> of Israel, for five years....

I have leased it from you from today
until the end of the year before the sabbatical year.
The rental, that I hereby pay to you,
every year: fine
and pure wheat, four *kor* and eight *seah*,
tithed, … which you
shall measure out on the roof of the storehouse in Herodium
every year. [This agreement] is binding for me in this form,
Eleazar ben ha-Shiloni on his own behalf,[22]
Shimon ben Kosiba by his word.[23]

The text of this agreement has not come down to us complete (the central passage is missing), but the most important points are clear: the lessee (Eleazar b. ha-Shiloni) leases a plot of land through an administrative officer (Hillel b. Garis) from Bar Kochba, the owner of the land. He pays rent in the form of grain, that is, natural produce, that has been tithed, i.e. from which the traditional tithe has been deducted. It remains unclear whether the rent was paid in its entirety in Bar Kochba's storehouse, or whether the administrative officer received the rent and in turn delivered only the tithe to Bar Kochba's storehouse.[24] What is certain is that Bar Kochba was the real lord of the land, ruling with absolute authority, although not to his own advantage but for the good of all. This quite clearly distinguishes Bar Kochba from his Hasmonean predecessors, not to mention the Herodian dynasty:

From Shim'on Bar Kosiba to the men of En-gedi, to Masabala and Yehonatan Bar Ba'ayan, peace.

You sit, eat and drink from the property of the House of Israel and care nothing for your brothers.[25]

The concept of the brother, which crops up on various occasions in the texts from the Dead Sea, seems to characterize the special relationship of the members of the House of Israel under Bar Kochba. This does not, however, mean that Bar Kochba did not assert a claim to absolute leadership, as can be seen from many of his letters. So, for instance, he orders Yehonatan and Masabala (both of whom were apparently the military commanders in En Gedi) to seize the wheat of a certain Tanchum b. Ishmael and deliver it to Bar Kochba: "And if you do not accordingly, you shall be punished severely".[26] At the same time, they are forbidden, under threat of punishment, to give refuge to the men of Tekoa, who had possibly ignored Bar Kochba's mobilization orders: "Regarding all men from Tekoa who are found in your locality—the houses in which they are living shall be burnt down and you [shall also be] punished".[27] It is apparently these same "shirkers" who are the subject of another letter: "See to it that all men from Tekoa and other places who are residing in your locality are sent to me without delay. And if you shall not send them, then let it be known that you shall be punished".[28] And the tone of a letter to another commander, Jeshua b. Galgula, is even more threatening. We do not know precisely why Bar Kochba was threatening him, but the threat itself is unmistakable: "May Heaven be my witness ... that I shall put your feet in fetters like I did to Ben Aphlul!"[29]

One final characteristic of the *Nasi* Bar Kochba was his concern to uphold religious precepts. So, for instance, he instructs his envoys to rest on the Sabbath and not to transport wheat until "after the Sabbath". Following his arrest, Eleazar b. Chitta is to be delivered to Bar Kochba "before the Sabbath". In the leasing agreements, which were issued in the name of Bar Kochba as the supreme "ruler of the country", the sabbatical year plays a major role. The most important document in this regard is an Aramaic letter in which a certain Judah b. Menashe is instructed to make arrangements for the delivery of palm branches, *etrogim*, myrtle and willow to Bar Kochba's camp.[30] This is quite clearly a reference to the "four species" of the festive bunch for the Feast of Tabernacles, so we can see that, even in the final phase of the war, Bar Kochba (he is specified as the sender of the letter) was concerned to ensure that the Feast of Tabernacles was celebrated in his camp. Moreover, Bar Kochba expressly exhorts the recipient of the letter to ensure that the *etrogim* are tithed.

Here we see evidence of a degree of ritual observance and rigorous adherence to the Torah which finds its closest parallel amongst the Zealot leaders of the first revolt and the "pious" of the early Maccabean uprising. In this respect, Bar Kochba was certainly not a representative of the Pharisaic-rabbinic tendency of Judaism—it is no accident that only R. Akiba's support is recorded in the sources, and that this is immediately contradicted—,[31] but rather of those groups who wished to put the Torah into full and undivided effect in both the religious and the sociopolitical senses.

9.3. The revolt

Little is known about the actual course of events during the revolt. The research concentrates on the following points:

1. Did the rebels conquer Jerusalem and perhaps even attempt to rebuild the Temple (now the third Temple) and resume sacrificial worship in this "new" capital of Bar Kochba's Messianic kingdom? To be sure, Jerusalem was still in ruins and would hardly have been particularly well fortified by the

Romans, yet the available sources give no clear indication of a Jewish occupation of Jerusalem. The few literary sources are all skimpy and late, and so
we must turn to the coins for evidence to support this theory.

Roughly speaking, the coins from the Bar Kochba revolt fall into the following categories:

(a) Coins with the inscription "Year One of the Redemption of Israel". These
    coins therefore originate from the first year of the revolt.

(b) Coins with the inscription "Year Two of the Liberation of Israel". These
    coins certainly belong to the second year of the revolt.

(c) Coins dating from the first and second years bearing only the inscription
    "Jerusalem".

(d) Coins with an inscription that can be translated as either "[Year X] of the
    Liberation of Jerusalem" or "For the Freedom/Liberation of Jerusalem".
    No date is given, but it seems certain that they can be dated to the third
    year of the revolt.

These coins have been used to infer that, in the first years of the revolt,
Jerusalem was in the hands of the rebels: the legends on the coins dating from
the first and second years proclaim the successful liberation or redemption of
Israel. At the same time, the coins from the first two years bearing the
inscription "Jerusalem" show that they were minted in Jerusalem itself and
that the rebels therefore had their own mint in Jerusalem. In the third year,
Jerusalem was lost once more to the Romans, and the legend "For the
Freedom of Jerusalem" is therefore to be translated as an appeal ("[Fight] for
the Liberation of Jerusalem!") which expresses the desire for the speedy
recapture of Jerusalem from the Romans.

Against this supposition, it may be objected that it is by no means certain
that the legends on the coins from the third year can be taken to represent an
appeal. Furthermore (and this is particularly telling), there have in the meantime been numerous major finds of coins from the Bar Kochba period in
Judaea (near Hebron, for instance), but out of the approximately fifteen thousand coins recovered during excavations in Jerusalem, only two (!) Bar
Kochba coins were found. For this reason, archaeologists and numismatists
have cast serious doubt on the theory that Bar Kochba's mint was situated in
Jerusalem, which (together with the lack of literary sources) undermines the
case for the reconquest of Jerusalem by Bar Kochba's troops.

Similar objections apply in respect of the supposed resumption of the
Temple cult. Here too, the coins are called upon for evidence, and particularly

those depicting the Temple facade and various other motifs borrowed from the Temple cult (festive bunch, trumpet, lyre, jug), some of which also bear the legend "Eleazar the Priest". Such arguments are just as unconvincing. As regards the depiction of the Temple, this is frequently to be found on coins dating from the third year, which can hardly be reconciled with the above-mentioned thesis that Jerusalem was lost again in the third year. The symbols from the Temple cult also occur so frequently on other coins (on those from the Hasmonean era, for example) that nothing whatsoever can be inferred from these. Temple and cultic symbols are in all probability to be understood as purely programmatic and with no actual historical implications in the sense of indicating possession of the Temple and the resumption of sacrificial worship.

The fact that the priest Eleazar is mentioned on some of the coins has given rise to some particularly wild speculation. Some researchers would like to see him as the High Priest of the Third Temple, construction of which would have begun immediately upon taking Jerusalem. Against this view speaks the fact that Eleazar is always referred to on the coins as "Priest" and never "High Priest". This is an important point, as the title of High Priest occurs frequently on the Hasmonean coins, and should warn against the ready assumption that Eleazar was the High Priest of the new Temple. Certainly, he was a leading figure to be placed alongside Bar Kochba, but his exact function during the uprising cannot be determined from the coins. His role may have been that of a priest or even a "priestly Messiah" to complement the "secular leader" Bar Kochba, but this permits no conclusions to be drawn regarding the construction of the Temple, or even the occupation of Jerusalem.

2. What was the overall area affected by the revolt? This question is concerned above all to establish whether the revolt was confined to Judaea in the narrow geographical sense, or whether—and this is what makes it so controversial, and more than a merely topographical problem—it also extended to other regions of the province of Judaea, and Galilee in particular. The problem is more than one of topography and geography since it touches on the relationship between Judaea and Galilee, and in the older research it was assumed that Galilee always stood a little to one side and showed less eagerness to follow the Torah than the more "conservative" Judaea. In this context, some researchers have a special interest in demonstrating that Galilee participated in the revolt.

One thing we can be sure of is that the town of Bethar (approx. 10 km south-west of Jerusalem) was an important centre of the revolt.[32] The other places in Galilee mentioned in the rabbinic literature in connection with the revolt are all dubious. On the other hand, the localities mentioned in the letters and documents from the Judaean Desert allow us to map out a clearly defined territory. With few exceptions, the places concerned are all located in the area circumscribed by Bethar to the north-west, Hebron to the south-west and the western coast of the Dead Sea to the east. The northernmost point that can be associated with the revolt is Wadi ed-Daliyeh, about 18 km north-west of Jericho. Numerous finds were made here from the time of the Bar Kochba revolt, above all items of practical use, but only one (badly preserved) coin and no skeletons or written documents as in the caves near En Gedi. The caves at Wadi ed-Daliyeh, like the caves to the west of the Dead Sea near En Gedi, had quite clearly been used by Jewish refugees. However, as we do not know where the refugees came from—they may equally well have come from Central Judaea or Samaria as from the Jordan Valley in the south—only very limited conclusions may be drawn from the finds at Wadi ed-Daliyeh regarding the area affected by the revolt.

To be sure, the area delimited by the clearly identifiable and localizable vicinities is not to be automatically equated with the overall area covered by the revolt, but it nonetheless certainly indicates the revolt's heartland. The localities in question are so clearly restricted to the territory of Judaea in the narrow sense, and largely concentrated in the region south of Jerusalem, that it would seem unlikely that the revolt extended beyond this area (as far as the actual fighting is concerned). In particular, there is as yet no reason to assume that the Jews of Galilee took part in the revolt.

3. There is also little information available concerning the actual course of the war. We know the name of the governor of the province of Judaea at the time the war broke out—Tineius Rufus—, and we know that the Romans must have found it extremely difficult to suppress the revolt. This is shown by the fact that several legions were involved in putting down the rebellion. These certainly included the *legio III Cyrenaica*, the *legio III Gallica*, the *legio X Fretensis* and the *legio VI Ferrata*, as well as numerous auxiliaries; the *legio X Fretensis* and probably the *legio VI Ferrata* were the two garrisons stationed in Judaea when the war broke out.[33] Not only was the governor of Syria, Publicius Marcellus, forced to intervene in the fighting, but Hadrian also summoned his foremost general, Julius Severus, to Palestine from Britain to assume overall command of the Roman troops.

The only precise information we have concerns the end of the war and comes from the rabbinic literature and the finds in the Judaean Desert. The rabbinic literature hands down an extensive series of traditional accounts detailing the conquest of Bethar. Unfortunately, the town has not yet been systematically excavated, but the conquest would appear to have taken a similar course to the conquest of Masada in 74 CE. According to rabbinic tradition, Bethar fell on the 9th of Av 135 CE, the same day traditionally associated with the destruction of both Temples. The rabbinic account of the conquest of Bethar is certainly not a historical report in the strict sense, but it gives some indication of the response to this event and the importance accorded to the fall of Bethar in the rabbinic tradition:

> They [= the Romans] continued to slay them [= the inhabitants of Bethar] until the horses sank up to their nostrils in blood. And the blood rolled boulders weighing forty *seah* [forwards] until [after] four miles it reached the sea ...

> They said: The brains of three hundred small children were found on one rock. [Likewise] three baskets were found containing phylacteries [with a capacity] of nine *seah* each. Others say: Nine [baskets with a capacity] of three *seah* each.

> It is taught: Rabban Shimon b. Gamaliel says: There were five hundred schools in Bethar, and in the smallest of them were not less than five hundred children. They used to say: If the enemy comes upon us, we shall go out to meet them with these pencils and bore out their eyes. When however sin caused this to happen, [the Romans] wound every one of them in his own scroll and burnt him ...

> Hadrian the blasphemer had a great vineyard of eighteen square miles, as much as the distance from Tiberias to Sepphoris. He surrounded it with a fence made from those slain at Bethar as high as a man with outstretched arms. And he commanded that they were not to be buried until another king arose and ordered their burial.[34]

The finds in the Judaean Desert (above all in Nachal Chever, south of En Gedi) come from the final phase of the war. The last of the rebels were starved out in the caves near En Gedi until they could be killed by the Romans, a tactic already successfully implemented by Herod. The excavations carried out in 1960 and 1961 turned up a large number of skeletons, as well as clothing, utensils and, above all, letters and documents that the rebels had taken into the caves with them and which now constitute our most important source for the revolt.

9.4. The consequences

The consequences of the revolt were perhaps even more catastrophic and far-reaching than those of the first war. As regards the Romans, Hadrian had himself acclaimed a second time as *Imperator*, but he did not stage a triumphal procession and only awarded the *ornamenta triumphalia* to his victorious general, Julius Severus. The cost of victory was so great for the Romans that, in his report to the Senate, Hadrian omitted the usual formula *mihi et legionibus bene* ("all is well with me and the legions").[35]

For the Jews of Palestine, however, both the immediate and the long-term consequences were certainly far worse. According to Cassius Dio:

> Fifty of their most important outposts and nine hundred and eighty-five of their most famous villages were razed to the ground. Five hundred and eighty thousand men were slain in the various raids and battles, and the number of those that perished by famine, disease and fire was past finding out. Thus nearly the whole of Judaea was made desolate, a result of which the people had had forewarning before the war. For the tomb of Solomon, which the Jews regard as an object of veneration, fell to pieces of itself and collapsed, and many wolves and hyenas rushed howling into their cities.[36]

Even if Dio's figures are somewhat exaggerated, the casualties amongst the population and the destruction inflicted on the country would have been considerable. According to Jerome, many Jews were also sold into slavery, so many, indeed, that the price of Jewish slaves at the slave market in Hebron sank drastically to a level no greater than that for a horse.[37] The economic structure of the country was largely destroyed. The entire spiritual and economic life of the Palestinian Jews moved to Galilee.

Jerusalem was now turned into a Roman colony with the official name *Colonia Aelia Capitolina* (*Aelia* after Hadrian's family name: P. Aelius Hadrianus; *Capitolina* after Jupiter Capitolinus).[38] The Jews were forbidden on pain of death to set foot in the new Roman city.[39] Aelia thus became a completely pagan city, no doubt with the corresponding public buildings and temples.[40] Whether, as Dio maintains, a temple dedicated to Jupiter Capitolinus was erected on the site of the destroyed Jewish Temple[41] has now been put into question. We can, however, be certain that a statue of Hadrian was erected in the centre of Aelia, and this was tantamount in itself to a desecration of Jewish Jerusalem. It is therefore justified to speak of a total paganization of Jerusalem.

It is, however, debatable whether the Palestinian Jews were subjected to systematic persecution either during the revolt or after it had been put down. The rabbinic sources suggest such a "Hadrianic persecution" accompanied by numerous prohibitions (in addition to the ban on circumcision, it is also maintained that there were prohibitions on the Sabbath, the Torah, and other aspects of the Jewish religion).[42] Upon closer examination of these sources, it would appear that the further away the sources are in time from the historical event of the Bar Kochba revolt, the more extreme the persecution becomes. The historical basis of the traditions concerning persecution is probably only the ban on circumcision, which the rabbis gradually blew up into a systematic and massive persecution of the Jews.

Notes

1. See p. 141 ff. above.
2. Vita Hadr. 14.2.
3. HR LXIX, 12.
4. According to Eusebius, HE IV, 6.1–4, this was not the cause but a result of the war.
5. BerR 64.10.
6. Suetonius, Domitian 7.1; Cassius Dio, HR XLVII, 2 f.
7. Ulpian, Digesta XLVIII, 8.4.2.
8. Modestinus, Digesta XLVIII, 8.11.1.
9. See p. 37 above.
10. t Shab 15 [16]. 9.
11. Cf. p. 151 ff. below.
12. With a *zayin*.
13. With a *samech* or *sin*.
14. j Taan 4.8, fol. 68d.
15. TO on Num. 24:17.
16. Ch. 24.
17. 7.18-21.
18. HE IV, 6.2. The English translation is taken from The Fathers of the Church, vol. 19, tr. Roy J. Deferrari (Washington, 1953).
19. Apol. I, 31.6. The English translation is taken from The Fathers of the Church, vol. 6, tr. Thomas B. Falls (Washington, 1984).
20. 1 QSb 5.23–28 [English translation G. Vermes, The Dead Sea Scrolls in English (2nd. ed., Middlesex, England, 1975), p. 209]; cf. also the text CD 7.18–21 cited on p. 149 above [Vermes, p. 104].
21. The later use of the title of Nasi by the rabbis in the sense of "patriarch" (see p. 168 ff. below) had not yet been introduced at the time of the Bar Kochba revolt.
22. I.e. in his own hand?
23. I.e. by proxy? Mur. 24 B, in: Milik, DJD II, p. 124 f.
24. It is also possible to read:"that *I* [i.e. the lessee] ... shall measure out"; the word in question was added by Milik.
25. Yadin, IEJ 11, 1961, p. 46 f.
26. Yadin, ibid. p. 41 f.
27. Yadin, Bar Kochba, p. 125.
28. Yadin, IEJ 11, 1961, p. 47 f.
29. Yadin, Bar Kochba, p. 137.
30. Yadin, ibid., p. 128 f.
31. See p. 149 above.

32. See p. 157 f. below.
33. See p. 142 above.
34. j Taan 4.8, fol. 69a.
35. Dio Cassius, HR LXIX, 14.3.
36. Ibid. The English translation is taken from Dio's Roman History, vol. VIII, tr. Earnest Cary (London-Cambridge, Massachusetts, 1925), pp. 449–451.
37. *In Zachariam* 11.5 (CCL LXXVIA, p. 851).
38. The province seems gradually to have become known as *Syria Palaestina*; at any rate, this is the name given to it in a document from the year 139 CE (CIL, XVI, 87).
39. Eusebius, HE IV, 6.3; Justin, Apol. I, 47.6; Dial. c. Tryph. 16; Tertullian, Adv. Jud. 13.
40. *Chronicon Paschale*, ed. Dindorf, p. 474.
41. HR LXIX, 12.1.
42. Cf. b Taan 18a and *passim*.

10. FROM THE BAR KOCHBA REVOLT TO THE ARAB CONQUEST OF PALESTINE

10.1. Usha and Beth Shearim

Just as Judaism reconstituted and reorganized itself in the previously insignificant town of Jabneh after the first Jewish war, a fresh start was made after the second revolt. The crucial difference in this case was that Judaea no longer served as the focal point of Palestinian Judaism. The centre now moved to Galilee, a region that had previously been of only marginal importance to Jewish life and whose inhabitants had never been regarded as particularly orthodox. The first place where the rabbis assembled after the catastrophe of the Bar Kochba revolt was the little town of Usha in Upper Galilee. Of this generation of rabbis, central importance must be accorded to R. Shimon b. Gamaliel II, R. Nathan and R. Meir, although their ranking in a hierarchy (Shimon b. Gamaliel as Patriarch and President of the Synhedrion and Nathan and Meir as his deputies) is almost certainly a later convention.

The rabbinic literature gives us a very stylized "report" which, although no doubt formulated at a much later date, nevertheless makes it clear that Shimon b. Gamaliel had already begun to assert the superior authority of the position of Patriarch:

> Our rabbis taught: When the *Nasi* [Patriarch] enters, all the people rise and do not resume their seats until he requests them to sit. When the *Ab-beth-din* [President of the Court of Justice] enters, one row rises on one side and another row on the other [and they remain standing] until he has sat down in his place. When the *Chacham* [Vice-President of the Synhedrion and foremost authority in doctrinal matters] enters, every one [whom he passes] rises and sits down [as soon as he passed] after the Sage has sat down in his place. ...

> R. Johanan said: That instruction was issued in the days of
> R. Shimon b. Gamaliel [II], when R. Shimon b. Gamaliel was the
> *Nasi*, R. Meir the *Chacham*, and R. Nathan the *Ab-beth-din*.
> Whenever R. Shimon b. Gamaliel entered all the people stood up
> for him; when R. Meir and R. Nathan entered all the people stood
> up.for them also. Said R. Shimon b. Gamaliel: Should there be no
> distinction between my [office] and theirs? And so he issued that
> ordinance.[1]

Relations with the Romans seem to have slowly improved; they probably recognized Shimon b. Gamaliel as the official representative of the Jews, while
Hadrian's successor, Antoninus Pius (138–161 CE), relaxed the ban on circumcision to allow the Jews to have their own sons circumcised. It remained
forbidden to enter Jerusalem, as is attested by a number of mainly Christian
writers, but this ban was very soon relaxed as well; certainly, the rabbinic
sources make no mention of such a ban, and there even appears to have been
an ascetically orientated Jewish group, the "Mourners for Zion" (*avle tsion*),
who were able to settle in Jerusalem. When the son of Shimon b. Gamaliel,
R. Judah ha-Nasi, moved to Beth Shearim, the golden age of rabbinic
Judaism after the Bar Kochba revolt began, leading ultimately to the codification of traditional doctrine in the great corpora of the Mishnah and the
Tosefta.

10.1.1. The Mishnah

The Mishnah is the literary work that uniquely expresses the way early rabbinic Judaism saw itself, as well as playing a central role in the future development of Judaism as a whole. Attempts to define the Mishnah as simply a
compendium of laws, a textbook for use in rabbinic academies or a codex of
established religious doctrine fall short of the mark and fail to do justice to its
all-embracing claims.

The primary aim of the Mishnah was to enable the Torah to be put into
practice in such a fashion and to such an extent as was both appropriate and
possible under the changed political and social circumstances in which
Judaism found itself in the second century CE. In concrete terms, this means
that the Mishnah formulates the rabbinic view of the world and reality following the loss of the Temple and (especially after the catastrophe of the Bar
Kochba revolt) in increasing cognizance of the fact that political autonomy—
and thus the realization of the political mission of the Torah in the wider
sense—would remain unattainable for a long time to come. The domination

of Edom, the Roman world power, was unbroken and had to be accepted as a fact that one had to come to terms with.

As a document of rabbinic Judaism, the Mishnah articulates solely the self-understanding of the dominant group amongst these Jews, that is, the rabbis, who considered themselves the appointed and authorized leaders of the people. Opinions to the contrary originating from other groups can be found in the Mishnah at best in fragments and traces that have been covered over by the unifying and homogenizing viewpoint and sheer creative genius of its editors. Recent research has shown that various distinct strata in the development and crystallization of the established Halachah (the individual "law" or complex of laws applicable in each case) can indeed be distinguished, but the formulation and editing of the material collected together in the Mishnah was only carried out in the final phase of the transmission process, that is, in the last generation of so-called Tannaitic Judaism under Judah ha-Nasi (from about 175 to the end of the second century CE).

The rabbinic view of the world and reality is expounded in six major "Orders" (*sedarim*) of the Mishnah, which are arranged according to subject matter. The first Order, *Zera'im* (Seeds), contains mainly regulations to do with the land and which could be put into effect under the prevailing political conditions (e.g. the tithing of crops, the sabbatical year, etc.). The second Order, *Mo'ed* (Festivals), is chiefly concerned with the celebration of the festive days such as the Sabbath and the major and minor festivals throughout the yearly cycle. The third Order, *Nashim* (Women), is concerned with the position of women in the patriarchal society of Palestine, while the fourth Order, *Neziqin* (Damages), codifies the civil and penal law, which is almost exclusively orientated to the dominant position of the man as *ba'al ha-bayyit* (head of the family and household) and thus focal point of the economic and social order.

Of particular interest are the fifth and sixth Orders, *Qodashim* (Holy Things) and *Tohorot* (States of Purity), in which the rules and regulations of the sacrificial cult and the laws of ritual purity are laid down. The inclusion of the cultic Halachah in the spectrum of legal regulations compiled in the Mishnah is initially surprising, for the Mishnah is after all the document of a Judaism to whom the destruction of the Temple, and thus of the centre of their cultic practices, must increasingly have appeared final and irrevocable. So what sense is there in the minutely detailed description of the sacrifice and even (in the tractate *Middot*—Measures) of the dimensions and architectonics of the Temple? The explanation that the authors and editors of the Mishnah wished to preserve these regulations for the time when the Temple would be rebuilt and the practice of the cult resumed is only partly true. To be sure, hope of the restitution of the Temple and the cult was never abandoned, but it was certainly never more utopian than after the Bar Kochba revolt, when Jerusalem was turned into a Roman colony and the Jews were forbidden to set foot in the city. The intention of the Mishnah was therefore something more than this. The cultic Halachah laid down in the Mishnah is not there to be complied with in *practice* (this had become impossible in the political circumstances), but compliance lies in writing it down and *studying* it. Concrete application of the Torah has been replaced in this instance by teaching and study. As only the rabbis are duly authorized to teach it, they are the true inheritors and guardians of the tradition, which they transpose to a new era and thereby keep alive. The fifth Order of the Mishnah is perhaps the clearest expression of the change that had taken place in the rabbi-dominated society of Palestinian Jewry in the second century CE, namely, the transition from the priests to the rabbinic scribes, from Temple to Torah, from cult to community, from sacred place to sacred people, from a cosmocentric and cultically orientated religious system to a social structure with man at the centre.

The dissolution of a society dominated by cult and priest, in which Jerusalem and the Temple constituted the centre of the cosmos and the practice of the cult guaranteed harmony between heaven and earth, is also evident in the sixth Order. If the observance of specific and precisely defined purity laws was originally a requirement of the cultic rituals of the Temple, then the ideal of the purity of the Temple and its sacrifices was now extended to the wider sphere of everyday life. It was no longer the sacrifice that had to be prepared and consumed in a state of purity, but the daily meal in each private household; no longer were the narrow confines of the Temple holy, but the entire land. This also meant that the official upholders and guarantors of purity and holiness, the priests, were replaced by the new "class" of rabbis, who did not reserve the state of purity for themselves alone, but transmitted it to the entire nation: anyone who observed the laws on purity (as formulated by the rabbis) was a priest, anyone could know and practise what formerly only the priests knew and practised, Israel was a nation of priests which no longer achieved harmony between heaven and earth by practising a cult but by implementing the Torah.

So, under the new political conditions of the period following the Bar Kochba revolt, there took place what was perhaps the most radical change ever in the consciousness and social structure of Judaism, the consequences of which were to extend well beyond the Jews of ancient Palestine to determine the future course of Judaism in the Middle Ages and up to the modern era. In the Mishnah (and in the Talmud, which was structured around it), the rabbis completed the work of their immediate predecessors, the Pharisees and the scribes, and with their revision of the meaning and mission of the Torah, laid the basis for the future development of Judaism.

10.1.2. Beth Shearim

The town of Beth Shearim in Lower Galilee (south-east of present-day Haifa), which became the centre of Palestinian Judaism for a brief period after the Patriarch Judah ha-Nasi settled there (from about 175 CE), is of interest above all on account of its catacombs. The necropolis of Beth Shearim was apparently the central burial place of the Jews of Palestine and (especially) the Diaspora in the third and fourth centuries CE, and is the only known example of its kind; excavations were carried out in 1935–40 and 1953–60.

The vast site consists of numerous catacombs with burial niches and sarcophagi. Many of the burial chambers are decorated with drawings, inscriptions and reliefs engraved in or carved out of the soft rock. There are many examples of traditional Jewish motifs, such as the Seven-Branched Lampstand, the Ark of the Covenant, the shofar, the lulab, the etrog and the incense pan (familiar to us from synagogue mosaics), as well as secular motifs such as human figures, animals, ships and geometrical patterns. The same goes for the sarcophagi, which feature predominantly pagan motifs, including even scenes from Greek mythology such as Leda and the Swan, the Battle of the Amazons and the mask of a bearded man possibly intended to represent Zeus.

The inscriptions on the walls of the burial chambers or on tablets are also written mostly in Greek (218 out of about 250), the remainder in Hebrew and Aramaic; Greek rather than Hebrew was no doubt the lingua franca of the Palestinian and Diaspora Jews during this period. A lengthy Greek epitaph in best Homeric style is certainly an exception rather than the rule and probably accompanied the tomb of a Diaspora Jew, yet the fact that it was allowed to stand, apparently without objection, in Beth Shearim is remarkable enough:

> Here I, son of Leontius, lie dead, Justus, son of Sappho,
> and after having plucked the fruits of all wisdom,
> I left the light and my unhappy parents, who mourn incessantly,
>   behind me,
> and my brothers. Woe unto me, in my Besara![2]
> After I am descended to Hades, I, Justus, lie here
> with many others, because all-powerful Fate willed it so.
> Console yourself, Justus, no-one is immortal![3]

The necropolis of Beth Shearim thus shows, together with other archaeological and literary evidence, the immense influence of Greek culture on ancient Judaism in general and Palestinian Jewry in particular. That this cannot have been merely a marginal phenomenon or something only reluctantly tolerated by the rabbis is demonstrated by the fact that the rabbis also allowed themselves to be buried in Beth Shearim. In one catacomb (No. 14), the inscriptions "Rabbi Simeon", "this is the grave of Rabbi Gamaliel" and "Anina[4] the Lesser" were found, from which it has been concluded that this was the catacomb of the Patriarch's family ("Simeon" and "Gamaliel" were probably the two sons of Judah ha-Nasi and "Anina" his pupil Chanina b. Chama).[5]

10.1.3. Judah ha-Nasi and the Patriarchs

The office of Patriarch enjoyed its finest hour under R. Judah (from about 175 to 217 CE). He alone bore the epithet ha-Nasi (= "the Patriarch" as such) and was also referred to as "our holy Rabbi"; when the sources speak of "Rabbi" without a surname, they always mean R. Judah ha-Nasi.

R. Judah was officially recognized as Patriarch by the Romans and ruled almost like a king. Prayers were offered in the synagogue for his well-being, and incense was burned after his death as if for royalty.[6] The fact that he was accorded equivalent status to a king not only indicates the political power of the Patriarch, but also points to quasi-Messianic ambitions (albeit in a diluted, "secularized" form that had come to terms with Roman supremacy). The claim that, as a descendant of Hillel, the Patriarch could trace his lineage to the House of David, would also date from this period.[7] This was no doubt nothing but propaganda for a patriarchal dynasty whose Davidic claim was intended to secure power at home while opposing similar claims to authority made elsewhere, and particularly those of the head of the Babylonian Diaspora (the exilarch), who had probably announced his Davidic descent earlier (and with greater justification). So it is not surprising that it is Abba Aricha (= Rab), founder of an academy in Babylon and one of R. Judah's pupils, who is accredited with the following interpretation of Gen. 25:23:

> *Two nations [Goyim] are in thy womb* (Gen. 25:23). ... Read not *Goyim* [nations] but *Ge'im* [proud ones]. This refers to Antoninus and Rabbi ...[8]

Antoninus is here the prototypical Roman emperor (and perhaps refers in this case to the emperor Caracalla), Rabbi is of course Judah ha-Nasi. The Babylonian pupil of the Patriarch and later president of the famous academy in Sura compares his master in dignity and power to the Roman emperor, thereby also acknowledging the sovereignty of the Palestinian Patriarch over the Jews of the Diaspora as well. A further (anonymous) text places the Patriarch on a level with Daniel, Mordechai, Esther and the Maccabees, thus stylizing him into a figure of national salvation and the direct precursor of the final epoch of Israel's history, the Messianic age.[9]

The Patriarch also seems to have cultivated relations with the Diaspora by regularly despatching envoys to strengthen contacts with Palestine and to consolidate his own central authority. One of their tasks was the promulgation of the calendar prescribed by the Patriarch, which would ensure that he had overall control in all religious matters; attempts by the Babylonian Jews to establish their own calendar were rigorously suppressed.[10] This influence on the Babylonian Diaspora in particular was no doubt welcome to the Romans as it helped pacify the region on the unruly eastern border of the empire.

The Patriarch's power was also founded on a solid economic base. The rabbinic literature mentions a ship "from the household of Rabbi" on board which there were "more than three hundred barrels [full] of fish",[11] which presupposes extensive trade relations. Another passage mentions "balsam-trees of the household of Rabbi" in the same breath as the "balsam-trees of Caesar's household".[12] It may therefore be conjectured that the emperor had granted the Patriarch land from the old "royal estates", including perhaps land in the Jordan Valley where the famous balsam plantations were situated. This would be a further indication that the Patriarch was gradually taking on the status of the former Jewish kings.

When and in what form the patriarchs first imposed a tax is uncertain. It is possible that, like the Hellenistic kings, they demanded a fixed sum as "crown tax" (*aurum coronarium*) upon taking office and also collected a more or less voluntary "messenger's tax" (*apostolē*) through their envoys in the Diaspora. The first clear evidence of money being collected by envoys is to be found in a decree by the Roman emperor Honorius in 399 CE, who briefly forbade the export of such funds to Palestine and claimed them for his treasury.[13]

The economic power of the Patriarch inevitably made him an advocate of the interests of the wealthy upper classes. A brief episode mentioned in the Talmud (in passing and in a quite different context) would seem to intimate as much:

> The son of Bonyis[14] once visited Rabbi. 'Make room', the latter called out, 'for the owner of a hundred *maneh*.' Another person entered, when he called out, 'Make room for the owner of two hundred *maneh*.'[15]

So, despite the general esteem in which he was held by the people, it should nevertheless come as no surprise that the rabbinic literature also contains some overt criticism of the Patriarch:

> Judah and Hezekiah, the sons of R. Hiyya, once sat at table with Rabbi and uttered not a word. Whereupon he said: Give the young men plenty of strong wine, so that they may say something. When the wine took effect, they began by saying: The son

> of David [i.e. the Messiah] cannot appear ere the two ruling
> houses in Israel shall have come to an end, viz., the Exilarchate in
> Babylon and the Patriarchate in Israel ...[16]

Here we find not merely the expression of a rather insignificant opposition limited to a few "isolated voices",[17] but evidence of a gradual development which was also characteristic of the Hasmonean dynasty, namely, the increasing compromising of the highest office-holder by political and economic power and the opposition to this of the pious orthodoxy (*chasidim*), who understood compliance with the Torah to extend beyond "purely religious" matters. In the eyes of these pious Jews, the arrangement reached by the ruling elite with the prevailing political conditions was a sham and would in the final analysis only delay the real and ultimate redemption which would arrive with the Messiah.

The fact that such discontent did not escalate further was due less to any special integrity on the part of the office-holder than to the political and, above all, economic developments in Palestine.[18] With Judah ha-Nasi, the office of Patriarch attained a status it was never to regain. According to tradition (although its basis in historical fact is disputed in the research), Judah prudently decreed in his last will and testament that there should be a division of powers, nominating his second eldest son Gamaliel (III) as Patriarch, but placing him on an equal footing with his eldest son Shimon, who was to be *chacham* (foremost authority on doctrinal matters) and R Chanina b. Chama, who was to be *Ab beth-din* (President of the Court of Justice).[19]

Little is known concerning the further history of the patriarchate. The patriarchs receive various mentions in Roman legislation and were granted a variety of privileges.[20] In a law from as late as 392 CE, they are referred to as the group of *virorum clarissimorum et inlustrium patriarcharum*,[21] whereby it should be noted that *illustris* was the official form of address for the highest class of official in the Roman empire. However, the patriarchate seems to have gone into rapid decline at the beginning of the fifth century. As is apparent from a law issued in 429 CE,[22] the institution of the patriarchate had by then already ceased to exist.

10.2. The crisis of the Roman empire in the third century

The economic and political crisis suffered by the Roman empire in the third century and in the first half of the fourth century CE played a major role in the development of Judaism in Palestine. This crisis was attributable to a variety of causes which, taken together, had catastrophic results and badly affected the Palestinian Jews. According to the research, the main reason for the crisis was the rapid escalation of centrifugal forces in the Roman empire, accompanied by a weakening of central authority. The clearest evidence of this weakening of central authority can be seen in the high turnover of emperors, which had already begun with the imperial family of Severus (as of 193 CE with Septimius Severus) and became particularly striking under the so-called "soldier emperors" (from 235 CE onwards). An emperor rarely died a natural death, and each change of power was accompanied by large-scale changes and upheavals in both central government and the provinces. The provinces gained increasingly in importance over the mother country, and the economic consequences of the migration of numerous industries from the mother country to the provinces, which had begun in the second century, now began to make themselves felt. This was accompanied—especially in the wake of the spread of Christianity—by the decline of the old religions, which had played a major role in uniting the various parts of the empire, and consequently a decline in worship of the emperor as the representative of imperial unity. Finally, there was a sharp increase in social conflict between the (well-to-do) urban population, one of the central pillars of the empire, and the mostly poor and exploited rural population.

The rabbinic literature contains numerous references to the effect of the crisis on the Jews of Palestine. The two most important, and mutually dependent consequences were the constantly increasing tax burden and inflation.

The taxes payable by the Jews of Palestine were, as before, the land tax (*tributum soli*), poll tax (*tributum capitis*), customs duties and the *anforta*, which was probably a charge to be paid by tenants of state-owned land. Of these fiscal charges, the *anforta* seems to have played a relatively minor role; the number of tenants of state-owned lands was not very great. The customs duties, on the other hand, were somewhat more important; at least, the customs officials and tax collectors are hardly portrayed any more sympathetically in the rabbinic literature than they were in the New Testament. The crown tax (*aurum coronarium*) likewise became increasingly onerous, especially since the emperor was always changing (and what was originally a voluntary donation had long since become a compulsory tax). The most swingeing of the long-standing taxes, however, was the poll tax, which was actually a tax on property, as it was levied according to the value of the property owned by each individual tax-payer.[23]

To these long-standing taxes was now added the so-called *annona militaris*. This *annona* was not a tax in the true sense of the word, but designated the obligation of a province to furnish the troops passing through it with provisions. This became an increasingly onerous burden the more frequently troops descended on a province, and this was the order of the day during the civil wars in the third century. Military expenditure far exceeded state revenues in the second half of the third century, leading to galloping inflation and an almost total collapse of the money economy. The public sector economy was once again run largely on the basis of payment in kind. The *annona* was particularly burdensome for the rural population, and they constituted the majority of the Jewish inhabitants of Palestine.

The other factor that led to a rapid deterioration of the economic situation was inflation. As the cash requirement rose steadily in the third century (due above all to the increase in military pay), the emperors were forced to make constant reductions in the silver value of the Roman denarius. This currency depreciation forced up prices, thereby increasing the money supply even further, so that the inflationary spiral turned ever faster. It has been calculated that the silver value of the denarius sank by a half in the two hundred years from Augustus to Septimius Severus, and that in the third century it dwindled to only 5% of its former value within about forty years. By the end of the third century, the so-called silver denarius consisted of pieces of copper with only a thin coating of silver.

Periods of inflation are usually accompanied by an increase in interest rates and a consequent growth in usurious practices. Although interest and usury are forbidden by the Torah,[24] the rabbis were forced to tolerate interest and even a specific form of usury, the so-called "agreed usury" (*ribbit qetsutsa*), in order to prevent the economy from collapsing. The following saying comes from R. Jochanan in the second half of the third century:

> What is interest and what is usury?[25] R. Yannai said: Usury is when [the case] goes to court.[26] R. Jochanan was asked: What does 'when [the case] goes to court' mean? He said to him [i.e. the questioner]: Were it [to be defined] thus,[27] we would leave nothing [in the way of business possibilities] for the great [i.e. the rich] of the land of Israel![28]

One consequence of the constantly increasing tax burden, especially in respect of the property tax and the *annona militaris*, was a mass migration from the country (*anachōrēsis*), especially of the poorer section of the population who were unable to offset the tax burden through other sources of income:

> A typical instance was that of the crown [*kelila* = *aurum coronarium*] for which the inhabitants of Tiberias were called upon to find the money. They came to Rabbi [Judah ha-Nasi] and said to him, 'Let the Rabbis give their share [of the taxes] with us.'[29] He refused. 'Then we will run away,' they said. 'You may,' he

replied. So half of them ran away [from the city]. The sum demanded was then imposed on the other half [alone].[30] The other half then came to Rabbi and asked him that the Rabbis might share with them. He again refused. 'We will run away,' they said. 'You may,' he replied. So they all ran away, leaving only a certain fuller. The money was then demanded of him, and he ran away, and the demand for the crown was then dropped.[31]

In the Talmudic period, the sole right, or rather the obligation to collect the taxes devolved upon the city council (boulē). The members of the council were saddled with liability for the amount due in taxes, which meant that it was mainly the wealthy citizens and landowners who were nominated to the city council. A Midrash accordingly interprets the vision in Daniel of the fourth and last kingdom, here equated with Rome, as follows:

... this alludes to the wicked State, which casts an envious eye upon a man's wealth, [saying], 'So-and-so is wealthy: we will make him a city magistrate [archōn]; So-and-so is wealthy: let us make him a councillor [bouleutēs].'[32]

In view of the economic decline and the increasing impoverishment of the population in the third century, it became almost impossible for the city councillors to collect the taxes. This meant that even sections of the rich upper classes were forced to leave the country in order to avoid financial ruin:

R. Jochanan said, 'If you have been nominated to the city council [boulē], let the Jordan be your border.'[33]

Since the rich landowners did not necessarily sell their estates when they emigrated, but simply let them lie fallow in anticipation of better times to come, the rabbinical judiciary had increasingly to deal with the problem of such abandoned land (agri deserti). Acts of chazaqah (usucapio), that is, the occupation of abandoned land by "squatters", evidently occurred with ever-increasing frequency in the course of the third century. Although, according to Talmudic law, such land became the property of the "squatters" after three years of continuous and unopposed occupation, towards the end of the third century the Rabbis seem to have tightened up the law and made it more difficult to occupy abandoned land in order to protect the rights of the landowners. This implies that even the emigration of wealthy landowners would no longer have been the exception, but a relatively frequent occurrence as of the end of the third century.

The economic crisis led to the abandonment of a large number of Jewish settlements in Palestine, initially in the border territories, but eventually in

Galilee as well. Agricultural production fell off, and famine and epidemics decimated the Jewish population:

> ... Thus said R. Jochanan, In the first year they ate what was stored up in the houses, in the second what was in the fields, in the third the flesh of clean animals, in the fourth the flesh of unclean animals, in the fifth the flesh of forbidden animals and reptiles, in the sixth the flesh of their sons and daughters and in the seventh the flesh of their own arms and thus the verse of Scripture was fulfilled, *They eat every man the flesh of his own arm* (Isa. 9:19).[34]

This interpretation by R. Jochanan refers to the seven-year famine mentioned in 2 Kgs. 8:1, but at the same time reflects the author's times (the second half of the third century). Another interpretation from the same period pithily summarizes the social crisis in third-century Palestine:

> Resh Laqish said to [R. Jochanan], '... it is written, *As if a man did flee from a lion, and a bear met him; or went into the house, and leaned his hand on the wall, and a serpent bit him* (Amos 5:19) ... When one goes out into the field and meets a bailiff, it is as though he had met a lion. When he enters the town, and is accosted by a tax-collector, it is as though he had met a bear. On entering his house and finding his sons and daughters in the throes of [or: dead from] hunger, it is as though he were bitten by a serpent!'[35]

The impoverishment of the Jewish population was virtually proverbial. The rabbinic literature contains jokes on the subject that are startlingly reminiscent of certain modern ones:

> They then take a camel into their theatres, put their [sack-like] shirts upon it,[36] and [the actors] ask one another, 'Why is it in mourning?' To which they reply, 'The Jews observe the law of the Sabbatical year and they have no vegetables, so they eat this camel's thorns, and that is why it is in mourning'! Next they bring a clown with shaven head into the theatre and ask one another, 'Why is his head shaven?' To which they reply, 'The Jews observe the Sabbath, and whatever they earn during the week they eat on the Sabbath. Since they have no wood to cook with, they break their bedsteads and use them as fuel; consequently they sleep on the ground and get covered with dust, and anoint themselves with oil [in order to get clean] which is very

expensive for that reason [and the clown has to shave his head as he cannot get any oil for his hair]!'[37]

In view of the deteriorating social conditions, it is not surprising that there are also increasing complaints during this period about "banditry", whereby these "bandits" are designated by the same term as in Josephus (*listis* = Gr. *lēstēs*):[38]

> R. Levi said, '... That is like a bandit who waits at a crossroads and robs the passers-by. One day a legionary came by who was busy collecting the taxes of a city. He held him up, robbed him and took away everything he had on him.'[39]

R. Levi certainly gives here an accurate picture of the times in which he lived (around 300 CE). The municipal authorities evidently found themselves compelled to arrange for shipments of money to be escorted by Roman troops, or to have soldiers actually collect the taxes. In any case, a marked increase in banditry is a typical sign of deteriorating social conditions. As an even later comment (from the middle of the fourth century) succinctly puts it:

> R. Shimon b. Abba [said] in the name of R. Chanina, 'Danger threatens on every side. When R. Jonah undertook a journey and [whilst *en route* had to spend the night] in an inn, he made his will [before leaving home].'[40]

Excessive taxation, inflation, famine, epidemics, widespread money-lending and usury, increasing theft and robbery: all this meant a dangerous widening of the gap between rich and poor and a consequent aggravation of social tensions. The relaxation of various halachic rulings concerning agriculture (particularly the sabbatical year), which had already begun under Judah ha-Nasi, was unable to do much to remedy this in the long term. The decline of the patriarchate and ultimately of Palestinian Judaism in general is certainly closely linked to these rapidly mounting economic problems. Only with the accession to power of Diocletian in 284 CE did the Roman empire begin to regain political and economic stability. Diocletian succeeded in bringing inflation under control and reformed the monetary system, as well as carrying out a reform of the administration;[41] by this time, however, the heyday of Palestinian Judaism was essentially over. Furthermore, another major force was now about to make itself felt, one that would supersede foreign rule by the detested Romans and replace it with one that was even more oppressive and would last even longer, namely, Christianity. The smoothness of this transition can be seen from the fact that the rabbis employed the same symbolic name, "Edom", for Christianity as they did for Rome.

10.3. Judaism and Christianity

10.3.1. Constantine the Great (324–337)

Constantine had become supreme ruler of the West following his famous victory at the Milvian Bridge in the year 312. After defeating the emperor of the East, Licinius, in 324 CE near Byzantium, he became the first Christian ruler of Palestine.

In 313, Constantine renewed the edict of toleration issued by Galerius in 311, thereby establishing parity for Christianity as an officially recognized religion (*religio licita*). For the Jews, this meant that Christianity was put on an equal footing with Judaism and was granted the same privileges (in particular, exemption from the obligation to participate in public sacrifices). Thus began the process which led to the eventual triumph of Christianity in Palestine, a triumph achieved at no little expense to Judaism. Under Constantine, Christian communities spread throughout Palestine, Christian pilgrimages became common (the earliest known account dates from the year 333 and was written by a pilgrim from Bordeaux), and Christian churches were erected at important Christian sites (including the Church of the Nativity in Bethlehem and the Church of the Holy Sepulchre in Jerusalem).

The Jews appear to have responded to this development with a revival of Messianic expectations; there are certainly a large number of Messianic references in the rabbinic literature of the time, in marked contrast to the lengthy period of silence on that score following the Bar Kochba revolt. The minor apocalypse in the Mishnah[42] is possibly a later addition and might therefore come from this period; the government's turn to "heresy" would then be the transition to Christian rule:

> In the footsteps of the Messiah insolence will increase and honour dwindle; the vine will yield its fruit [abundantly] but wine will be dear; the government will turn to heresy and there will be none [to offer them] reproof; the meeting-place [of scholars] will be used for immorality; Galilee will be destroyed, Gablan [= Golan] desolated, and the dwellers on the frontier will go about [begging] from place to place without anyone to take pity on them; the wisdom of the learned will degenerate, fearers of sin will be despised, and the truth will be lacking; youths will put old men to shame, the old will stand up in the presence of the young, a son will revile his father, a daughter will rise against her mother, a daughter-in-law against her mother-in-law, and a man's enemies will be the members of his household [Mic. 7:6]; the face of the generation will be like the face of a dog, a son will not

feel ashamed before his father. So upon whom is it for us to rely?
Upon our Father who is in Heaven.

The Aramaic translation of the Bible even plays directly on the hoped-for
fall of Edom = Rome and the destruction of the new capital city,
Constantinople, as well as Caesarea, the metropolis of the young Christianity:

> The Edomites shall be driven out—and the sons of Gabla like-
> wise—from Israel, their enemy, and Israel shall become mighty
> through [their] wealth which they shall inherit. And a ruler shall
> arise from the House of Jacob and annihilate and destroy the
> remainder who have fled from Constantinople, the sinful city, and
> devastate and lay in ruins the rebellious city of Caesarea, the
> mighty city of the nations.[43]

However, it is most unlikely that these new Messianic expectations were converted into concrete political activity in the form of an uprising against Rome.
According to Chrysostom, as well as later Christian chronicles clearly influenced by the Church Father, the Jews started a rebellion under Constantine
and were punished by the emperor by having their ears cut off.[44] These
accounts are legendary and almost certainly of no historical value, especially
since such a rebellion is mentioned nowhere else in earlier sources.

It was no doubt also at this time that initial attempts at Christian missionary
work were made amongst the Jews; many rabbinic texts contain indications of
some sort of Christian-Jewish "dialogue" going on in the background. These
Christian missions met with very little success, however. The most famous
such case is recorded by Epiphanius.[45] According to him, a certain Joseph, a
close friend of the Patriarch Hillel II, was supposed to have converted to
Christianity (because he discovered the magic power of the name of Jesus, a
common motif!). He was consequently expelled from the Jewish community,
went to the emperor's court and received from Constantine the title of *comes*,
that is, a special confidant of the emperor who was employed on official missions. In this capacity, he was supposedly despatched to Galilee to help spread
Christianity, although he met with little success. This story also contains a
number of legendary features, but its gist, the conversion of an apparently
well-known Jew to Christianity, may well be authentic.

However much the political changes introduced by Constantine may have
affected Judaism, there can nevertheless be no talk of a "Jewish policy", let
alone a specifically anti-Jewish one. Constantine certainly passed a number
of laws on Jewish matters, but these were, like most Roman laws, ad hoc
decisions arising from concrete instances and not the expression of a systematic policy regarding the Jews.

The matter of the Jewish mission and conversion to Judaism had already been a sore point under the pagan Roman emperors. In his famous rescript issued after the Bar Kochba revolt, Antoninus Pius had forbidden the circumcision of non-Jews, a measure aimed at combatting Jewish proselytism.[46] This prohibition of circumcision continued to be upheld under Roman law and was expressly renewed by Septimius Severus in 201 CE.[47] So Constantine was following the precedent set by his pagan predecessors when he passed a number of laws which further reinforced this prohibition within the specific context of Judaeo-Christian relations.

In a law dating from 21st October 335, Constantine forbade the circumcision of Christian slaves (in other words, their conversion to Judaism), and declared any slave circumcised despite this prohibition a free man:

> If any Jew should ... circumcise a Christian slave ... he shall not retain in slavery such circumcised person. But the person who endured such treatment shall obtain the privilege of freedom.[48]

In a law issued on 8th October 315, Constantine had already forbidden in a more general form the harassment of Jews who had converted to Christianity as well as the conversion of Christians to Judaism:

> It is Our will that Jews and their elders and patriarchs shall be informed that if, after the issuance of this law, any of them should dare to attempt to assail with stones or with any other kind of madness ... any person who has fled their feral sect and has resorted to the worship of God, such assailant shall be immediately delivered to the flames and burned, with all his accomplices. Moreover, if any person from the people[49] should betake himself to their nefarious sect and should join their assemblies, he shall sustain with them the deserved punishments.[50]

There was also nothing new about the question of Jews sitting on the municipal councils and their appointment to public office. Jews had long enjoyed a number of privileges such as exemption from military service and, above all, from the obligation to offer sacrifice to the pagan gods and to participate in the emperor cult. As public offices and public cult were originally closely interconnected, exemption from participation in the official sacrificial cult also implied exemption from public office. When Caracalla enacted his *Constitutio Antoniana* in 212, under which the Jews were granted Roman citizenship, he started a process which was not wholly to the Jews' advantage. To be sure, as Roman citizens, the Jews now enjoyed the same rights as their fellow-citizens in addition to their former privileges, but they also came under the same obligations, including participation in the curiae. As the members of the curiae were responsible and bore liability for tax revenues,[51] this was a dubious honour which was to be evaded if possible. When the question of participation in the sacrificial cult finally became redundant under Constantine, there were no further grounds (from the Roman point of view) for exempting the Jews from sitting on the municipal councils. In 321, Constantine, supreme ruler of the West, passed a law obliging the Jews to participate in the curiae. The decree is addressed to the "Decurions of Cologne" (councillors of Cologne) and was apparently issued in response to a specific enquiry by the councillors:

> By a general law We permit all municipal senates to nominate Jews to the municipal council (*ad curiam*). But in order that something of the former rule may be left them as a solace, We extend to two or three persons from each group the perpetual privilege of not being disturbed by any nominations.[52]

The Jewish cult officials, on the other hand, retained their privileges. After conquering the Orient, Constantine passed at least two laws in which he placed the Jewish religious officials on a par with the Christian and pagan priests and exempted them from service on the curiae:

> We command that priests, rulers of the synagogues, fathers of the synagogues, and all others who serve the synagogues shall be free from every compulsory public service of a corporal nature.[53]

One direct result of the Christianization of Palestine was the fact that the Patriarch was deprived of the right to carry out an annual rescheduling of the lunisolar Jewish calendar, which had to be continually readjusted to the seasons of the annual summer-based cycle by means of complicated calculations; the influence and authority of the Patriarch in the Diaspora was based to a large extent on precisely this privilege. This happened as a result of the dispute over Easter between the so-called "quartodecimanes" (those Christians who wanted to celebrate Easter on 14/15 Nisan to coincide with the Jewish Passover) and those Christians who wanted to establish Resurrection Sunday as the obligatory date for Easter. In 325, Constantine (in accord with the Council of Nicaea) decided for the Sunday and forbade the Patriarch to send messengers to proclaim the date of the Jewish Passover in the Diaspora, thereby depriving the quartodecimanes of the basis for their Easter celebrations. As a result, the Patriarch Hillel II decided in 358/359 CE to introduce a fixed calendar in order to ensure a uniform Jewish date for Passover.

It is uncertain whether Constantine also changed the law concerning Jewish access to Jerusalem and allowed the Jews to enter Jerusalem (only) on the 9th of Av, the day on which the Temple was destroyed. There is no such law in the Codex Theodosianus, and the earliest testimony we have comes from Eutychius, the Patriarch of Alexandria, in the tenth century.[54] This report is possibly only a later reformulation of Hadrian's original ban following the Bar Kochba revolt. Speculation as to whether Constantine reinforced or relaxed Hadrian's edict (which was not rigidly enforced for very long anyway) would therefore only be futile.

10.3.2. Constantius II (337–361)

Upon the death of Constantine the Great, his empire was divided amongst his three sons, Constantine, Constantius and Constans. Constantius (II) received the Orient, while the two other brothers shared the West between them (in 340, Constans defeated his older brother Constantine II and became sole ruler of the West). Following the death of Constans (in 350) and the defeat of a usurper (in 351), Constantius took control of the entire empire.

The most important law concerning the Jews is a double law which was issued on the 13th of August 339 and addressed to Euagrius, the *praefectus praetorio* of the Orient:

> In so far as pertains to the women who were formerly employed in Our imperial weaving establishment (*gynaeceum*) and who have been led by the Jews into the association (*consortium*) of their turpitude (*turpitudo*), it is Our pleasure that they shall be restored to the weaving establishment. It shall be observed that Jews shall not hereafter unite Christian women to their villainy (*flagitium*); if they should do so, however, they shall be subject to the peril of capital punishment.[55]

After Constantine I had already made it more difficult to convert to Judaism, mixed marriages between Christian women and Jews were now forbidden. There are good economic reasons underlying the fact that the women receive special mention. The imperial *gynaeceum* is a reference to state-owned textile factories, and in particular silk mills, which were evidently in competition with Jewish textile concerns. Women who had "migrated" to Jewish concerns were to be forced back into state-owned factories, even if they had entered into a mixed marriage with a Jew. It is striking how only negative terms (*consortium, turpitudo, flagitium*) are used to refer to mixed marriages between Jews and Christians.

The second part of the law is concerned with slaves:

> If any Jew should suppose that he should purchase the slave of
> another sect (*secta*) or people (*natio*), such slave shall be imme-
> diately vindicated to the fisc (*fiscus*). If the Jew should purchase
> a slave and circumcise him, he shall be penalized not only with
> the loss of the slave, but he shall also be visited with capital
> punishment.[56]

Here too, Constantine's legislation is tightened up. The purchase of non-
Jewish slaves is not actually specifically forbidden, but is made impossible in
practice, for such a slave becomes the property of the state. The circumcision
of a non-Jewish slave leads not merely to the slave receiving his freedom (as
under Constantine I), but to punishment by death. This law also had a concrete economic rationale. Slaves were an indispensable part of the economic
order in antiquity, and the de facto prohibition of non-Jewish slaves must
have been a severe blow to the economic life of the Jews.

The tendency of Constantius II to tighten up on already existing laws finds
further expression in a law dated 3rd July 353,[57] and thus from the period of
his autocracy. If the subject of previous legislation was simply mixed marriages between Christian women and Jews, then this law now decrees that, in
the event that a person converts from Christianity to Judaism, "his property
shall be vindicated to the ownership of the fisc".[58] Here too, theological considerations are no doubt combined with economic ones.

In 351, when Constantius had become supreme ruler following the death of
Constans, he adopted his nephew Gallus and appointed him Caesar of the
East. Under this Gallus, a local Jewish revolt seems to have broken out in
Palestine, but little information on this has come down to us.

The main sources are the late Roman historian Sextus Aurelius Victor (second half of the fourth century) and his contemporary, the Church Father
Jerome. In his *Caesares*, Sextus Aurelius Victor mentions a revolt (*seditio*) of
the Jews who appointed "maliciously" a certain Patricius to a kind of kingship (*in regni speciem*).[59] According to Jerome, the rebels attacked a Roman
garrison and looted their arsenal. The revolt was soon suppressed by Gallus,
and the cities of Sepphoris/Diocaesarea, Tiberias and Lod/Diospolis and
numerous other communities were burned down and several thousand people
killed.[60]

Many commentators consider that a Midrashic interpretation of the biblical
verse Zeph. 1:10 is an allusion to these events:

> *And it shall come to pass in that day, saith the Lord, that there
> shall be the noise of a cry from the fish gate* (Zeph. 1:10)—that is

Acco, which lies near to the fishes. *And an howling from the second*—that is Lod, which was Jerusalem's suburb. *And a great crashing from the hills*—that is Sepphoris, which lies on hills. *Howl, ye inhabitants of* [the valley] (Zeph. 1:11)—that is Tiberias, which is deep as a valley.[61]

The names of the above-mentioned localities fit in very well with the places mentioned by Sextus Aurelius Victor, all excepting Acco, which was strongly fortified and had a predominantly non-Jewish population. This casts doubt on the value of the rabbinic source, which can hardly be dispelled by referring simply to "battles that were fought in the vicinity of this city" (when these battles were supposedly the only ones of note in this instance!).[62]

The other cities, Sepphoris, Tiberias and Lod, were important industrial centres of Palestinian Judaism. Whether this in itself provides sufficient basis for the assumption that the revolt was initiated by manual workers and manufacturers "who were the ones most severely affected by Constantius' edicts against the keeping of non-Jewish slaves",[63] is likewise extremely questionable. Inadequate enough as they already are in other respects, the sources tell us nothing whatsoever about the causes of the revolt.

Practically nothing is known either about the consequences. We only know that Beth Shearim was destroyed shortly after 350, and it may be that this was as a result of the revolt. The few rabbinic texts that mention the Roman general Ursicinus[64] are not especially negative and may not necessarily refer to the revolt, but simply come from a period (from 350 or 351 onwards) when Ursicinus was in Palestine as supreme commander during the Persian War.

The inadequacies of the sources have given rise to the suspicion that no such revolt of the Jews ever took place, and that Patricius was not a Jewish Messianic pretender, but on the contrary, a Roman officer who put himself forward as anti-emperor (which was not an uncommon occurrence at the time). This would explain both the Latin name of the "rebel leader"[65] and the local acts of destruction in Palestine mentioned in the sources. It is even conceivable that some Jewish communities—no doubt hoping for an improvement in the situation of the Jews—gave their support to the anti-emperor. It is therefore by no means certain that there ever was a Jewish revolt under Gallus.

10.3.3. The restoration under Julian the Apostate (361–363)

The government of Emperor Julian, called *Apostata* ("the Apostate") by the Christians, was a brief and relatively insignificant interlude for the Jews of Palestine, although for a little while it revived hopes of a national rebirth.

Julian was Constantine the Great's nephew and the step-brother of Gallus, and was appointed Caesar in Gaul by Constantius at the end of 355. In spring 360, the troops acclaimed him as Augustus. He did not have to oppose Constantius on the battlefield as the latter died suddenly in November 361. Julian thus became supreme ruler and went to Constantinople in December 361.

In that same year, Julian issued the first "edicts of toleration", in which he promoted the pagan cults and restrained the influence of Christianity. As the follower of a Hellenistic-syncretistic religion (tinged with Neoplatonism), he attempted to breathe new life into the pagan institutions, especially the sacrificial cult, and to abolish the privileges enjoyed by the Christians in state and society. To this end, he permitted the "heretical" bishops who had been banished by his predecessors to return to their bishoprics in the not unfounded hope that the ensuing religious controversy would weaken the Church.

His attitude to Judaism was ambivalent. On the one hand, he saw Judaism as the source of the Christianity he opposed, and refuted the Jews' claim to be the chosen people. On the other hand, the Jewish Temple cult confirmed his predilection for sacrificial ritual and must therefore have seemed useful to him in his fight against Christianity. There was also the political consideration that the Mesopotamian Jews could be useful allies in his campaign against the Persians if he were to pursue emphatically pro-Jewish policies. So Julian's Jewish policy was characterized by a mixture of religious and political motives which cannot easily be separated.

When Julian decided in 362 to go to war against the Persians, one of his reasons for doing so would appear to be that, by achieving a victory over the Persians and a "final" pacification of the eastern border of the empire, he hoped to validate his new policies and prove the power of the pagan gods. In July 362, he arrived in Antioch, where he immediately came into conflict with the inhabitants and their evidently indulgent lifestyle, and, amongst other things, closed down their largest Christian church. According to Christian sources[66]—Jewish sources are completely silent on the matter—he received a Jewish delegation in Antioch and, in an official audience, granted them permission to rebuild the Temple.

The initiative for this seems clearly to have come from the emperor rather than from the Jews.[67] The Jewish Patriarch (Hillel II) was apparently not present at the audience, and the rabbinic literature has retained only the merest echo (if any) of this venture. This is hardly surprising if one considers the development of rabbinic Judaism since the Bar Kochba revolt. The rabbis, with the Patriarch at their head, had largely established themselves as the dominant group in Jewish society in Palestine and, in their self-created rabbinic literature, had a powerful propaganda instrument at their disposal to

secure their religious and political influence. The rebuilding of the Temple
would greatly increase the influence of the priests, and so would help back
into power the group whose power base had been eliminated with the
destruction of the Temple in 70 CE, and who the rabbis had succeeded with
such determination and success.[68]

Julian's granting of permission to rebuild the Jewish Temple in Jerusalem
(a largely Christian city!), with all its religious and political implications,
therefore seems not to have met with anything like the unanimous approval
of all the Palestinian Jewry. According to Christian authors, widespread
enthusiasm was to be found only in the Diaspora, from where a large number
of Jews immediately set out for Jerusalem.[69] In any case, it is completely
inappropriate to regard Julian as a "forerunner of Zionism".[70] It is uncertain
whether Julian sent a letter to the Patriarch; doubts have also been raised as to
the authenticity of his famous letter "To the Community of the Jews",[71] in
which he mentions his promise to rebuild Jerusalem, repeals the taxes
imposed on the Jews by Constantius, and calls on the Patriarch to stop levy-
ing the *apostolē* tax.[72]

In March 363, Julian set out on his campaign against the Parthians. At
about the same time, preliminary work must have begun in Jerusalem on the
reconstruction of the Temple. A high-ranking imperial official, Alypius of
Antioch, had been appointed to supervise the building work. However, in
May of that same year, building already seems to have come to a halt. The
reasons for this are mysterious. The Christian sources give reports of earth-
quakes and a fire that fell from heaven, as well as numerous miracles accompanying these happenings.[73] The Roman historian Ammianus Marcellinus,
perhaps the most reliable source,[74] mentions "fearsome balls of flame"
(*metuendi globi flammarum*) which repeatedly flared up "near to the founda-
tions" of the Temple and burned some of the workers to death;[75] the church
historian Rufinus likewise mentions the fire and also speaks of an earthquake.[76] It is often suggested that the fire was the main reason why work was
halted and that the Christians must bear the blame for causing the fire as they
wished to sabotage the building work. This is certainly not out of the question, but the most probable explanation is that there was an earthquake (no
rare event during this period) that then caused a fire to break out. It goes
without saying that the Christians attributed the events to the direct intervention of God.

After this unhappy beginning, the building work was not resumed. Alypius
apparently sent a report to the emperor and waited for his decision. This
report will not have reached Julian, for the emperor was severely wounded in
June 363 and died shortly afterwards. With the subsequent Christian restoration, the project of rebuilding the Temple fell through; one may speculate as

to what would have happened if Julian had managed to realize his plan, but history clearly and definitively took a different direction.

10.3.4. Theodosius I (379–395) and II (408–450)

In 379, Emperor Gratianus appointed Theodosius I ("the Great") Augustus of the East. One of his main aims was to preserve the political and religious unity of the empire. Even before his baptism at the end of 380, he issued an edict (on 28th February 380) prohibiting Arianism and prescribing the Athanasian form of "Catholicism" for all the peoples of the empire;[77] together with the subsequent banning of all pagan cults,[78] this was the decisive step towards the establishment of Christianity as the official state religion.

We can see from these edicts that Theodosius I's legislation on religious matters was aimed mainly at the Christian heretics and the pagans. The Jews are first mentioned in two laws dating from 384 and 388, neither of which adds significantly to the previous legislation of the Christian emperors. On 22nd September 384, the Jews are forbidden to purchase Christian slaves and "contaminate" them with their "Jewish religious rites" (*Iudaicis sacramentis*), that is, circumcision.[79] This had already been decreed by Constantine I and Constantius; an additional provision (Christian slaves who were already in Jewish possession before the edict was issued are to be "redeemed from this unworthy servitude" by payment of a suitable price) shows that the strict laws of Constantine I and Constantius had proved difficult to implement in practice.

The same applies for the question of mixed marriages. Constantius had decreed, primarily on economic grounds, that *Christian women who were married to a Jew should be returned to the imperial gynaeceum*.[80] In a decree dated 14th March 388, Theodosius renewed the prohibition of mixed marriages and increased its severity by equating mixed marriages with adultery, which was a capital offence.[81]

These basic laws, which adhere closely to established precedent, were followed by three decrees which, while not to be interpreted as a sudden expression of philosemitism on the part of the emperor, nevertheless fully represented the interests of the Jews. The background was a power struggle over religious policy between the emperor and Ambrose, the bishop of Milan. At Callinicum on the Euphrates, the local bishop had presided over the burning of a synagogue. When Theodosius ordered the synagogue to be rebuilt, Ambrose threatened not to celebrate mass in the emperor's presence (which in practical terms was equivalent to excommunication). Theodosius had to give in and withdraw his threats of punishment. This gave encouragement to Christian circles in the East to step up their anti-Jewish activities. The emperor's three decrees are therefore to be understood as reactions to these excesses, and were intended both to be of benefit to the Jews and (above all) to strengthen his own authority.

The first law, issued on 18th February 390,[82] concerns the obligation on the Jews and Samaritans to act as shipmasters for the transportation of goods for the state. Such an obligation was indeed held to exist for the Jews and Samaritans as an "entire group" (*universum corpus*), but not for each specific person in every particular instance. The degree of obligation was dependent on financial circumstance, and poor people and petty tradesmen were to remain exempt.

Of greater importance was the second law of 17th April 392,[83] which guaranteed the Jews a limited degree of autonomy in judicial matters. The law was a response to complaints by Jewish authorities that former members of their faith who had been expelled from the Jewish community had been forcibly reinstated by the Roman authorities. Theodisius consequently forbade this "zealous group of persons in the aforesaid superstition" (*in ea superstitione sedulus coetus*) to "obtain the power of undeserved reconciliation (*indebita reconciliatio*)". No state authority (and no fraudulent imperial rescript) should be allowed to sabotage the decisions of the Jewish primates who, by the decision of the patriarchs (*virorum clarissimorum et inlustrium patriarcharum*), had the right to pronounce sentence in matters concerning the Jewish religion (*habere sua de religione sententiam*).

The third law, issued on 29th September 393,[84] also criticizes Christian malpractices. It starts off by stating categorically: "It is sufficiently established that the sect of the Jews is forbidden by no law" (*Iudaeorum sectam nulla lege prohibitam satis constat*) and then continues: "Hence We are gravely disturbed that their assemblies have been forbidden in certain places." Theodosius orders the addressees of this edict to use all the official means at their disposal to combat the excesses of those who, "in the name of the Christian religion", presume to destroy the synagogues.

In view of such legislation, it is hardly appropriate to regard the "great assault on the Jews and Judaism"[85] as beginning with Theodosius I. None of the Christian emperors was actively pro-Jewish, but, as the edicts of Theodosius I demonstrate, the law could still come down in their favour if it was politically convenient to do so. However, the underlying negative tendency could only get stronger the more the emperor in question was prepared to concede to the growing self-assurance of Christianity as its influence spread throughout the empire.

Theodosius II, who became supreme ruler in the East in 408 CE following the brief reign of Arcadius, began his Jewish legislation with a decree issued on 29th May 408,[86] which raised objections to the celebration of the Feast of

Purim, in which the Jews allegedly held the Christians up to ridicule. In a law dated 20th October 415,[87] the Patriarch Gamaliel VI is strongly rebuked for founding new synagogues and for allowing Christian slaves to be circumcised, and is commanded to free such slaves in accordance with the law of Constantine I[88] and to demolish any synagogues "in desert places", provided that this can be done "without sedition". At the same time, the decree stipulates that legal disputes between Jews and Christians may from now on only be settled in civil courts. The underlying intention was clearly to avoid any semblance of authority being exercized by Jews over Christians.

Attacks on synagogues by Christians became so frequent under Theodosius II that most of the imperial edicts were concerned with this problem. On 6th August 420, Theodosius II issued an edict to the effect that synagogues and the private residences of Jews were not to be indiscriminately damaged or burnt down.[89] This prohibition was backed up in three consecutive decrees issued in 423 alone. New sites were to be offered for the replacement of synagogues that had already been converted into churches. However, as it still remained forbidden to build new synagogues or to enlarge those already in existence, the overall deterioration in the situation brought about by the violent actions of the Church was now effectively condoned, at least in law.[90] How far this actually corresponded to the reality of the situation in Palestine is, however, a different matter. The archaeological finds from the Byzantine period indicate that a lot of building work was carried out and that the situation was by no means as bad as it would appear from the legislation. The legislation concerning synagogues is pithily summarized in the third Novel of Theodosius II, which dates from 31st January 438.[91] The building of new synagogues remains prohibited; any new synagogues built in contravention of this prohibition shall become the property of the Church. Synagogues in a state of disrepair may be restored, but any improvement to the building in excess of the requirements of preservation is to be punished with a fine of fifty pounds of gold (!).

The law issued in October 415 had already indicated the existence of a conflict with the Patriarch, and Theodosius II took advantage of the opportunity provided by the lack of a direct successor to Gamaliel VI to abolish the patriarchate upon the latter's death. A law issued on 30th May 429[92] speaks of the "extinction of the patriarchate" (*excessus patriarcharum*). Supreme authority was now divided amongst the primates of the Synhedria in both parts of Palestine[93] and the remaining provinces; the tax that had formerly been collected for the Patriarch was now to go to the state.

With the abolition of the Patriarchate, the last remnants of a central Jewish authority were eliminated. This severely weakened both the internal unity of Palestine and the Diaspora and the external representation of Judaism in respect of the state authorities. Judaism was now nothing more than a marginal phenomenon for the Christian state, which could be dealt with according to local circumstances, and which was therefore increasingly at the mercy of local rulers.

10.3.5. Justinian I (527–565)

The period between Theodosius II and the accession to power of Justinian I was a relatively peaceful one for the Jews of Palestine.[94] It was a time of relative economic prosperity, to which the many pilgrims and associated public and private investments in the "Holy Land" no doubt made a significant contribution. Moreover, the Byzantine emperors' political energies were focussed almost exclusively on the conflict between orthodoxy and the Monophysites, which had led to a schism in the Church at the Council of Chalcedon (451). Following these disputes, Juvenal, the orthodox bishop of Jerusalem, was elevated to the patriarchate and thus achieved primacy over the Church in Palestine. The Jews of Palestine did not take part in the two great Samaritan uprisings against Byzantine rule in 485 and 529.

Justinian wanted to revive the idea of unity of empire and considered himself the guardian of orthodoxy. In order to gain control of the West, he had to combat the Monophysites, but in so doing he ran the risk of encouraging separatist movements in the Monophysite churches of the East (particularly in Egypt and Syria). In negotiating this dilemma, he took an increasingly hard line in his policies concerning the Monophysites, especially after the death of his wife Theodora (in 548), who was sympathetic to their cause. The legislation affecting the Jews, which was stepped up once more under Justinian, must be seen against this background. Justinian extended the notion of heresy to cover not only the Christian "heretics", but all non-orthodox groups, including the Jews (and the Samaritans). This new attitude finds initial expression in a Novel dating from 535 (although only Africa is concerned in this case), in which heretics and Jews are forbidden to practice their cult.[95]

Justinian's legislation concerning the Jews affected their civil rights as well as matters of religion. As regards civil rights, Justinian renewed the law forbidding Jews to keep Christian slaves, a law that his predecessors had already repeatedly revised with increasing severity.[96] In a Novel issued in 527, he decreed that Jews were to set free their Christian slaves and pay a penalty of thirty pounds of gold.[97] In 533, the legislation concerning slaves achieved new heights of severity: the Jews were to set free their slaves without compensation if they underwent baptism.[98] Like all such legislation concerning slaves enacted by the Christian emperors, this decree was not simply a matter of religious policy, but was also issued for economic reasons. It made it almost impossible for the Jews to practise a trade as, once they had become Christians, slaves could demand their freedom at any time. It would seem that many Jews tried to forestall this by having themselves baptized, but they were still only allowed to keep their slaves if they had had themselves baptized *before* the slaves; the law expressly prohibits a "conversion" by a Jewish slave-owner after his slaves have already been baptized.

Jewish participation on the municipal councils also appears to have been the subject of new discriminatory measures. In his tax reforms, the emperor Anastasius (491–518) had evidently exempted the municipal councillors from personal liability for taxes and appointed special treasury officials to act as tax-collectors. This meant there were no longer any economic grounds for retaining Jews in the curiae, and in a Novel issued in 537,[99] Justinian decreed that Jews were to be removed from all important offices in the municipal administration. They were only to be permitted to hold lower positions "where the burden of office was greater than the honour".[100]

In contractual law, the Jews—unlike pagans and (other) heretics!—were granted the right of attestation, that is, they could act as witnesses to wills and contracts. On the other hand, Justinian was the first to deny Jews the right to appear before a court as witnesses against an (orthodox) Christian.[101]

In his self-appointed role as guardian of orthodoxy, Justinian also felt himself under a greater obligation than his predecessors to intervene in the internal affairs of the Jewish religion. The most well-known example of this is to be found in his Novel CXLVI from 553, which is primarily aimed at the Jews of the Diaspora, but is nevertheless a typical example of Justinian's religious policy and was no doubt conceived as a statement of principle. The occasion was a dispute which broke out amongst the members of the synagogue of Constantinople over the question as to whether only the Hebrew text should be used when reciting from the Scriptures in the synagogue service, or whether it was also permissible to use the Greek translation. Justinian not only permitted the use of the Greek translation (preferably the Septuagint used by the Christians), but also took advantage of the opportunity to specify what the Jews were supposed to believe; the resurrection of the dead, the existence of angels and the Last Judgement were declared binding articles of faith under penalty of severe punishment. At the same time, use of the *deuterōsis*,[102] that is, the entire tradition of interpretation, was forbidden in the synagogue. The traditional interpretation of the Bible (especially in the Midrashim) had clearly become an integral part of the synagogue service, so that Justinian's law constituted a direct intervention in the fundamental teachings of the Jewish religion (no doubt in the intention of promoting Christian doctrine). The prohibition on *deuterōsis* by Justinian is commonly regarded as one of the reasons why synagogal poetry (*Piyyut*) flourished in the Byzantine era.

All in all, Justinian took the legislation on Jews enacted by his Christian predecessors and made it tougher. Significantly, the compilation of his constitutions promulgated in 534 (Codex Iustinianus)[103] adopts practically none of the laws concerning the protection of synagogues from the Codex Theodosianus, even though the frequency of Christian attacks had certainly not diminished. Fundamentally new was the emperor's interference in the internal affairs of the Jewish religion in Novel CXLVI.[104] The long-term consequences of the Codex Iustinianus were considerable. Its codification of legislation on Jewish matters served as the basis for all future legal practice and remained in force until after the Middle Ages.

10.4. The Persian conquest

The period after Justinian was characterized by increasing tension between the Byzantine rulers and the Jews. Under Justin II (565–578) a further Samaritan-Jewish revolt broke out in Palestine (in 578). The emperors Maurice (582–602) and Phocas (602–610) attempted to convert the Jews forcibly to Christianity, at first in individual actions, later (under Phocas) in what appears to be a large-scale campaign. But these measures, the logical culmination of the policies initiated by Constantine, met with little success. A new and final war between Persia and the Roman-Byzantine Empire was to prove a turning point, leading to the end of Roman (since 63 BCE) and Christian (since 324 CE) rule in Palestine.

The final war between Persia and Byzantium began in 603 under the Persian king Chosroes II and the Byzantine emperor Phocas, who had acceded to power following the assassination of his predecessor Maurice. By 606, the Persians had advanced as far as Syria, and were thus in close proximity to Palestine. In 610, Heraclius became the new emperor of Byzantium, and in 611 the Persians conquered Antioch and blocked the overland route between Byzantium and Palestine. In 613, they took Damascus and were at the gates of Palestine.

The Jews of Palestine, who had been suffering under the pressure of an ever-worsening legal situation and the threat of compulsory baptism, looked on the Persians as liberators of the country from Byzantine tyranny. An entire apocalyptic literature sprang up again (in particular, the apocalypses of Zerubbabel and Elias) in which the new Messianic hopes were articulated. Even as the Persians were approaching Palestine, the Jews appear to have risked an open revolt against the Christians and to have allied themselves with the Persians. Jewish requests for (above all) the return of Jerusalem met with a positive response from the Persians, both for reasons of principle (the Persian state under the Sassanians was extremely tolerant in religious matters) and on tactical grounds. At any rate, the Persian advance, which had to pass through densely populated Jewish territory, was carried out extraordinarily rapidly. In one offensive at the beginning of 614, the Persians advanced from Damascus to Jerusalem, taking in Tiberias, Sepphoris, Caesarea and Lod *en route*. We do not know the exact course of events in Jerusalem, as neither of the two main sources[105] provides us with a clear picture. It would seem that the city initially surrendered (like Caesarea before it), but that shortly afterwards (in early May?) there was an attempted revolt. The Persians conquered Jerusalem once and for all at the end of May 614, and this time they destroyed a large number of churches, ransacked the city and caused carnage amongst the Christian population. They subsequently handed over the city to the Jews who, hoping for a restoration similar to that following the edict of the Persian king Cyrus in 538 BCE, proceeded to set up a Jewish administration.

Unfortunately, we know very little about the period of Jewish self-rule in Jerusalem. The Zerubbabel apocalypse would appear to allude to these events, but it adheres so closely to the established conventions of the apocalyptic tradition that it is difficult to establish the concrete historical implications. According to the Zerubbabel apocalypse, forty years before the coming of the Messiah ben David, the "suffering Messiah" will appear. Behind the heavily symbolic name of Nehemiah (ben Chushiel), an allusion to the "first" great restorer under Persian sovereignty, we may perhaps find the Jewish leader of the new Messianic kingdom, to whom it is said the whole of Israel will flock from the Diaspora and once again offer up communal sacrifices.[106] The gathering in of the dispersed and the resumption of the sacrificial cult in the reconstructed Temple are so much part of the traditional Messianic scenario that one may hardly take this as concrete evidence of a revival of the Jewish sacrificial cult in liberated Jerusalem.

The Christian sources naturally comment on events purely from a Christian viewpoint. They report a persecution of the Christians in Jerusalem, with the Jews taking their revenge for the long years of Christian oppression. After the greater part of the Christian population of Jerusalem had been deported to Persia together with the relic of the True Cross, the remainder were handed over to the Jews and presented with the choice of conversion to Judaism or death. Almost all of them chose a martyr's death. The account written (in Arabic) by the monk Strategius of Mar Saba is typical for its mixture of anti-Jewish polemic and historical information:

As those (Christians) who had been in hiding now emerged, the commanding officers (of the Persians) inquired after their trade, and each replied accordingly. They chose the best of them for transportation to their country as captives. They imprisoned the remaining men in the cistern of Mamila, about two arrow-throws away from the city and half a mile from the Tower of David. They appointed sentries to watch over them in this cistern. Who, O my friends, would be capable of describing the misery of these Christians on that day, for they were so many that one trod on the other, just like cattle driven into a pen for slaughtering. That is exactly what happened to those poor unfortunates! They had nothing to eat or drink. Most of them died since God had abandoned them. In their great misery, they longed for death—just as men normally desire to live—and cried out loud: O Lord, let us not fall into the hands of these unbelievers, let us not perish, O our Lord. We believe in you, O Lord, look upon us and do not let our cries for help go unheard! Have mercy on us and either save us or let us soon die so that we may be delivered from this punishment!

At that time the Jews were in favour with the King of Persia. They had been delighted at the murder (of the Christians) and relished their misfortune. The Jews now went to that cistern where those poor unfortunates were being held and said: If any of you wishes to become a Jew, let him come forward and we shall buy his freedom from the Persians. But they were unable to satisfy their pernicous desire, for the children of baptism preferred death to such an abhorrent life, did not give up their faith, and their fate will not be that of the Jews in hell-fire! When the Jews saw that their hopes would be unfulfilled, they became so angry with them that they ran to the Persians in order to buy a large number (of Christians) from them, who they then slaughtered, just as one might buy cattle to slaughter. All those slaughtered, however, they go as martyrs to their Lord, for they have died for their faith. So that is what those unbelievers did to those who believe in the Messiah, and they killed them. So the cistern became a cistern of blood. The dying, however, called out to the Jews: You asked us to become Jews, unbelievers like yourselves, but we have become God's martyrs, we who believe in the Messiah. Because of this persecution we have suffered we shall be accusers (on the Day of Judgement) and demand the severest punishment for you in the world to come. It was not the Persians who killed us, but you, you Jews, who shall be damned. You killed the Lord of the World and his prophets in exactly the same way, and exactly as you bought the death of the Lord of Glory with your money, so you now buy the death of his servants with your money. May you receive due punishment on that terrible day!

After the withdrawal of the Persians from the city of Jerusalem, the Jews—may God's curse be upon them!—gathered together and destroyed the churches with their unclean hands. But none of you should be surprised at all this, for where there is so much sin, there is much suffering and the enemy is powerful![107]

The radical Messianic government of the Jews in Jerusalem was, however, to be of only short duration. After conquering Jerusalem, the Persians planned attacks on Egypt and Constantinople, which they besieged for almost ten years without success (from 615 onwards). In Palestine, they managed to take Acco with the aid of the city's Jewish inhabitants. However, they failed to capture the equally important coastal city of Tyre, where the local authorities had interned their Jewish fellow-citizens. The unsuccessful siege of Tyre (617?) seems to have led to a shift in Persian policy. The Persians realized that the Jews were unable to provide them with the necessary military assistance in their further war against Byzantium and that they could not hold Palestine with only Jewish support when the overwhelming majority of the population was Christian. So, probably in that very same year (617), they took Jerusalem back from the Jews and returned the city to the Christians. The following passage from the Zerubbabel apocalypse is probably an allusion to this:

In the fifth year (of the rule) of Nehemia ben Chushiel and the assembly of the Holy People, Shiroi[108] the king of Persia shall advance against Nehemia and against Israel, and there shall reign great distress in Israel ... Shiroi shall run through Nehemia ben Chushiel ..., and Israel shall be dispersed into the desert.[109]

In 622, Heraclius began a successful counter-offensive against the Persians, and by 627/28 had managed to advance into the Persian heartland. In 628, Chosroes II was deposed and assassinated by his son, and a vicious struggle for the succession broke out in Persia. In these circumstances, it did not prove difficult for Heraclius to win back the occupied provinces and the relic of the True Cross and set free the Christian prisoners. On 21st March 629, he marched triumphantly into Jerusalem and returned the relic of the True Cross to the Church of the Holy Sepulchre. He had promised the Jews of Palestine an amnesty in Tiberias,[110] but was unable to hold to this. At the insistence of the leaders of the Christians, who had not forgotten the period of Jewish rule from 614 to 617, he once more expelled the Jews from Jerusalem and had to allow large numbers of them to be executed.

But the days of Byzantine-Christian rule in Palestine were also numbered. By 632, the newly emergent great power of the Arabs was on the advance, leading to the fall of Tiberias (and consequently Galilee) in 636 and the capture of Jerusalem in 638. The fall of Jerusalem to the Arabs marked a significant turning-point in the history of Palestine. The era of early and rabbinic Judaism, characterized by confrontation with the Greeks and Romans— latterly in the guise of Christianity—was now at an end. Edom was succeeded by Ishmael, the confrontation with Islam.

Notes

1. b Hor 13b.
2. = Beth Shearim.
3. Schwabe-Lifshitz, Beth She'arim II, p. 45.
4. = Graecized form of "Chanina".
5. See p. 170 below.
6. t Shab 7[8].18. According to this source, however, this same rite had already been carried out for Gamaliel II.
7. j Taan 4.2, fol. 68a.
8. b AZ 11a.
9. b Meg 11a.
10. j Ned 6.13, fol. 40a; b Ber 63a.
11. j AZ 2.10, fol. 42a.
12. b Ber 43a.
13. CT XVI, 8.14; the decree was repealed in 404 (CT XVI, 8.17).
14. Who was very rich.
15. b Er 85 bf.
16. b San 38a.
17. Avi-Yonah, Geschichte, p. 56.
18. See p. 171 ff. below.
19. b Ket 103b.
20. See note 53 below and CT XVI, 8.11,13,15.
21. CT XVI, 8.8; see p. 186 f. below.
22. See p. 187 below.
23. See p. 106 above.
24. Cf. Lev. 25:35–37; Deut. 23:20.
25. Cf. Mishnah BM 5.1.
26. I.e. when legal proceedings are instituted for usury.
27. I.e. if one were to proceed according to R. Yannai's definition.
28. I.e. an accusation of usury is an insufficient criterion for usury. High, and apparently even excessive interest is allowed, provided that it has been mutually agreed; j BM 5.1, fol. 10a.

29. The rabbis were usually exempted from taxes.
30. Or: "Half of the sum demanded was then remitted." However, the irony of the story comes out more clearly in the above translation.
31. b BB 8a.
32. BerR 76.6. The English translation is taken from Midrash Rabbah, vol. II, tr. Rabbi Dr. H. Freedman, The Soncino Press, London, 1939.
33. I.e.: Flee across the Jordan! j MQ 2.3, fol. 81b.
34. b Taan 5a.
35. b San 98b.
36. I.e. as a sign of mourning.
37. EchaR, Pet. 17, p. 14. The English translation is taken from Midrash Rabbah: Lamentations, tr. Rev. Dr. A. Cohen, The Soncino Press, London, 1939.
38. See p. 109 above.
39. PRK, ed. Mandelbaum, p. 410 f.
40. j Ber 4.4, fol. 8b.
41. The borders of the province of *Syria Palaestina* were also altered (leading to the loss of some territories in the north and the gain of parts of the province of *Arabia* in the south). Diocletian visited Palestine in 286 and 297 CE.
42. m Sot 9.15.
43. TPsJ Num. 24:18 f.
44. Orat. adv. Iud. V, 11 (PG XLVIII, col. 900).
45. Panharion haer. XXX, 4–12 (GCS XXV, p. 338 ff.).
46. See p. 146 above.
47. HA, Sept. Sev. 17.1.
48. CT XVI, 9.1. The English translation is taken from The Theodosian Code and Novels and the Sirmondian Constitutions, tr. Clyde Pharr, Princeton University Press, New Jersey, 1952.
49. I.e. Christians.
50. CT XVI, 8.1. The prohibition was repeated on 22nd October 335; cf. XVI, 8.5.
51. See p. 173 above.
52. CT XVI, 8.3 (11/12/321).
53. CT XVI, 8.4 dated 1/12/331 (330?). Cf. also the law of 29/11/330 (CT XVI, 8.2), in which the patriarchs and priests (*presbyteri*) are exempted "from all compulsory public services that are incumbent on persons".
54. Eutychius, Annales I, 465 (PG CXI, col. 1012).
55. CT XVI, 8.6. The ascription to Constantius is uncertain; the law may also have originated with his brother and co-regent Constantine II.
56. CT XVI, 9.2.
57. Or 357?
58. CT XVI, 8.7. Cf. also CT XVI, 8.1 and 5 above under Constantine I.
59. Historiae abbreviatae (= De Caesaribus), 42.9-12 (Ed. Fr. Pichelmayr, Leipzig 1911, repr. 1970, p. 128).
60. Jerome, Chronicon, GCS XXIV/XXXIV, p. 238.
61. PesR 8, p. 29b.
62. Avi-Yonah, Geschichte, p. 184.
63. Ibid., p. 183.
64. j Yeb 16.3, fol. 15c; j Shebi 4.2, fol. 35a; j Ber 5.1, fol. 9a and *passim*.
65. The claim that the name was also common amongst the Jews in the fourth century (as made by Avi-Yonah, Geschichte, p. 181 with reference to J.-B. Frey,

Corpus Inscriptionum Iudaicarum, vol. 1, Rome 1936, Index), can hardly be upheld on the basis of a single piece of evidence—and a reconstructed one at that—in Frey (No. 350).

66. Cf. Chrysostom, Orat. adv. Iud. V, 11 (PG XLVIII, col. 900); Rufinus, Hist. eccl. X, 38 (GCS IX/2, p. 997); Sozomenos, Hist. eccl. V, 22 (GCS L, p. 229 ff.).

67. Cf. also Gregory of Nyssa, Orat. V contra Iulianum, 3–4 (PG XXXV, col. 668).

68. See p. 134 above.

69. Ephrem, Vier Lieder über Julian den Apostaten I, 16 ff. (Bibliothek der Kirchenväter XXXVII, p. 217 f.); Gregory of Nyssa, Oratio V contra Iulianum, 3–4 (PG XXXV, col. 668); Rufinus, Hist. eccl. X, 38 (GCS IX/2, p. 997); Chrysostom, Orat. adv. Iud. V, 11 (PG XLVIII, col. 901) and passim.

70. As does Avi-Yonah, Geschichte, p. 197.

71. Ed. W. C. Wright, The Works of the Emperor Julian, III, London 1969, p. 176 ff. (No. 51).

72. See p. 169 above.

73. Ambrosius, Ep. XL, 12 (PL XVI, col. 1105); Gregory of Nyssa, Orat. V contra Iulianum, 4 (PG XXXV, col. 668 f.); Chrysostom, Orat. adv. Iud. V, 11 (PG XLVIII, col. 901) and passim.

74. Although he was not an eyewitness, he accompanied Julian on his campaign and may have had access to official reports.

75. Res Gestae XXIII, 1.3 (Ed. W. Seyfarth, Berlin 1970, p. 67).

76. Hist. eccl. X, 39–40 (GCS IX/2, p. 998).

77. CT XVI, 1.2.

78. Edicts of 24/2/391 and 8/11/392 (CT XVI, 10.10 and 12).

79. CT III, 1.5.

80. See p. 180 above.

81. CT III, 7.2. At the same time, he further increased the law's severity by extending the right of accusation to the "voices of the public", whereas Constantine I had restricted this to next of kin (CT IX, 7.2).

82. CT XIII, 5.18.

83. CT XVI, 8.8.

84. CT XVI, 8.9.

85. The title of the corresponding chapter in Avi-Yonah, Geschichte, p. 209.

86. CT XVI, 8.18.

87. CT XVI, 8.22.

88. See p. 178 above.

89. CT XVI, 8.21.

90. CT XVI, 8.25 (15/2/423); XVI, 8.26 (9/4/423); XVI, 8.27 (8/6/423).

91. Cf. also CI I, 9.18.

92. CT XVI, 8.29.

93. This refers to the administrative units of the province of Palestine which had existed under joint military command since the end of the fourth century: Palaestina prima with Judaea, Samaria, Peraea and Caesarea as administrative centre, and Palaestina secunda with Galilee, the Decapolis and Scythopolis as administrative centre. The Arabian parts of the province, Palaestina tertia (with Petra as its centre), had virtually no Jewish inhabitants.

94. The Palestinian Jews were not involved in the conflict between the royal house of Himyar in South Arabia, which had converted to Judaism, and Byzantium

under Justin I (518–527). The Christian Abyssinians overthrew the Jewish King Dhu Nuwas in 525 CE, following which the Himyarites came under Byzantine (and subsequently Persian) influence.

95. Nov. XXXVII, 8. Cf. also the law enacted in 518 by Justin I (possibly in collaboration with Justinian), CI I, 5.12 § 2.
96. See pp. 178, 181, 185 and 187 above.
97. CI I, 10.2.
98. CI I, 3.54 (56) §§ 8–11.
99. Nov. XLV, praefatio.
100. Avi-Yonah, Geschichte, p. 248. However, this interpretation of the law is disputed.
101. CI I, 5.21 issued in 531.
102. Literally: "repetition".
103. Supplemented later by *novellae*.
104. Further evidence of the deterioration in the general climate can be found in the fact that the Jews of Caesarea took part in a Samaritan uprising against the Christian population in 556.
105. Sebeus, ch. XXIV, tr. F. Macler, Histoire d'Héraclius par l'Évêque Sebéos, traduite de l'Arménien et annotée, Paris, 1904, p. 68 f.; Strategius of Mar Saba, cf. A. Couret, La prise de Jérusalem par les Perses en 614, Orléans, 1896, p. 29 f.; P. Peeters, "La prise de Jérusalem par les Perses", in: icl., Recherches d'Histoire et de Philologie Orientales, vol. I, Brussels, 1951, p. 93 ff.
106. Sefer Zerubavel, ed. J. Even-Schemuel, in: *Midreshe Ge'ullah*, p. 78.
107. Strategius of Mar Saba, ed. Peeters, p. 95 f.
108. = Chosroes?
109. Even-Schemuel, *Midreshe Ge'ullah*, pp. 78, 80.
110. Eutychius, Annales II, 240 ff. (PG CXI, col. 1089 f.).

BIBLIOGRAPHY

General

Abel, F.-M., *Géographie de la Palestine*, I–II, Paris, 1933–38.
— *Histoire de la Palestine depuis la conquête d'Alexandre jusqu'à l'invasion arabe*, I–II, Paris, 1952.
Al(l)on, G., *Geschichte der Juden im Lande Israel im Zeitalter der Mischnah und des Talmud* (Heb.), I (4th ed.), Tel Aviv, 1967; II (2nd ed.), Tel Aviv, 1961. Engl. tr.: *The Jews in their Land in the Talmudic Age (70–640 C.E.)*, I, Jerusalem, 1980; II, Jerusalem, 1984.
— *Studien zur Geschichte Israels* (Heb.), I–II (2nd ed. 1967), Tel Aviv, 1957–58. Engl. tr.: *Jews, Judaism and the Classical World*, Jerusalem, 1977.
Applebaum, S., *Judea in Hellenistic and Roman Times*. Historical and Archaeological Essays (Studies in Judaism in Late Antiquity 40), Leiden, 1989.
Avi-Yonah, M., *Geschichte der Juden im Zeitalter des Talmud*, Berlin, 1962.
— *The Holy Land from the Persian to the Arab Conquest: Historical Geography*, Grand Rapids, Mich.,1966.

Baer, Y., *Among the Nations* (Heb.), Jerusalem, 1955.
Baras, Z., Safrai, S., Tsafrir, Y., Stern, M. (eds.), *Eretz Israel from the Destruction of the Second Temple to the Muslim Conquest* (Heb.), Jerusalem, 1982.
Baron, S. W., *A Social and Religious History of the Jews*, I–II (2nd. ed.), New York, 1952.
Baumann, U., *Rom und die Juden: Die römisch-jüdischen Beziehungen von Pompeius bis zum Tode des Herodes (63 v. Chr.–4 v. Chr.)*, Frankfurt a.M.–Berne–New York, 1986.
Ben-David, A., *Jerusalem und Tyros. Ein Beitrag zur palästinensischen Münz- und Wirtschaftsgeschichte (126 a.C.–57 p.C.)*, Tübingen, 1969.
— Talmudische Ökonomie, I, Hildesheim, 1974.
Bengtson, H., *Die Strategie in der hellenistischen Zeit*, I–III, Munich, 1937–52.
— *Griechische Geschichte von den Anfängen bis in die römische Kaiserzeit*, HAW III/4 (4th ed.), Munich, 1969.
Bevan, E., *Jerusalem under the High-Priests*, London, 1924 (repr. 1952).
Bi(c)kerman(n), E., *From Ezra to the Last of the Maccabees*, New York, 1962.
Bickerman, E., *The Jews in the Greek Age*, Cambridge MA—London, 1988.
Bietenhard, H., "Die syrische Dekapolis von Pompeius bis Traian", in: *ANRW* II.8, Berlin–New York, 1977, pp. 220–261.

Cohen, B., *Jewish and Roman Law. A Comparative Study*, I–II, New York, 1966.
Cohen, S.A., *The Three Crowns. Structures of Communal Politics in Early Rabbinic Jewry*, Cambridge/New York, 1990.
Cohen, S. J. D., *From the Maccabees to the Mishnah*, Philadelphia, 1987.

Davies, W.D. and Finkelstein, L. (eds.), *The Cambridge History of Judaism*. Vol II: The Hellenistic Age, Cambridge, 1989.
De Geus, C. H. J., "Idumaea", *JEOL* 26, 1979–1980, pp. 53–74.
Duncan-Jones, R., *The Economy of the Roman Empire*, Cambridge, 1974.

Efron (Ephron), J. (Y.), "The Sanhedrin of the Second Temple" (Heb.), in: *Commentationes Benzioni Katz dedicatae*, ed. S. Perlman and B. Shimron, Tel Aviv, 1967, pp. 167–204.
— *Studies of the Hasmonean Period* (Heb.), Tel Aviv, 1980. Engl. tr.: *Studies on the Hasmonean Period*, Leiden, 1987.

Feldman, L.H., *Jew & Gentile in the Ancient World. Attitudes and Interactions from Alexander to Justinian*, Princeton NJ, 1993.
Freyne, S., *Galilee from Alexander the Great to Hadrian 323 B.C.E. to 135 C.E.*, Wilmington, Del.–Notre Dame, Ind., 1980.
Fuks, G., "The Jews of Hellenistic and Roman Scythopolis", *JJS 33*, 1982, pp. 407–416.

Ghiretti, M., "Lo 'status' della Giudea dall'età Augustea all'età Claudia", *Latomus* 44, 1985, pp. 751–766.
Gil, M., "Land Ownership in Palestine under Roman Rule", *RIDA* 17, 1970, pp. 11–53.
Glatzer, N. N., *Geschichte der talmudischen Zeit*, Berlin, 1937.
Goldschmid, L., "Les impôts et droits de douane en Judée sous les Romains", *REJ* 34, 1897, pp. 192–217.
Goodenough, E.R., *Jewish Symbols in the Greco-Roman Period*, edited and abridged by J. Neusner, Princeton NJ, 1992.
Grabbe, L.L., *Judaism from Cyprus to Hadrian*, I–II, Minneapolis, 1992.
Gunneweg, A. H. J., *Geschichte Israels bis Bar Kochba*, Stuttgart, 1972.

Hachlili, R., *Ancient Jewish Art and Archeology in the Land of Israel*, Leiden, 1988.
Hadas-Lebel, M., *Flavius Joseph. Eyewitness to Rome's First-Century Conquest of Judea*, translated by Richard Miller, New York, 1933.
Heichelheim, F. M., in: T. Frank, *An Economic Survey of Ancient Rome*, IV: *Roman Syria*, Baltimore, 1938, pp. 121–257.
Heinen, H., "Die politischen Beziehungen zwischen Rom und dem Ptolemäerreich von ihren Anfängen bis zum Tag von Eleusis (273–168 BC)", in: *ANRW* I.1, Berlin–New York 1972, pp. 633–659.
Hengel, M., *Judentum und Hellenismus* (2nd ed.), Tübingen, 1973.
— *Juden, Griechen und Barbaren*, Stuttgart, 1976.
Hengel, M., *The 'Hellenization' of Judaea in the First Century after Christ*, London, 1990.
Herzfeld, L., *Handelsgeschichte der Juden des Altertums* (2nd ed.), Braunschweig, 1894.

Hoenig, S. B., *The Great Sanhedrin*, Philadelphia, 1953.
Horsley, R. A., "High Priests and the Politics of Roman Palestine. A Contextual Analysis of the Evidence in Josephus", JSJ 17, 1986, pp. 23–55.

Jagersma, H., *A History of Israel from Alexander the Great to Bar Kochba*, London, 1985.
Jeremias, J., *Jerusalem zur Zeit Jesu* (3rd ed.), Göttingen, 1962. English translation: *Jerusalem in the Time of Jesus*, 1975.
Jones, A. H. M., *The Cities of the Eastern Roman Provinces* (2nd ed.), Oxford, 1971.
— *The Roman Economy*, Oxford, 1974.
Juster, J., *Les Juifs dans l'empire romain*, I–II, Paris, 1914.

Kanael, B., "Altjüdische Münzen", *JNG* 17, 1967, pp. 159–298.
Kasher, A., "Gaza during the Greco–Roman Era", *The Jerusalem Cathedra* 2, 1982, pp. 63–78.
— *The Jews in Hellenistic and Roman Egypt. The Struggle for Equal Rights*, Tübingen, 1985.
Kasher, A., *Jews and Hellenistic Cities in Eretz-Israel*, Tübingen, 1990.
Kasher, A., Oppenheimer, A., and Rappaport, U. (eds.), *Synagogues in Antiquity* (Hebrew), Jerusalem, 1987.
Kippenberg, H. G., *Religion und Klassenbildung im antiken Judäa*, Göttingen, 1978.
Kippenberg, H. G. and Wewers, G. A., *Textbuch zur neutestamentlichen Zeitgeschichte*, Göttingen, 1979.
Klausner, J., *A History of the Second Temple* (Heb.), I–V (4th ed.), Jerusalem, 1954.
Klein, S., *Galiläa von der Makkabäerzeit bis 67*, Palästina-Studien, No. 4, Wien 1928.
Krauss, S., *Talmudische Archäologie*, I–III, Leipzig, 1910–12.

Launey, M., *Recherches sur les armées hellénistiques*, I–II, Paris, 1949–50.
Leaney, A. R. C. and Neusner, J., "The Roman Era", in: *Israelite and Judaean History*, ed. J. H. Hayes and J. M. Miller, London, 1977, pp. 605–677.
Levine, L. I., *Caesarea under Roman Rule*, lleiden, 1975.
— *The Rabbinic Class of Roman Palestine in Late Antiquity*, Jerusalem–New York, 1989.
Levine, L. I., *The Galilee in Late Antiquity*, New York—Jerusalem, 1992.
Lifshitz, B., "Études sur l'histoire de la province romaine de Syrie", in: *ANRW* II.8, Berlin–New York, 1977, pp. 3–30.
— "Jérusalem sous la domination romaine. Histoire de la ville depuis la conquête de Pompée jusqu'à Constantin (63 a.C.–325 p.C.)", in: *ANRW* II.8, Berlin–New York, 1977, pp. 444–489.
— "Césarée de Palestine, son histoire et ses institutions", in: *ANRW* II.8, Berlin–New York, 1977, pp. 490–518.
Linder, A., *The Jews in Roman Imperial Legislation*, Detroit, 1987.
Loftus, F., "The Anti-Roman Revolts of the Jews and the Galileans", *JQR* 68, 1977, pp. 78–98.
Lohse, E., *Umwelt des Neuen Testaments* (3rd ed.), Göttingen, 1977.

Maier, J., *Grundzüge der Geschichte des Judentums im Altertum*, Darmstadt, 1981.

Maier, J. and Schreiner, J. (eds.), *Literatur und Religion des Frühjudentums*, Würzburg, 1973.

Mantel, H., *Studies in the History of the Sanhedrin*, Cambridge, Mass., 1961.

— "The Nature of the Great Synagogue", HTR 60, 1967, pp. 69–91.

Marquardt, J., *Römische Staatsverwaltung* (3rd ed.), I–II, Darmstadt, 1957.

Masada I: The Aramaic and Hebrew Ostraca and Jar Inscriptions, Yigael Yadin and Joseph Naveh; *The Coins of Masada*, Yaakov Meshorer (The Yigael Yadin Excavations 1963–1965, Final Reports), Israel Exploration Society, Jerusalem, 1989.

Masada II: The Latin and Greek Documents, Hannah M. Cotton and Joseph Geiger, with a contribution of J. D. Thomas (The Yigael Yadin Excavations 1963–1965, Final Reports), Israel Exploration Society, Jerusalem, 1989.

Masada III: The Buildings, Stratography and Architecture, Netzer, E. (The Yigael Yadin Excavations 1963–1965, Final Reports), Israel Exploration Society, Jerusalem, 1991.

McCracken Flesher, P. V. (ed.), *New Perspectives on Ancient Judaism*, Vol. V (Society and Literature in Analysis Studies in Judaism), Lanham—New York—London, 1990.

McLaren, J. S., *Power and Politics in Palestine: The Jews and the Governing of their Land*, Sheffield, 1991.

Mendels, D., *The Land of Israel as a Political Concept in Hasmonean Literature*, Tübingen, 1987.

Mendels, D., *The Rise and Fall of Jewish Nationalism: Jewish and Christian Ethnicity in Ancient Palestine within the Greco-Roman Period*, New York—London, 1992.

Meshorer, Y., *Jewish Coins of the Second Temple Period*, Tel Aviv, 1967.

Meyers, E. M., Netzer, E. and Meyer, C. L., *Sepphoris*, Winona Lake, 1992.

Miller, S. S., *Studies in the History and Tradition of Sepphoris*, Leiden, 1984.

Momigliano, A., "Richerche sull' organizzazione della Giudea sotto il dominio romano (63 a.C.–70 d.C.)", ASNSP 3, 1934, pp. 183–221; Amsterdam, 1967, pp. 347–396.

Mommsen, T., *Judaea und die Juden*, Berlin, 1936.

Moore, G. F., *Judaism in the First Centuries of the Christian Era* (7th ed.), I–III, Cambridge, Mass., 1954.

Mor, M. and Rappaport, U., *Bibliography of Works on Jewish History in the Hellenistic and Roman Periods, 1976–1980*, Publications of the Zalman Shazar Center, Jerusalem, 1982.

Oesterley, W. O. E., *The Jews and Judaism during the Greek Period*, London, 1941 (repr. New York–London, 1970).

Oppenheimer, A., *The 'Am ha-'Aretz. A Study of the Jewish People in the Hellenistic-Roman Period*, Leiden, 1977.

— *Galilee in the Mishnaic Period* (Heb.), Jerusalem, 1991.

Otzen, B., *Judaism in Antiquity. Political Development and Religious Current from Alexander to Hadrian*. Sheffield, 1990.

Peterson, E., *Der Monotheismus als politisches Problem. Beitrag zur Geschichte der politischen Theologie im Imperium Romanum*, Leipzig, 1935.

Piatelli, D., "An Inquiry into the Political Relations between Rome and Judaea from 161 to 4 B.C.E.", *Israel Law Review* 14, 1979, pp. 195–236.

Pöhlmann, R. von, *Geschichte der sozialen Frage und des Sozialismus in der antiken Welt* (3rd ed.), I–II, Munich, 1925.

Préaux, C., *Le monde hellénistique*, I–II, Paris, 1978.

Rabello, A. M., "The Legal Conditions of the Jews in the Roman Empire", in: *ANRW* II.13, Berlin–New York, 1980, pp. 662–762.

Rajak, T., *Josephus. The Historian and His Society*, London, 1983.

Rappaport, U., *A History of Israel in the Period of the Second Temple* (Heb., 2nd ed.), Tel Aviv, 1982.

— "Bibliography of Works on Jewish History in the Hellenistic and Roman Periods, 1946–1970", in: *Studies in the History of the Jewish People and the Land of Israel*, II, Haifa, 1972, pp. 247–321.

— (in collaboration with M. Mor), *Bibliography of Works on Jewish History in the Hellenistic and Roman Periods, 1971–1975*, The Institute for Advanced Studies, Jerusalem, 1976.

Reicke, B., *Neutestamentliche Zeitgeschichte* (2nd ed.), Berlin, 1968.

Reifenberg, A., *Ancient Jewish Coins* (2nd ed.), Jerusalem, 1947.

Rostovtzeff, M., "Geschichte der Steuerpacht in der römischen Kaiserzeit bis Diokletian", *Ph. S* 9, 1904, pp. 331–512.

— *Gesellschafts- und Wirtschaftsgeschichte der hellenistischen Welt*, I–III, Darmstadt, 1955–56 (repr. 1962).

— *The Social and Economic History of the Roman Empire*, I–II (2nd ed.), Oxford, 1957 (repr. 1963).

Roth, O., *Rom und die Hasmonäer*, Leipzig, 1914.

Roth-Gerson, L., *The Greek Inscriptions from the Synagogues in Eretz-Israel* (Heb.), Jerusalem, 1987.

Russell, D. S., *The Jews from Alexander to Herod*, London, 1967.

Sacchi, P., *Storia del mondo giudaico*, Turin, 1976.

Safrai, S. and Stern, M. (eds.), *Compendium Rerum Judaicarum ad Novum Testamentum*, I/1.2: *The Jewish People in the First Century*, Assen–Amsterdam, 1974–76.

Safrai, S., "Das Zeitalter der Mischna und des Talmuds (70–640)", in: H. H. Ben-Sasson (ed.), *Geschichte des jüdischen Volkes*, I, Munich, 1978, pp. 377–469.

— *Das jüdische Volk im Zeitalter des Zweiten Tempels*, Neukirchen–Vluyn, 1978.

Safrai, Z., "The Administration Structure of Judaea in the Roman Period" (Heb.), in: *Studies in the History of the Jewish People and the Land of Israel*, IV, ed. U. Rappaport, Haifa, 1978, pp. 103–136. Abridged English version in: *Immanuel* 13, 1981, pp. 30–38.

Saldarini, A. J., *Pharisees, Scribes and Sadducees in Palestinian Society*, Wilmington DE, 1988.

Schäfer, P., "The Hellenistic and Maccabean Periods", in: *Israelite and Judaean History*, ed. J. H. Hayes and J. M. Miller, London, 1977, pp. 539–604.

Schalit, A., *Roman Administration in Palestine* (Heb.), Jerusalem, 1937.

— (ed.), *The Hellenistic Age*, New Brunswick, 1972 (*WHJP* I/6).

Schlatter, A., *Geschichte Israels von Alexander dem Großen bis Hadrian* (3rd. ed.), Stuttgart, 1925.

Schürer, E., *The History of the Jewish People in the Age of Jesus Christ (175 B.C.–A.D. 135), A New English Version*, rev. and ed. by G. Vermes and F. Millar, I–III, Edinburgh, 1973–86.

Schwartz, J. J., *Lod (Lydda), Israel. From its Origins through the Byzantine Period 5600 B.C.E.–640 C.E.*, Oxford, 1991.

Schwartz, S., *Josephus and Judaean Politics*, Leiden—New York—Kopenhagen—Cologne, 1990.
Shatzman, I., *The Armies of the Hasmonaeans and Herod. From Hellenistic to Roman Frameworks*, Tübingen, 1991.
Sherwin-White, A. N., *Roman Foreign Policy in the East 168 B.C. to A.D. 1*, London, 1984.
Smallwood, E. M., *The Jews under Roman Rule*, London, 1976.
Smith, M., *Palestinian Parties and Politics that Shaped the Old Testament*, New York, 1971.
Stemberger, G., *Das klassische Judentum*, Munich, 1979.
— *Die römische Herrschaft im Urteil der Juden*, Darmstadt, 1983.
Stern, M., *Greek and Latin Authors on Jews and Judaism*, I–III, Jerusalem, 1974–84.
— "Die Zeit des Zweiten Tempels", in: H. H. Ben Sasson (ed.), *Geschichte des jüdischen Volkes*, I, Munich, 1978, pp. 231–373.
— (ed.), *The History of Eretz Israel*, III: *The Hellenistic Period and the Hasmonean State (332–37 B.C.E.)* (Heb.), Jerusalem, 1981.
Sullivan, R. D., "The Dynasty of Judaea in the First Century", in: *ANRW* II.8, Berlin–New York, 1977, pp. 296–354.

Talmon, S. (ed.), *Jewish Civilization in the Hellenistic–Roman Period*, Sheffield, 1991.
Tarn, W. W. and Griffith, G. T., *Hellenistic Civilization* (3rd ed.), Cleveland–New York, 1961.
Tcherikover, V., *Hellenistic Civilization and the Jews* (2nd ed.), Philadelphia–Jerusalem, 1961.
Tcherikover, V. and Fuks, A., *Corpus Papyrorum Judaicarum*, I–III, Cambridge, Mass., 1957–64.
Tsafrir, Y., "The Desert Forts of Judea in Second Temple Times" (Heb.), *Qadmoniot* 8, 1975, pp. 41–53.
— "The Desert Fortresses of Judaea in the Second Temple Period", *The Jerusalem Cathedra* 2, 1982, pp. 120–145.

Will, E., *Histoire politique du monde héllenistique*, I–II, Nancy, 1966–1967.

Zeitlin, S., *The Rise and Fall of the Judaean State*, I–II, Philadelphia, 1962–1967 (2nd ed. 1968).
Zucker, H., *Studien zur jüdischen Selbstverwaltung im Altertum*, Berlin, 1936.

1. Alexander the Great and the Diadochi

Abel, F.-M., "Alexandre le Grand en *Syrie et en Palestine*", *RB* 43, 1934, pp. 528–545; 44, 1935, pp. 42–61.
Auscher, D., "Les relations entre Grèce et la Palestine avant la conquête d'Alexandre", *VT* 17, 1967, pp. 8–30.

Bull, R. J. and Wright, G. E., "Newly Discovered Temples on Mount Gerizim in Jordan", *HTR* 58, 1965, pp. 234–237.

Coggins, R. J., *Samaritans and Jews. The Origins of Samaritanism Reconsidered*, Oxford, 1975.

Cross, F. M., "Aspects of Samaritan and Jewish History in Late Persian and Hellenistic Times", *HTR* 59, 1966, pp. 201–211.
— "Papyri of the Fourth Century BC from Dâliyeh: A Preliminary Report on their Discovery and Significance", New Directions, 1969, pp. 45–69.

Dexinger, F., "Limits of Tolerance in Judaism: The Samaritan Example", in: *Jewish and Christian Self-Definition*, II: *Aspects of Judaism in the Graeco–Roman Period*, ed. E. P. Sanders, Philadelphia, 1981, pp. 88–114, 327–338.

Golan, D., "Josephus, Alexander's Visit to Jerusalem, and Modern Historiography", in Rappaport, U. (ed.), *Josephus Flavius. Historian of Eretz-Israel in the Hellenistic-Roman Period. Collected Papers* (Heb.), Jerusalem, 1982, pp. 29–55.
Gutman, Y. (Gutmann, J.), "Alexander the Macedonian in Palestine" (Heb.), *Tarbiz* 11, 1940, pp. 271–294.

Hammond, H. G. L., *Alexander the Great: King, Commander and Statesman*, Park Ridge, N. J., 1981.

Kasher, A., "Some Suggestions and Comments Concerning Alexander Macedon's Campaign in Palestine" (Heb.), *Bet Miqra* 20, 1974/75, pp. 187–208.
Kindler, A., "Silver Coins Bearing the Name of Judea from the Early Hellenistic Period", *IEJ* 24, 1974, pp. 73–76.
Kippenberg, H. G., *Garizim und Synagoge*, Berlin–New York, 1971.

Momigliano, A., "Flavius Josephus and Alexander's Visit to Jerusalem", *Athenaeum* 57, 1979, pp. 442–448.

Rahmani, L. Y., "Silver Coins of the Fourth Century B.C. from Tel Gamma", *IEJ* 21, 1971, pp. 158–160.
Rappaport, U., "The Coins of Judea at the End of the Persian Rule and the Beginning of the Hellenistic Period" (Heb.), in: *Jerusalem in the Second Temple Period*, A. Schalit Memorial Volume, Jerusalem, 1980, pp. 7–21.
— "The First Judean Coinage", *JJS* 32, 1981, pp. 1–17.

Schur, N., *History of the Samaritans*, Frankfurt A. M.—Bern, 1989.

Wacholder, B. Z., "The Beginning of the Seleucid Era and the Chronology of the Diadochoi", in: F. E. Greenspahn, E. Hilgert, B. L. Mack (eds.), *Nourished with Peace. Studies in Hellenistic Judaism in Memory of Samuel Sandmel*, Chico, CA 1984, pp. 183–211.
Wright, G. E., "The Samaritans at Shechem", *HTR* 55, 1962, pp. 357–366.

2. Palestine under Ptolemaic Rule

Abel, F.-M., "La Syrie et la Palestine au temps de Ptolémée Ier Soter", *RB* 44, 1935, pp. 559–581.

Bagnall, R.S., *The Administration of the Ptolemaic Possessions outside Egypt*, Leiden, 1976.

Bar-Kochva, B., "Zeno's Version of the Battle of Panium (Polybius 16 16.18–19)" (Heb.), in: *Studies in the History of the Jewish People and the Land of Israel*, III, ed. B. Oded et al., Haifa, 1974, pp. 43–57.
— "The Battle of Raphia (217 B.C.)" (Heb.), in: *Studies in the History of the Jewish People and the Land of Israel*, IV, ed. U. Rappaport, Haifa, 1978, pp. 41–58.
Bengtson, H., "Die ptolemäische Staatsverwaltung im Rahmen der hellenistischen Administration", *MH* 10, 1953, pp. 161–177.
Bevan, E. R., *A History of Egypt under the Ptolemaic Dynasty*, London, 1927.
Bouché-Leclercq, A., *Histoire des Lagides*, I–IV, Paris, 1903–07.

Cross, F. M., "An Aramaic Ostracon of the Third Century B.C.E. from Excavations in Jerusalem" (Heb.), EI 15, 1981, pp. 67*–69*.
Cuq, E., "La condition juridique de la Coelé-Syrie au temps de Ptolémée V Épiphane", *Syria* 8. 1927, pp. 143–162.

Fraser, P. M., *Ptolemaic Alexandria*, I–III, London, 1972.
Fuks, G., "Tel Anafa—A Proposed Identification", SCI 5, 1979/80, pp. 178–184.

Galili, E., "Raphia, 217 B.C.E., Revisited", SCI 3, 1976/77, pp. 52–126.
Goldstein, J. A., "The Tales of the Tobiads", in: *Christianity, Judaism and other Greco-Roman Cults*, FS M. Smith, ed. J. Neusner, III, Leiden, 1975, pp. 85–123.

Ieselsohn, D., "A New Coin Type with Hebrew Inscription", *IEJ* 24, 1974, pp. 77–78.

Kasher, A., "Anti-Jewish Persecutions in Alexandria in the Reign of Ptolemy Philopator, According to III Maccabees" (Heb.), in: *Studies in the History of the Jewish People and the Land of Israel*, IV, ed. U. Rappaport, Haifa, 1978, pp. 59–76.

Landau, Y. H., "A Greek Inscription Found Near Hefzibah", *IEJ* 16, 1966, pp. 54–70.
Lenger, M. Th., *Corpus des Ordonnances des Ptolémées*, Brussels, 1964.
Lifshitz, B., "Der Kult des Ptolemaios IV Philopator in Jafa", *ZDPV* 78, 1962, pp. 82–84.

Mazar, B., "The House of Tobias" (Heb.), *Tarbiz* 12, 1940/41, pp. 109–123.
— "The Tobiads", *IEJ* 7, 1957, pp. 137–145, 229–238.
McCown, C. C., "The 'Araq el-Emir and the Tobiads", BA 20, 1957, pp. 63–76.
McLean Harper, G., "A Study in the Commercial Relations between Egypt and Syria in the Third Century B.C.", *AJP* 49, 1928, pp. 1–35.
Mittmann, S., "Zenon im Ostjordanland" in: *Archäologie und Altes Testament*, FS K. Galling, ed. A. Kuschke and E. Kutsch, Tübingen, 1970, pp. 199–210.

Préaux, C., *L'économie royale des Lagides*, Brussels, 1939.

Stern, M., "Notes on the Story of Joseph the Tobiad (Josephus, Ant. XII, 154 ff.)" (Heb.), *Tarbiz* 32, 1962, pp. 35–47.

Taeubler, E., "Jerusalem 201 to 199 B.C.E.", *JQR* 37, 1946/47, pp. 1–30; 125–137; 249–263.

Tcherikover, V., "Palestine in the Light of the Zenon Papyri" (Heb.), *Tarbiz* 4, 1933, pp. 226–247, 354–365; 5, 1934, pp. 37–44.
— "Palestine under the Ptolemies (A Contribution to the Study of the Zenon Papyri)", *Mizraim* 4–5, 1937, pp. 9–90.
Thissen, H.-J., *Studien zum Raphiadekret*, Meisenheim am Glan, 1966.

Weinberg, S. S., "Tel Anafa: The Hellenistic Town", *IEJ* 21, 1971, pp. 86–109.
Westerman, W. L., "Enslaved Persons who are Free", *AJP* 59, 1938, pp. 1–30.

3. Palestine under Seleucid Rule

Abel, F.-M., "Topographie des campagnes machabéennes", *RB* 32, 1923, pp. 495–521; 33, 1924, pp. 201–217, 371–387; 34, 1925, pp. 194–216; 35, 1926, pp. 206–222, 510–533.
— "La fête de Hanoucca", *RB* 53, 1946, pp. 538–546.
Alt, A., "Zu Antiochos' III. Erlaß für Jerusalem", *ZAW* 57, 1939, pp. 283–285.
Avigad, N., "A Bulla of Jonathan the High Priest", *IEJ* 25, 1975, pp. 8–12.
Avi-Yonah, M., "The Battles in the Books of the Maccabees" (Heb.), in: *J. Lewy (Y. Levi) Memorial Volume*, ed. J. Gutman and M. Schwabe, Jerusalem, 1949, pp. 13–24.

Baer, Y., "The Persecution of the Monotheistic Religion by Antiochos Epiphanes" (Heb.), *Zion* 33, 1968, pp. 101–124.
Bar Kochva, B., "The Status and Origin of the Garrison at the Akra on the Eve of the Religious Persecutions" (Heb.), *Zion* 38, 1973, pp. 32–47.
— "The Battle of Bet-Zekharyah" (Heb.), *Zion* 39, 1974, pp. 157–182.
— *The Seleucid Army*, Cambridge, 1976.
— (ed.), *The Seleucid Period in Eretz Israel. Studies on the Persecutions of Antiochus Epiphanes and the Hasmonean Revolt* (Heb.), Tel Aviv, 1979/80.
— *Judas Maccabeus. The Jewish Struggle against the Selucids* Cambridge, 1989.
Ben Dov, M., "Die seleukidische Akra—südlich des Tempelberges" (Heb.), *Kathedra* 18, 1980/81, pp. 22–35.
Bevan, E. R., *The House of Seleucus*, I–II, London, 1902 (repr. 1966).
Bi(c)kerman(n), E., "La charte séleucide de Jérusalem", *REJ* 100, 1935, pp. 4–35; see also Bi(c)kerman(n), Studies in Jewish and Christian History, II, Leiden, 1980, pp. 44–85.
— "Un document relatif à la persécution d'Antiochus IV Epiphane", *RHR* 115, 1937, pp. 188–221; see also *Studies*, pp. 105–135.
— *Der Gott der Makkabäer*, Berlin, 1937.
— *Institutions des Séleucides*, Paris, 1938.
— "Héliodore au Temple de Jérusalem", *AIPh* 7, 1939–1944, pp. 5–40; see also *Studies*, pp. 159–191.
— "Une proclamation séleucide relative au temple de Jérusalem", *Syria* 25, 1946–48, pp. 67–85; see also *Studies*, pp. 86–104.
Bilde, P., Engberg-Pedersen, T., Hannestad, L. and Zahle, J. (eds.), *Religion and Religious Practice in the Seleucid Kingdom*, Aarhus, 1990.
Bouché-Leclercq, A., *Histoire des Séleucides*, I–II, Paris, 1913–14.

Bringmann, K., *Hellenistische Reform und Religionsverfolgung in Judäa. Eine Untersuchung zur jüdisch-hellenistischen Geschichte (175–163 v. Chr.)*, Göttingen, 1983.

Briscoe, J., "Eastern Policy and Senatorial Politics 168–146 B.C.", *Hist* 18, 1969, pp. 49–70.

Büchler, A., *Die Tobiaden und die Oniaden im II. Makkabäerbuche und in der verwandten jüdisch-hellenistischen Literatur*, *JITL* 6, 1898/99.

Bunge, J. G., *Untersuchungen zum zweiten Makkabäerbuch*, diss., Bonn, 1971.

— "Zur Geschichte und Chronologie des Untergangs der Oniaden und des Aufstiegs der Hasmonäer", *JSJ* 6, 1975, pp. 1–46.

— "Die sogenannte Religionsverfolgung Antiochus IV. Epiphanes und die griechischen Städte", *JSJ* 10, 1979, pp. 155–165.

Burgmann, H., "Antichrist–Antimessias. Der Makkabäer Simon?", *Judaica* 36, 1980, pp. 152–174.

— "Das umstrittene Intersacerdotium in Jerusalem 159–152 v. Chr.", *JSJ* 11, 1980, pp. 135–176.

Callaway, P. R., *The History of the Qumran Community. An Interpretation*, Sheffield, 1988.

Davies, P., "Hasidim in the Maccabean Period", JJS 28, 1977, pp. 127–140.

Derfler, S. L., *The Hasmonean Revolt: Rebellion or Revolution*, Lewinston, 1989.

Eisenman, R., *Maccabees, Zadokites, Christians and Qumran. A New Hypothesis of Qumran Origins*, Leiden, 1983.

Fischer, T., "Zu den Beziehungen zwischen Rom und den Juden im 2. Jh. v. Chr.", *ZAW* 86, 1974, pp. 90–93.

— "Zur Seleukideninschrift von Hefzibah", *ZPE* 33, 1979, pp. 131–138.

— *Seleukiden und Makkabäer. Beiträge zur Seleukidengeschichte und zu den politischen Ereignissen in Judäa während der 1. Hälfte des 2. Jahrhunderts v. Chr.*, Bochum, 1980.

Giovannini, A. and Müller, H., "Die Beziehungen zwischen Rom und den Juden im 2. Jh. v. Chr.", *MH* 28, 1971, pp. 156–171.

Habicht, C., "Royal Documents in Maccabees II", *HSCP* 80, 1976, pp. 1–18.

Harrington, D. J., *The Maccabean Revolt. Anatomy of a Biblical Revolution*, Wimigton DE, 1988.

Heinemann, I., "Wer veranlaßte den Glaubenszwang der Makkabäerzeit?", *MGWJ* 82, 1938, pp. 145–172.

Hölscher, G., "Die Feldzüge des Makkabäers Judas", *ZDPV* 29, 1906, pp. 133–151.

Kasher, A., "Athenians in the Persecutions of Antiochus IV Epiphanes" (Heb.), *Tarbiz* 51, 1981–1982, pp. 537–542.

Katzoff, R., "Jonathan and Late Sparta", *AJP* 106, 1985, pp. 485–489.

Keil, V., "Onias III. — Märtyrer oder Tempelgründer?", *ZAW* 97, 1985, pp. 221–233.

Kolbe, W., *Beiträge zur syrischen und jüdischen Geschichte*, Stuttgart, 1926.

Kreissig, H., "Der Makkabäeraufstand. Zur Frage seiner sozialökonomischen Zusammenhänge und Wirkungen", *StC* 4, 1962, pp. 143–175.

Lapp, P. W., "Soundings at 'Araq el-Emir (Jordan)", *BASOR* 165, 1962, pp. 16–34.
— "The Second and Third Campaigns at 'Arâq el Emir", *BASOR* 171, 1963, pp. 8–39.
Lebram, J. C. H., "König Antiochus im Buch Daniel", *VT* 25, 1975, pp. 737–772.
Liebmann-Frankfort, T., "Rome et le conflit judéo-syrien (164–151 avant notre ère)", *AC* 38, 1969, pp. 101–120.

Mendels, D., "A Note on the Tradition of Antiochus IV's Death", *IEJ* 31, 1981, pp. 53–56.
Millar, F., "The Background to the Maccabean Revolution. Reflections on Martin Hengel's 'Judaism and Hellenism' ", *JJS* 29, 1978, pp. 1–21.
Mittwoch, A., "Tribute and Land-Tax in Seleucid Judaea", *Bibl* 36, 1955, pp. 352–361.
Mørkholm, O., *Antiochus IV of Syria*, Copenhagen, 1966.
Momigliano, A., "I Tobiadi nella preistoria del moto maccabaico", *AAST* 67, 1931–32, pp. 165–210.
— *Prime linee di storia della tradizione maccabaica* (2nd. ed.), Amsterdam, 1968.

Otzen, B. (ed.), *Archaeology and History in the Dead Sea Scrolls. The New York Conference in Memory of Yigael Yadin*, Sheffield, 1990.

Plöger, O., "Hyrkan im Ostjordanland", ZDPV 71, 1955, pp. 70–81. Reprinted in Plöger, *Aus der Spätzeit des AT, Studien*, Göttingen, 1971, pp. 90–101.
— "Die Feldzüge der Seleukiden gegen den Makkabäer Judas", ZDPV 74, 1958, pp. 155–188. Reprinted in *Aus der Spätzeit des AT*, pp. 134–164.
— "Die makkabäischen Burgen", in: *Aus der Spätzeit des AT*, pp. 102–133.

Rajak, T., "Roman Intervention in a Seleucid Siege of Jerusalem?", *GRBS* 22, 1981, pp. 65–81.
Rappaport, U., "Ascalon and the Coinage of Judaea" (Heb.), in: *Studies in the History of the Jewish People and the Land of Israel*, IV, ed. U. Rappaport, Haifa, 1978, pp. 77–88.
Rowley, H. H., "Menelaus and the Abomination of Desolation", in: *Studia Orientalia Ioanni Pedersen dedicata*, Copenhagen, 1953, pp. 303–315.

Schmitt, H. H., *Untersuchungen zur Geschichte Antiochos' des Großen und seiner Zeit*, Wiesbaden, 1964.
Shatzman, I., *The Armies of the Hasmoneans and Herod. From Hellenistic to Roman Frameworks*, Tübingen, 1991.
Shotwell, W. A., "The Problem of the Syrian Akra", *BASOR* 176, 1964, pp. 10–19.
Sordi, M., "Il valore politico del trattato fra i Romani e i Giudei nel 161 a.C.", *Acme* 5, 1952, pp. 509–519.
Stegemann, H., *Die Entstehung der Qumrangemeinde*, diss., Bonn, 1971.
Stein, S., "The Liturgy of Hanukkah and the first two Books of the Maccabees", *JJS* 5, 1954, pp. 100–106, 148–155.
Stern, M., "The Death of Onias III (II Macc. 4.30–8)" (Heb.), *Zion* 25, 1960, pp. 1–16.
— "The Hasmonaean Revolt and its Place in the History of Jewish Society and Religion", *CHM* 11, 1968, pp. 92–106.
— *The Documents on the History of the Hasmonaean Revolt* (Heb., 2nd ed.), Tel Aviv, 1972.

Tcherikover, V., "Antiochia in Jerusalem" (Heb.), in: *J. N. Epstein Jubilee Volume*, Jerusalem, 1950, pp. 61–67.
— "Was Jerusalem a 'Polis'? ", *IEJ* 14, 1964, pp. 61–78.
Timpe, D., "Der römische Vertrag mit den Juden von 161 v. Chr.", *Chiron* 4, 1974, pp. 133–152.
Tsafrir, Y., "The Location of the Seleucid Akra in Jerusalem", *RB* 82, 1975, pp. 501–521.
— "Zur Lokalisierung der seleukidischen Akra in Jerusalem" (Heb.), *Kathedra* 14, 1979/80, pp. 17–40.

Wibbing, S., "Zur Topographie einzelner Schlachten des Judas Makkabäus", *ZDPV* 78, 1962, pp. 159–170.
Will, E., "Rome et les Séleucides", in: *ANRW* I.1, Berlin–New York 1972, pp. 590–632.
Willrich, H., *Juden und Griechen vor der makkabäischen Erhebung*, Göttingen, 1895.
Wirgin, W., "Judah Maccabee's Embassy to Rome and the Jewish–Roman Treaty", *PEQ* 101, 1969, pp. 15–20.
— "Simon Maccabeus' Embassy to Rome. Its Purpose and Outcome", *PEQ* 106, 1974/75, pp. 141–146.

4. The Hasmonean Dynasty

Abel, F.-M., "Le siège de Jérusalem par Pompée", *RB* 54, 1947, pp. 243–255.
— "Hellénisme et orientalisme en Palestine au déclin de la période séleucide", *RB* 53, 1946, pp. 385–402.
Alfrink, B., "L'idée de résurrection d'après Daniel XII,2.3", *Bibl* 40, 1959, pp. 335–371.

Bammel, E., "Die Neuordnung des Pompeius und das römisch–jüdische Bündnis", *ZDPV* 75, 1959, pp. 76–82.
Bar-Adon, P., "The Hasmonean Fortress and the Status of Khirbet Qumran" (Heb.), *EI* 15, 1981, pp. 349–352.
Barag, D., "The Beginning of Hasmonean Coinage", *INJ* 4, 1980, pp. 8–21.
Baumgarten, A. I., "Josephus and Hippolytus on the Pharisees", *HUCA* 55, 1984, pp. 1–25.
Beckwith, T., "The Pre-History and Relationship of the Pharisees, Sadducees and Essenes: A Tentative Reconstruction", *RdQ* 11, 1982, pp. 3–46.
Bellinger, A. R., "The End of the Seleucids", *TCAAS* 38, 1949, pp. 51–102.
Ben-David, A., "When Did the Maccabees Begin to Strike their First Coins?", *PEQ* 124, pp. 93–103.
Buehler, W. W., *The Pre-Herodian Civil War and Social Debate*, diss., Basel, 1974.
Burr, V., "Rom und Judäa im 1. Jahrhundert v. Chr. (Pompeius und die Juden)", in: *ANRW* I.1, Berlin–New York, 1972, pp. 875–886.

Efron, J., *Studies on the Hasmonean Period*, New York—Kopenhagen—Cologne, 1987.
Efron, Y., "Shimon ben Shetah and King Yannai" (Heb.), in: *In Memory of G. Alon: Essays in Jewish History and Philology*, Tel Aviv, 1970, pp. 69–132.

Finkelstein, L., *The Pharisees: The Sociological Background of their Faith* (3rd ed.), I–II, Philadelphia, 1962.

Fischer, T., *Untersuchungen zum Partherkrieg Antiochos' VII. im Rahmen der Seleukidengeschichte*, diss., Munich, Tübingen, 1970.

— "Zum jüdischen Verfassungsstreit vor Pompejus (Diodor 440,2)", *ZDPV* 91, 1975, pp. 46–49.

— "Johannes Hyrkan I. auf Tetradrachmen Antiochos' VII.?", *ZDPV* 91, 1975, pp. 191–196.

— "Rom und die Hasmonäer. Ein Überblick zu den politischen Beziehungen 164–37 v. Chr.", *Gymnasium* 88, 1981, pp. 139–150.

Foerster, G., "The Conquest of John Hyrcanus I. in Moab and the Identification of Samaga-Samoge" (Heb.), *EI* 15, 1981, pp. 353–355.

Friedländer, I., "The Rupture between Alexander Jannai and the Pharisees", *JQR* 4, 1913/14, pp. 443–448.

Hanson, R. S., "Toward a Chronology of the Hasmonean Coins", *BASOR* 216, 1974, pp. 21–23.

Herford, T., *The Pharisees*, London 1924.

Kampen, J., *The Hasideans and the Origins of Pharisaism. A Study in 1 and 2 Maccabees*, Atlanta-Georgia, 1989.

Kanael, B., "The Beginning of the Maccabean Coinage", *IEJ* 1, 1950/51, pp. 170–175.

— "The Greek Letters and Monograms on the Coins of Jehohanan the High Priest", *IEJ* 2, 1952, pp. 190–194.

— "Notes on Alexander Jannaeus' Campaigns in the Coastal Region" (Heb.), *Tarbiz* 24, 1954/55, pp. 9–15.

Kindler, A., "Rare and Unpublished Hasmonean Coins", *IEJ* 2, 1952, pp. 188–189.

— "The Jaffa Hoard of Alexander Jannaeus", *IEJ* 4, 1954, pp. 170–185.

— "Addendum to the Dated Coins of Alexander Jannaeus", *IEJ* 18, 1968, pp. 188–191.

Kreissig, H., "Zur Rolle der religiösen Gruppen in den Volksbewegungen der Hasmonäerzeit", *Klio* 43–45, 1965, pp. 174–182.

Lauterbach, J. Z., "The Pharisees and their Teaching", *HUCA* 6, 1929, pp. 96–139.

Le Moyne, J., *Les Sadducéens*, Paris, 1972.

Lévi, I., "Les sources talmudiques de l'histoire juive. I. Alexandre Jannée et Simon ben Schétah. II. La rupture de Jannée avec les Pharisiens", *REJ* 35, 1897, pp. 213–223.

Levine, L. I., "The Hasmonean Conquest of Strato's Tower", *IEJ* 24, 1974, pp. 62–69.

— "The Political Struggle between Pharisees and Sadducees in the Hasmonean Period" (Heb.), in: *Jerusalem in the Second Temple Period*, A. Schalit Memorial Volume, Jerusalem, 1980, pp. 61–83.

Luria, B. Z., *King Yannai* (Heb.), Jerusalem, 1960.

Maffucci, P., "Il problema storico dei Farisei prima del 70 D.C. Rassegna critica di un secolo di studi", *RivBib* 26, 1978, pp. 353–399.

Mantel, H., "The Sadducees and the Pharisees", in: *Society and Religion in the Second Temple Period*, VIII, Jerusalem, 1977, pp. 99–123, 346–351.

Marcus, R., "The Pharisees in the Light of Modern Scholarship", *JR* 32, 1952, pp. 153–164.

Mason, S., *Flavius Josephus on the Paharisees: A Composition-Critical Study*, Leiden—New York—Kopenhagen—Cologne, 1991.

Meshorer, Y., "The Beginning of the Hasmonean Coinage", *IEJ* 24, 1974, pp. 59–61.

Michel, A. and Le Moyne, J., "Pharisiens", *DBS* 7, 1966, pp. 1022–1115.

Naveh, J., "Dated coins of Alexander Janneus", *IEJ* 18, 1968, pp. 20–25.

Neusner, J., "Josephus's Pharisees", in: *Ex Orbe Religionum*, FS G. Widengren, I, Leiden, 1972, pp. 224–244.

— *The Rabbinic Traditions about the Pharisees before 70*, I–III, Leiden, 1971.

— *From Politics to Piety. The Emergence of Pharisaic Judaism* (2nd ed.), New York, 1979.

Nickelsburg, G. W. E., *Resurrection, Immortality and Eternal Life in Intertestamental Judaism*, Cambridge, Mass., 1972.

Peters, J. P. and Thiersch, H., *Painted Tombs in the Necropolis of Marissa*, London, 1905.

Pucci, M., "An Unknown Source on a Possible Treaty between Hyrcanus I and the Parthians" (Heb.), *Zion* 46, 1981, pp. 331–338.

Rabin, C., "Alexander Jannaeus and the Pharisees", *JJS* 7, 1956, pp. 3–11.

Rahmani, L. Y., "Jason's Tomb", *IEJ* 17, 1967, pp. 61–100.

Rappaport, U., "The Hellenistic Cities and the Judaisation of Palestine in the Hasmonean Age" (Heb.), in: *Commentationes Benzioni Katz dedicatae*, ed. S. Perlman and B. Shimron, Tel Aviv, 1967, pp. 219–230.

— "La Judée et Rome pendant le règne d'Alexandre Jannée", *REJ* 127, 1968, pp. 329–345.

— "On the Meaning of Heber ha-Yehudim" (Heb.), in: *Studies in the History of the Jewish People and the Land of Israel*, III, ed. B Oded et al., Haifa, 1974, pp. 59–67.

— "The Emergence of Hasmonean Coinage", *AJS Review* 1, 1976, pp. 171–186.

— "The First Jewish Coinage", *JJS* 32, 1981, pp. 1–17.

Reich, R., "Archeological Evidence of the Jewish Population at Hasmonean Gezer", *IEJ* 31, 1981, pp. 48—52.

Rivkin, E., "Defining the Pharisees", *HUCA* 40–41, 1969/70, pp. 205–249.

— *A Hidden Revolution*, Nashville, 1978.

Schalit, A., "Alexander Yannai's Conquests in Moab" (Heb.), EI 1, 1951, pp. 104–121. German translation: "Die Eroberungen des Alexander Jannäus in Moab", in: *Theokratia* I, Leiden, 1969, pp. 3–50.

Schoeps, H. J., "Die Opposition gegen die Hasmonäer", *ThLZ* 81, 1956, col. 663–670.

Sievers, J., *The Hasmoneans and their Supporters. From Mattathias to the Death of John Hyrcanus I*, Atlanta, 1990.

Silva, M., "The Pharisees in Modern Jewish Scholarship. A Review Article", *WThJ* 42, 1980, pp. 395–405.

Stemberger, G., "Das Problem der Auferstehung im Alten Testament", *Kairos* 14, pp. 273–290.

Stern, M., "The Relations between Judea and Rome during the Rule of John Hyrkanus" (Heb.), *Zion* 26, 1961, pp. 1–22.

— "The Political Background of the Wars of Alexander Jannai" (Heb.), *Tarbiz* 33, 1963/64, pp. 325–336.

Strobel, A., "Machärus. Geschichte und Ende einer Festung im Lichte archäologisch–typographischer Beobachtungen", in: *Bibel und Qumran*, FS H. Bardtke, ed. S. Wagner, Berlin, 1968, pp. 198–225.

5. Herod the Great

Al(l)on, G., "The Attitude of the Pharisees to the Roman Government and the House of Herod", *ScrHie* 7, 1961, pp. 53–78. Reprinted in Al(l)on, *Jews, Judaism and the Classical World*, pp. 18–47.
Avi-Yonah, M. and Baras, Z. (eds.), *The Herodian Period*, New Brunswick, 1975 (*WHJP* I/7).

Bammel, E., "Die Bruderfolge im Hochpriestertum der Herodianisch–römischen Zeit", *ZDPV* 70, 1954, pp. 147–153.
— "The Organization of Palestine by Gabinius", *JJS* 12, 1961, pp. 159–162.
Bernegger, P. M., "Affirmation of Herod's Death in 4 B.C.", *JTS* 34, 1983, pp. 526–531.
Bi(c)kerman(n), E., "The Warning Inscriptions of Herod's Temple", *JQR* 37, 1947, pp. 387–405. Reprinted in *Studies*, pp. 210–224.
Braund, D. C., "Gabinius, Caesar, and the publicani of Judaea", *Klio* 65, 1983, pp. 241–244.
Broshi, M., "The Role of the Temple in the Herodian Economy", *JJS* 38, 1987, pp. 31–37.
Büchler, A., "The Priestly Dues and the Roman Taxes in the Edicts of Caesar", in: *Studies in Jewish History. The Adolph Büchler Memorial Volume*, ed. I. Brodie and J. Rabbinowitz, London–New York–Toronto, 1956, pp. 1–23.

Corbishley, T., "The Chronology of the Reign of Herod the Great", *JTS* 36, 1935, pp. 22–32.
Corbo, V., "L'Herodion de Gebal Fureidis", *SBFLA* 13, 1962/63, pp. 219–277; 17, 1967, pp. 65–121.

Fiensy, D. A., *The Social History of Palestine in the Herodian Period. The Land Is Mine*, Lewinston, 1991.
Filmer, W. E., "The Chronology of the Reign of Herod the Great", *JTS N.S.* 17, 1966, pp. 283–298.

Gilboa, A., "On the Trial of Herod" (Heb.), in: *Jerusalem in the Second Temple Period, A. Schalit Memorial Volume*, Jerusalem, 1980, pp. 98–107.
Grant, M., *Herod the Great*, London, 1971.

Harder, G., "Herodes-Burgen und Herodes-Städte im Jordangraben", *ZDPV* 78, 1962, pp. 49–63.
Herzfeld, L., "Wann war die Eroberung Jerusalems durch Pompejus, und wann die durch Herodes?", *MGWJ* 4, 1855, pp. 109–115.
Hollis, F. J., *The Archaeology of Herod's Temple*, London, 1934.

Kanael, B., "The Partition of Judea by Gabinius", *IEJ* 7, 1957, pp. 98–106.

Ladouceur, D. J., "The Death of Herod the Great", *CP* 76, 1981, pp. 25–34.

Meyshan, J., "The Symbols on the Coinage of Herod the Great and their Meanings", *PEQ* 91, 1959, pp. 109–121.
Momigliano, A., "Herod of Judaea", *CAH* X, Cambridge, 1934, pp. 316–339.

Netzer, E., "The Hasmonean and Herodian Palaces at Jericho" (Heb.), *Qadmoniot* 7, 1974, pp. 27–36.
— "The Hasmonean and Herodian Winter Palaces at Jericho", *IEJ* 25, 1975, pp. 89–100.
— "The Hippodrome that Herod Built at Jericho" (Heb.), *Qadmoniot* 13, 1980, pp. 104–107.

Otto, W., *Herodes*, Stuttgart, 1913.

Perowne, S., *The Life and Times of Herod the Great*, London–Nashville, 1956/59.
Pritchard, J. B., *The Excavation at Herodian Jericho 1951*, AASOR 32–33, Philadelphia, 1958.

Rabello, A. M., "Hausgericht in the House of Herod the Great?" (Heb.), in: *Jerusalem in the Second Temple Period, A. Schalit Memorial Volume*, Jerusalem, 1980, pp. 119–135.

Sandmel, S., *Herod: Profile of a Tyrant*, Philadelphia, 1967.
Schalit, A., *König Herodes. Der Mann und sein Werk*, Berlin, 1969.
Segal, A., "Herodium", *IEJ* 23, 1973, pp. 27–29.
Sherwin-White, A. N., *Roman Society and Roman Law in the New Testament*, Oxford, 1963.
Smallwood, E. M., "Gabinius' Organisation of Palestine", *JJS* 18, 1967, pp. 89–92.
Sperber, D., "A Note on a Coin of Antigonus Mattathias", *JQR* 54, 1963/64, pp. 250–257.
Stern, M., "Herod's Policy and Jewish Society at the End of the Second Temple" (Heb.), *Tarbiz* 35, 1966, pp. 235–253.
— "Social and Political Realignments in Herodian Judaea", *The Jerusalem Cathedra* 2, 1982, pp. 40–62.

6. From Herod to the First Jewish War

Aberbach, M., "The Conflicting Accounts of Josephus and Tacitus Concerning Cumanus' and Felix' Terms of Office", *JQR* 40, 1949, pp. 1–14.
Applebaum, S., "The Zealots: The Case for Revaluation", *JRS* 60, 1970, pp. 155–170.
— "Judaea as a Roman Province; the Countryside as a Political and Economic Factor", in: *ANRW* II.8, Berlin–New York, 1977, pp. 355–396.
Avi-Yonah, M., "The Foundation of Tiberias", *IEJ* 1, 1951, pp. 160–169.
— "The Third and Second Walls of Jerusalem", *IEJ* 18, 1968, pp. 98–125.

Balsdon, J. P. V. D., "The Chronology of Gaius' Dealings with the Jews", *JRS* 24, 1934, pp. 13–24.

Bammel, E., "Die Blutgerichtsbarkeit in der römischen Provinz Judäa vor dem ersten jüdischen Aufstand", in: B. Jackson (ed.), *Studies in Jewish Legal History in Honour of David Daube*, *JJS* 25, 1974, pp. 35–49.

Baumbach, G., "Zeloten und Sikarier", *ThLZ* 90, 1965, col. 727–740.

— "Das Freiheitsverständnis der zelotischen Bewegung", in: *Das ferne und nahe Wort*, FS L. Rost, ed. F. Maass, Berlin, 1967, pp. 11–18.

Baumgarten, J. M., "Exclusion from the Temple: Proselytes and Agrippa I", *JJS* 33, 1982, pp. 215–225.

Bilde, P., "The Roman Emperor Gaius Caligula's Attempt to Erect His Statue in the Temple of Jerusalem", *StTh* 32, 1978, pp. 67–93.

Black, M., "Judas of Galilee and Josephus' 'Fourth Philosophy' ", in: *Josephus–Studien*, FS O. Michel, Göttingen, 1974, pp. 45–54.

Blinzler, J., "Die Niedermetzelung von Galiläern durch Pilatus", *NT* 2, 1957, pp. 24–29.

Borg, M., "The Currency of the Term 'Zealot' ", *JTS N.S.* 22, 1971, pp. 504–512.

Brandon, S. G. F., *Jesus and the Zealots*, Manchester–New York, 1967.

Brann, M., "Biographie Agrippa II.", *MGWJ* 19, 1870, pp. 433–444, 529–548; 20, 1871, pp. 13–28.

Bruce, F. F., "Herod Antipas, Tetrarch of Galilee and Peraea", *ALUOS* 5, 1963–65, pp. 6–23.

Büchler, A., *Die Priester und der Cultus im letzten Jahrzehnt des Jerusalemischen Tempels*, Vienna, 1895.

— "Familienreinheit und Familienmakel in Jerusalem vor dem Jahre 70", in: FS A. Schwarz, Berlin–Vienna, 1917, pp. 133–162. Reprinted in *Studies in Jewish History*, London–New York–Toronto, 1956, pp. 160–178.

Burr, V., *Tiberius Julius Alexander*, Bonn, 1955.

Edwards, O., "Herodian Chronology", *PEQ* 114, 1982, pp. 29–42.

Farmer, W. R., *Maccabees, Zealots, and Josephus*, New York, 1956.

— "Judas, Simon and Athronges", *NTS* 4, 1958, pp. 147–155.

Hengel, M., *The Zealots: Investigations into the Jewish Freedom Movement in the Period from Herod I until 70 AD*. Edinburgh, 1989.

— "Zeloten und Sikarier", in: *Josephus–Studien*, FS O. Michel, Göttingen, 1974, pp. 175–196.

Herrenbrück, F., *Jesus und die Zöllner*, diss. MS, Tübingen, 1979.

— "Wer waren die Zöllner?", *ZNW* 72, 1981, pp. 178–194.

Herz, J., "Großgrundbesitz in Palästina im Zeitalter Jesu", *PJB* 24, 1928, pp. 98–113.

Hoehner, H. W., *Herod Antipas*, Cambridge, 1972.

Horsley, R. A., "Popular Messianic Movements around the Time of Jesus", *CBQ* 46, 1984, pp. 471–495.

Isaac, B., "Bandits in Judaea and Arabia", *HSCP* 88, 1984, pp. 171–203.

Jones, A. H. M., "Procurators and Prefects", in: *Studies in Roman Government and Law*, Oxford, 1960, pp. 115–125.

— *The Herods of Judaea* (2nd ed.), London, 1967.

Kennard, J. S., "Judas of Galilee and his Clan", *JQR* 36, 1945/46, pp. 281–286.
Kingdon, P., "The Origins of the Zealots", *NTS* 19, 1972, pp. 74–81.
Kraeling, C. H., "The Episode of the Roman Standards at Jerusalem", *HTR* 35, 1942, pp. 263–289.
Kreissig, H., *Die sozialen Zusammenhänge des judäischen Krieges. Klassen und Klassenkampf im Palästina des 1. Jahrhunderts v.u.Z.*, Berlin, 1970.

Lémonon, J.-P., *Pilate et le gouvernement de la Judée*, Paris, 1981.
Lohse, E., "Die römischen Statthalter in Jerusalem", *ZDPV* 74, 1958, pp. 69–78.

Maier, P. L., "The Episode of the Golden Roman Shields at Jerusalem", *HTR* 62, 1969, pp. 111–114.
Meshorer, Y., "A New Type of Coins of Agrippa II", *IEJ* 21, 1971, pp. 164–165.
Meyshan, J., "The Coinage of Agrippa the First", *IEJ* 4, 1954, pp. 186–200.
— "A New Coin Type of Agrippa II and its Meaning", *IEJ* 11, 1961, pp. 181–183.

Perowne, S., *The Later Herods*, 1956.
Prandi, L., "Una nuova ipotesi sull'iscrizione di Ponzi Pilato", *Civiltà classica e christiana* 2, 1981, pp. 25–35.

Rhoads, D. M., *Israel in Revolution: 6–74 C.E. A Political History Based on the Writings of Josephus*, Philadelphia, 1976.
Rowley, H. H., "The Herodians in the Gospels", *JTS* 41, 1940, pp. 14–28.

Schwartz, D. R., "Ishmael ben Phiabi and the Chronology of Provincia Judaea" (Heb.), *Tarbiz* 52, 1982–1983, pp. 177–200.
— "Josephus and Philo on Pontius Pilate", in: Rappaport, U. (ed.), *Josephus Flavius. Historian of Eretz-Israel in the Hellenistic–Roman Period. Collected Papers* (Heb.), Jerusalem, 1982, pp. 217–236.
— "Pontius Pilate's Suspension from Office: Chronology and Sources" (Heb.), *Tarbiz* 51, 1981–1982, pp. 383–398.
Schwartz, D. R., *Agrippa I: The Last King of Judaea*, Tübingen, 1990.
Seyrig, M., "Les ères d'Agrippa II", *RN* 6, 1964, pp. 55–65.
Smallwood, E. M., "The Date of the Dismissal of Pontius Pilate from Judaea", *JJS* 5, 1954, pp. 12–21.
— "The Chronology of Gaius' Attempt to Desecrate the Temple", *Latomus* 16, 1957, pp. 3–17.
— "High Priests and Politics in Roman Palestine", *JTS* 13, 1962, pp. 14–34.
Smith, M., "Zealots and Sicarii: Their Origins and Relation", *HTR* 64, 1971, pp. 1–19.
Stern, M., "The Description of Palestine by Pliny the Elder and the Administrative Division of Judea, at the End of the Second Temple" (Heb.), *Tarbiz* 37, 1967/68, pp. 215–229.
Swain, J. W., "Gamaliel's Speech and Caligula's Statute", *HTR* 37, 1944, pp. 341–349.

Turner, E. G., "Tiberius Iulius Alexander", *JRS* 44, 1954, pp. 54–64.

Vermes, G., *Jesus the Jew*, London–New York, 1973.

Winter, P., *On the Trial of Jesus* (2nd ed.), Berlin, 1975.

Zeitlin, S., "Zealots and Sicarii", *JBL* 81, 1962, pp. 395–398.
— "Who were the Galileans?", *JQR* 64, 1973/74, pp. 189–203.

7. The First Jewish War

Aberbach, M., *The Roman Jewish War*, London, 1966.
Al(l)on, G., "The Burning of the Temple", in: *Jews, Judaism and the Classical World*, Jerusalem, 1977, pp. 252–268.
Applebaum, S., "The Struggle for the Soil and the Revolt of 66–73 C.E." (Heb.), *EI* 12, 1975, pp. 125–128.

Baer, Y., "Jerusalem in the Times of the Great Revolt" (Heb.), *Zion* 36, 1971, pp. 127–190.
Büchler, A., "On the Provisioning of Jerusalem in the Year 69–70 C.E.", in: *Studies in Jewish History*, ed. I. Brodie and J. Rabbinowitz, London–New York–Toronto, 1956, pp. 99–125.

Cohen, S. J. D., "Masada: Literary Tradition, Archaeological Remains, and the Credibility of Josephus", *JJS* 33, 1982, pp. 385–405.

Drexler, H., "Untersuchungen zu Josephus und zur Geschichte des jüdischen Aufstandes", *Klio* 19, 1925, pp. 277–312.

Eck, W., "Die Eroberung von Masada und eine neue Inschrift des L. Flavius Silva Nonius Bassus", *ZNW* 60, 1969, pp. 282–289.
— *Senatoren von Vespasian bis Hadrian*, Munich, 1970.

Feldmann, L. H., "Masada: A Critique of Recent Scholarship", in: FS M. Smith, ed. J. Neusner, III, Leiden, 1975, pp. 218–248.
Furneaux, R., *The Roman Siege of Jerusalem*, New York, 1972.

Geva, H., "The Camp of the Tenth Legion in Jerusalem: An Archaeological Reconsideration", *IEJ* 34, 1984, pp. 239–254.
Gichon, M. "Cestius Gallus's March on Jerusalam" (Heb.), in: Jerusalem in the Second Temple Period, A. Schalit Memorial Volume, Jerusalem, 1980, pp. 283–319.
Gichon, M., "Cestius Gallus's Campaign in Judaea", *PEQ* 113, 1981, pp. 39–62.
Goodman, M., "The First Jewish Revolt: Social Conflicts and the Problems of Debt", *JJS* 33, 1982, pp. 417–427.
— *The Ruling Class of Judaea. The Origins of the Jewish Revolt against Rome A.D. 66–70*, Cambridge, 1987.

Har-El, M., "The Zealot's Fortresses in Galilee", *IEJ* 22, 1972, pp. 123–130.
Horsley, R. A., "Banditry and the Revolt against Rome, A.D. 66–70", *CBQ* 43, 1981, pp. 409–432.

Jones, B. W., "Titus in the East, A.D. 70–71", *RMP N.F.* 128, 1985, pp. 346–352.

Kadman, L., *The Coins of the Jewish War of 66–73 C.E.*, Jerusalem–Tel Aviv, 1960.
Kasher, A. (ed.), *The Great Jewish Revolt* (Heb.), Jerusalem, 1983.
Kindler, A., "Numismatic Remarks on Jewish Minting of the End of the Second Temple Period" (Heb.), in: *Jerusalem in the Second Temple Period, A. Schalit Memorial Volume*, Jerusalem, 1980, pp. 271–282.
Kingdon, P., "Who were the Zealots and their Leaders in AD 66?", *NTS* 17, 1970, pp. 68–72.

Price, J. J., *Jerusalem under Siege. The Collapse of the Jewish State 66–70 C.E.*, Leiden—New York—Cologne, 1992.

Rappaport, U., "The Relations between Jews and Non-Jews and the Great War against Rome" (Heb.), *Tarbiz* 47, 1978, pp. 1–14.
— "John of Gischala: From Galilee to Jerusalem", *JJS* 33, 1982, pp. 479–493.
— "John of Gischala", in: U. Rappaport (ed.), *Josephus Flavius. Historian of Eretz-Israel in the Hellenistic–Roman Period. Collected Papers* (Heb.), Jerusalem, 1982, pp. 203–215.
— "John of Gischala in Galilee", *The Jerusalem Cathedra* 3, 1983, pp. 46–57.
Richmond, I. A., "The Roman Siegeworks of Masada, Israel", *JRS* 52, 1962, pp. 142–155.
Roth, C., "An Ordinance against Images in Jerusalem, AD 66", *HTR* 49, 1957, pp. 169–177.
— "The Zealots in the War of 66–73", *JSS* 4, 1959, pp. 332–355.
— "The Debate on the Loyal Sacrifices, AD 66", *HTR* 52, 1960, pp. 93–97.
— "The Historical Implications of the Jewish Coinage of the First Revolt", *IEJ* 12, 1962, pp. 33–46.
— "The Pharisees in the Jewish Revolution of 66–73", *JSS* 7, 1962, pp. 63–80.
— "The Constitution of the Jewish Republic of 66–70", *JSS* 9, 1964, pp. 295–319.

Safrai, Z., "Vespasian's Campaigns of Conquest in Judea" (Heb.), in: *Jerusalem in the Second Temple Period, A. Schalit Memorial Volume*, Jerusalem, 1980, pp. 320–339.
Schalit, A., "Josephus and Justus. Studien zur vita des Josephus", *Klio* 26, 1933, pp. 66–95.
— "Die Erhebung Vespasians nach Flavius Josephus, Talmud und Midrasch. Zur Geschichte einer messianischen Prophetie", in: *ANRW* II.2, Berlin–New York, 1975, pp. 208–327.

Weiler, I., "Titus und die Zerstörung des Tempels von Jerusalem—Absicht oder Zufall?", *Klio* 50, 1968, pp. 139–158.

Yadin, Y., "The Excavation of Masada—1963/64. Preliminary Report", *IEJ* 15, 1965, pp. 1–120.
— *Masada*, London, 1966. German translation: Hamburg, 1967.
Yankelevitch, R., "The Auxiliary Troops from Caesarea and Sebaste—A Decisive Factor in the Rebellion against Rome" (Heb.), *Tarbiz* 49, 1979–1980, pp. 33–42.

Zeitlin, S., "The Sicarii and Masada", *JQR* 57, 1967, pp. 251–270.

8. Between the Wars: From 74 to 132 AD

Al(l)on, G., "Rabban Johanan B. Zakkai's Removal to Jabneh", in: *Jews, Judaism and the Classical World*, Jerusalem, 1977, pp. 269–313.
— "The Patriarchate of Rabban Johanan ben Zakkai", in: *Jews, Judaism and the Classical World*, Jerusalem, 1977, pp. 314–343.
Applebaum, S., *Jews and Greeks in Ancient Cyrene*, Leiden, 1979.

Bi(c)kerman(n), E., "La châine de la tradition pharisienne", *RB* 59, 1952, pp. 44–54.
Reprinted in *Studies in Jewish and Christian History*, II, Leiden, 1980, pp. 256–269.
Büchler, A., *The Economic Conditions of Judea After the Destruction of the Second Temple*, London, 1912.

Flusser, D., "The Jewish–Christian Schism", *Immanuel* 16, 1982–1983, pp. 32–49; 17, 1983–1984, pp. 30–39.
Fuks, A., "Aspects of the Jewish Revolt in A.D. 115–117", *JRS* 51, 1961, pp. 98–104.

Goldenberg, R., "The Deposition of Rabban Gamaliel II" An Examination of the Sources", *JJS* 23, 1972, pp. 167–190.
Goodblatt, D., "The Origins of Roman Recognition of the Palestinian Patriarchate" (Heb.), in: *Studies in the History of the Jewish People and the Land of Israel*, IV, ed. U. Rappaport, Haifa, 1978, pp. 89–102.
— "The Story of the Plot against R. Simeon b. Gamaliel II" (Heb.), *Zion* 49, 1984, pp. 349–374.
Green, W. S. (ed.), *Persons and Institutions in Early Rabbinic Judaism*, Missoula, 1977.

Horbury, W., "The Benediction of the *Minim* and Early Jewish–Christian Controversy", *JTS N.S.* 33, 1982, pp. 19–61.

Isaak, B. and Roll, I., "Legio II Traiana in Judaea", *ZPE* 33, 1979, pp. 149–156.

Kanter, S., *Legal Traditions of Gamaliel II*, Missoula, 1980.
Kaplan, J., "Evidence of the Trajanic Period at Jaffa" (Heb.), *EI* 15, 1981, pp. 412–416.
Kimelman, R., "*Birkat Ha-Minim* and the Lack of Evidence for an Anti-Christian Jewish Prayer in Late Antiquity", in: *Jewish and Christian Self-Definition*, II, ed. E. P. Sanders et al., London, 1981, pp. 226–244.

Lepper, F. A., *Trajan's Parthian War*, Oxford, 1948.
Levine, L. I., "The Jewish Patriarch (Nasi) in Third Century Palestine", in: *ANRW* II.19.2, Berlin–New York, 1979, pp. 649–688.

Neusner, J., *A Life of Yohanan ben Zakkai* (2nd ed.), Leiden, 1970.
— *Development of a Legend: Studies on the Traditions Concerning Yohanan ben Zakkai*, Leiden, 1970.
— " 'Pharisaic–Rabbinic' Judaism: A Clarification", *HR* 12, 1973, pp. 250–270.
— *First-Century Judaism in Crisis: Yohanan ben Zakkai and the Renaissance of Torah*, Nashville, 1975.

— "The Formation of Rabbinic Judaism: Yavneh (Jamnia) from A.D. 70 to 100", in:
   ANRW II.19.2, Berlin–New York, 1979, pp. 3–42.
— *Beyond Historicism, After Structuralism: Story as History in Ancient Judaism, The
   1980 Harry Spindel Memorial Lecture*, Bowdoin College, Brunswick, Maine,
   1980.

Pucci, M., "Il movimento insurrezionale in Giudea (117–118 D.C.)", *SCI* 4, 1978,
   pp. 63–76.
— "Alexandria ad Aegyptum: 117–119 A.D.", *SCI* 5, 1979/80, pp. 195–205.
— "C.P.J. II 158 e la rivolta ebraica al tempo di Traiano", *ZPE* 51, 1983, pp. 95–103.
— *La rivolta ebraica al tempo di Traiano*, Pisa, 1981.

Rea, J. R., "The Legio II Traiana in Judaea?", *ZPE* 38, 1980, pp. 220–221.
Rokeah, D. (ed.), *Jewish Rebellions in the Time of Trajan* (Heb.), Jerusalem, 1978.
Rosenfeld, B. Z., "The Crisis of the Patriarchate in Eretz Israel in the Fourth Century"
   (Heb.), *Zion* 53, 1988, pp. 239–257.
— "The Standing and Activities of Rabban Gamaliel Prior to his Move to Yavneh"
   (Heb.), *Zion* 55, 1990, pp. 151–169.

Saldarini, A. J., "Johanan ben Zakkai's Escape from Jerusalem. Origin and Development of a Rabbinic Story", *JSJ* 6, 1975, pp. 189–204.
Schäfer, P., "Die sog. Synode von Jabne. Zur Trennung von Juden und Christen im
   1./2. Jh. n. Chr.", in: Schäfer, *Studien zur Geschichte und Theologie des rabbinis-
   chen Judentums*, Leiden, 1978, pp. 45–64.
— "Die Flucht Johanan b. Zakkais aus Jerusalem und die Gründung des 'Lehrhauses'
   in Jabne", in: *ANRW* II.19.2, Berlin–New York, 1979, pp. 43–101.
Smallwood, E. M., "Palestine c. A.D. 115–118", *Hist* 11, 1962, pp. 500–510.
Stemberger, G., "Die sogenannte 'Synode von Jabne' und das frühe Christentum",
   Kairos 19, 1977, pp. 14–21.

Thoma, C., "Auswirkungen des jüdischen Krieges auf das rabbinische Judentum", *BZ*
   12, 1968, pp. 186–210.
Thompson, L. A., "Domitian and the Jewish Tax", *Hist* 31, 1982, pp. 329–342.

Urbach, E. E., "The Derasha as a Basis of the Halakha and the Problem of the
   Soferim" (Heb.), *Tarbiz* 27, 1958, pp. 166–182.
— "Class Status and Leadership in the World of the Palestinian Sages", *PIASH* 2,
   1968, pp. 38–74.

Veltri, G., "Enteignung des Landes oder Pax Romana? Zur politischen Geschichte der
   Juden nach 70 (Josephus, Bell 7, §§ 216–218)", *FJB* 16, 1988, pp. 1–22.

Ziegler, K.-H., *Die Beziehungen zwischen Rom und dem Partherreich*, Wiesbaden,
   1964.

9. The Bar Kochba Revolt

The Documents from the Bar-Kokhba Period in the Cave of Letters—Greek Papyri,
   edited by Naphtali Lewis; *Aramaic and Nabatean Signatures and Subscriptions*,
   edited by Yigael Yadin and Jonas C. Greenfield, Jerusalem, 1990.

Abramsky, S., *Bar Kochba. Prince of Israel* (Heb.), Tel Aviv, 1961.
Applebaum, S., "The Agrarian Question and the Revolt of Bar Kokhba" (Heb.), *EI* 8, 1967, pp. 283–287.
— *Prolegomena to the Study of the Second Jewish Revolt (A.D. 132–135)*, Oxford, 1976.
— "The Second Jewish Revolt (A.D. 131–135)", *PEQ* 116, 1984, pp. 35–41.

Bar-Adon, P., *The Cave of the Treasure. The Finds from the Caves in Nahal Mishmar*, Jerusalem, 1980, pp. 205–211 (The Bar Kokhba Period).
Barnard, L. W., "Hadrian and Judaism", *JRH* 5, 1969, pp. 285–298.
Ben-Shalom, I., "Der Status Bar Kochbas als Haupt der Nation und die Unterstützung des Aufstands durch die Weisen" (Heb.), *Kathedra* 29, 1983, pp. 13–28.
Bowersock, G. W., "A Roman Perspective on the Bar Kochba War", in: *Approaches to Ancient Judaism*, ed. W. S. Green, II, Ann Arbor, Mich., 1980, pp. 131–141.
Büchler, A., "Die Schauplätze des Bar Kochba-Krieges und die auf diesen bezogenen jüdischen Nachrichten", *JQR* 16, 1903/04, pp. 143–205.

Devir, Y., *Bar Kochba. The Man and the Messiah* (Heb.), Jerusalem, 1964.

Ephrati, J. A., "From Jabneh to Usha" (Heb.), *Sinai* 77, 1974/75, pp. 37–61.

Fitzmyer, J. A., "The Bar Cochba Period", in: *The Bible in Current Catholic Thought*, ed. J. L. McKenzie, New York, 1962, pp. 133–168.

Geiger, J., "The Ban on Circumcision and the Bar Kokhba Revolt" (Heb.), *Zion* 41, 1976, pp. 139–147.
Goodblatt, D., "A Contribution to the Prosopography of the Second Revolt: Yehudah bar Menasheh", *JJS* 38, 1987, pp. 38–55.

Henderson, B. W., *The Life and Principate of the Emperor Hadrian*, London, 1923.
Herr, M. D., "Persecutions and Martyrdom in Hadrian's Days", *ScrHie* 23, 1972, pp. 85–125.
— "The Causes of the Bar Kochba Revolt" (Heb.), *Zion* 43, 1978, pp. 1–11.
Huteau-Dubois, L., "Les sursauts du nationalisme juif contre l'occupation romaine. De Massada à Bar Kokhba", *REJ* 127, 1969, pp. 133–209.

Isaac, B., "Roman Colonies in Judea: The Foundation of Aelia Capitolina" (Heb.), in: *Jerusalem in the Second Temple Period, A. Schalit Memorial Volume*, Jerusalem, 1980, pp. 340–360. English translation: "Roman Colonies in Judaea: The Foundation of Aelia Capitolina", *Talanta* 12–13, 1980–1981, pp. 31–54.
Isaac, B. and Oppenheimer, A., "The Revolt of Bar Kokhba: Ideology and Modern Scholarship", *JJS* 36, 1985, pp. 33–60.
Isaac, B. and Roll, I., "Judaea in the Early Years of Hadrian's Reign", *Latomus* 38, 1979, pp. 54–66.

Kadman, L., *The Coins of Aelia Capitolina*, Jerusalem, 1956.
Kanael, B., "Notes on the Dates Used During the Bar Kokhba Revolt", *IEJ* 21, 1971, pp. 39–46.
Kindler, A., "The Coinage of the Bar Kokhba War", in: *Numismatic Studies and Researches*, II: *The Dating and Meaning of Ancient Jewish Coins and Symbols. Six Essays in Jewish Numismatics*, Tel Aviv–Jerusalem, 1958, pp. 62–80.

Lapp, P. W. and N. L., *Discoveries in the Wâdî ed-Dâliyeh*, Cambridge, Mass., 1974.
Lieberman, S., "The Martyrs of Caesarea", *AIPh* 7, 1939–44, pp. 395–446.
— "On Persecution of the Jewish Religion" (Heb.), in: *S. Baron Jubilee Volume*, Hebrew section, Jerusalem, 1974/75, pp. 213–245.

Mantel, H., "The Causes of the Bar Kokba Revolt", *JQR* 58, 1967/68, pp. 224–242, 274–296; 59, 1968/69, pp. 341–342.
Meshorer, Y., "A Coin Hoard of Bar-Kochba's Time", *The Israel Museum Journal* 4, 1985, pp. 43–50.
Mildenberg, L., "The Elazar Coins of the Bar Kochba Rebellion", *HistJud* 11, 1949, pp. 77–108.
— "Bar Kochba in Jerusalem?", *SchM* 27, No. 105, 1977, pp. 1–6.
— "Bar Kokhba Coins and Documents", *HSCP* 84, 1980, pp. 311–335.
— *The Coinage of the Bar Kokhba War*, Aarau–Frankfurt a.M.–Salzburg, 1984.
Milik, J. T., Benoit, P., de Vaux, R., Discoveries in the Judaean Desert, II: *Les Grottes de Murabba'ât*, Oxford, 1961.
Mor, M., "The Bar-Kokhba Revolt and Non-Jewish Participants", *JJS* 36, 1985, pp. 200–209.

Oppenheimer, A. (ed.), *The Bar Kokhva Revolt* (Heb.), Jerusalem, 1980.
Oppenheimer, A. and Rappaport, U. (eds.), *The Bar Kokhva Revolt. A New Approach* (Heb.), Jerusalem, 1984.

Rabello, A. M., "Il problema della 'Circumcisio' in diritto Romano fino ad Antonino Pio", in: *Studi in onore di Arnaldo Biscardi*, II, Milan, 1982, pp. 187–214.
Reifenberg, A., "Der Thoraschrank auf den Tetradrachmen des zweiten jüdischen Aufstandes", *JPOS* 11, 1931, pp. 51–54.
Rokeah, D., "Comments on the Revolt of Bar Kokhba" (Heb.), *Tarbiz* 35, 1965/66, pp. 122–131.

Schäfer, P., "R. Aqiva und Bar Kokhba", in: Schäfer, *Studien zur Geschichte und Theologie des rabbinischen Judentums*, Leiden, 1978, pp. 65–121.
— *Der Bar Kokhba-Aufstand. Studien zum zweiten jüdischen Krieg gegen Rom*, Tübingen, 1981.
— "Hadrian's Policy in Judaea and the Bar Kokhba Revolt: A Reassessment", in: *A Tribute to Geza Vermes. Essays on Jewish and Christian Literature and History*, ed. P. R. Davies and R. T. White, Sheffield, 1990, pp. 281–303.
Schlatter, A., *Die Tage Trajans und Hadrians*, Gütersloh, 1897.
Smallwood, E. M., "The Legislation of Hadrian and Antoninus Pius against Circumcision", *Latomus* 18, 1959, pp. 334–347.
— "Addendum", *Latomus* 20, 1961, pp. 93–96.
Strathmann, D. H., "Der Kampf um Beth-Ter", *PJB* 23, 1927, pp. 92–123.

Thornton, M. K., "Hadrian and his Reign", in: *ANRW* II.2, Berlin–New York, 1975, pp. 432–476.

Yadin, Y., "The Expedition to the Judean Desert, 1960: Expedition D", *IEJ* 11, 1961, pp. 36–52.
— "Expedition D—The Cave of the Letters", *IEJ* 12, 1962, pp. 227–257.
— *The Finds from the Bar Kokhba Period in the Cave of Letters*, Jerusalem, 1963.

— *Bar Kochba. Archäologen auf den Spuren des letzten Fürsten von Israel*, Hamburg, 1971.

Yeivin, S., *The Bar Kochba War* (Heb., 2nd ed.), Jerusalem, 1957.

Zickermann, E., "Chirbet el-jehud (bettîr)", *ZDPV* 29, 1906, pp. 51–72.

10. From the Bar Kochba Revolt to the Arab Conquest of Palestine

Adler, M., "The Emperor Julian and the Jews", *JQR* O.S. 5, 1893, pp. 591–651.
Avi-Yonah, M., "The Economics of Byzantine Palestine", *IEJ* 8, 1958, pp. 39–51.

Baer, Y., "Israel, the Christian Church and the Roman Empire from the Time of Septimius Severus to the Edict of Toleration of A.D. 313" (Heb.), *Zion* 21, 1956, pp. 1–49. English translation: *ScrHie* 7, 1961, pp. 79–149.
Baumgarten, A. I., "Rabbi Judah I and his Opponents", *JSJ* 12, 1981, pp. 135–172.
Bietenhard, H., "Kirche und Synagoge in den ersten drei Jahrhunderten", *ThZ* 4, 1948, pp. 174–192.
— *Caesarea, Origenes und die Juden*, Stuttgart, 1974.
Bowder, D., *The Age of Constantine and Julian*, London, 1978.
Browe, P., "Die Judengesetzgebung Justinians", *AnGr* 8, 1935, pp. 109–146.
Büchler, A., *The Political and Social Leaders of the Jewish Community of Sepphoris in the Second and Third Centuries*, London, n.d.
— *Der galiläische 'Am Ha'ares des zweiten Jahrhunderts*, Vienna, 1906 (reprinted Hildesheim, 1968).
— "The Patriarch R. Judah I and the Graeco–Roman Cities of Palestine", in: *Studies in Jewish History*, London–New York–Toronto, 1956, pp. 179–244.

Couret, A., *La prise de Jérusalem par les Perses en 614*, Orléans, 1896.
Crawford, M., "Finance, Coinage and Money from the Severans to Constantine", in: *ANRW* II.2, Berlin–New York, 1975, pp. 560–593.

Goodman, M., *State and Society in Roman Galilee, A.D. 132–212*, Totowa, New Jersey, 1983.

Hadas-Lebel, M., "La fiscalité romaine dans la littérature rabbinique jusqu'à la fin du IIIe siècle", *REJ* 143, 1984, pp. 5–29.
Hak, M., "Is Julian's Proclamation a Forgery?" (Heb.), *Yavne* 2, 1940, pp. 118–139.
Hillkowitz, K., "The Participation of the Jews in the Conquest of Jerusalem by the Persians in 614 A.D." (Heb.), *Zion* 4, 1938/39, pp. 307–316.
Hruby, K., *Die Stellung der jüdischen Gesetzeslehrer zur werdenden Kirche*, Zürich, 1971.

Klein, R. (ed.), *Julian Apostata*, Darmstadt, 1978.
Krauss, S., "Die jüdischen Apostel", *JQR* 17, 1905, pp. 370–383.

Langenfeld, H., *Christianisierungspolitik und Sklavengesetzgebung der römischen Kaiser von Konstantin bis Theodosus II.*, Bonn, 1976.
Levy, Y. H., "The Emperor Julian and the Rebuilding of the Temple at Jerusalem" (Heb.), *Zion* 6, 1940/41, pp. 1–32. Reprinted in *Studies in Jewish Hellenism* (Heb.), Jerusalem, 1960, pp. 221–254.

224 Bibliography

Lieberman, S., "Roman Legal Institutions in Early Rabbinics and in the Acta Martyrum", *JQR* 35, 1944/45, pp. 1-57.
— "Palestine in the Third and Fourth Centuries", *JQR* 36, 1945/46, pp. 329-370; 37, 1946/47, pp. 31-54.
Linder, A., "The Roman Imperial Government and the Jews under Constantine" (Heb.), *Tarbiz* 44, 1974/75, pp. 95-143.

Maier, J., *Jüdische Auseinandersetzung mit dem Christentum in der Antike*, Darmstadt, 1982.
Marmorstein, A., "Judaism and Christianity in the Middle of the Third Century", *HUCA* 10, 1935, pp. 223-263. Reprinted in *Studies in Jewish Theology*, London, 1950, pp. 179-224.
Mazar (Maisler), B., *Beth She'arim. Report on the Excavations During 1936–40, I: The Catacombs I–IV*, Jerusalem, 1957.

Noethlichs, K.-L., *Die gesetzgeberischen Maßnahmen der christlichen Kaiser des vierten Jahrhunderts gegen Häretiker, Heiden und Juden*, diss., Cologne, 1971.

Parkes, J., *The Conflict of the Church and the Synagogue*, London, 1934.
Peeters, P., "La prise de Jérusalem par les Perses", in: Peeters, *Recherches d'Histoire et de Philologie Orientales*, I, Brussels, 1951, pp. 78-116.
Pharr, C., *The Theodosian Code*, Princeton, 1952.

Rabello, A. M., "La première loi de Théodose II C. Th. XVI, 8, 18 et la fête de Pourim", *RHD* 55, 1977, pp. 545-558.
— "On the Relations between Diocletian and the Jews", *JJS* 2, 1984, pp. 147-167.
Reichardt, K. D., "Die Judengesetzgebung im Codex Theodosianus", *Kairos* 20, 1978, pp. 16-39.
Rokeah, D., "Jews and their Law in the Pagan–Christian Polemic in the Roman Empire" (Heb.), *Tarbiz* 40, 1970/71, pp. 462-471.
— *Jews, Pagans and Christians in Conflict*, Jerusalem–Leiden, 1982.

Safrai, S., "The Practical Implementation of the Sabbatical Year after the Destruction of the Second Temple" (Heb.), *Tarbiz* 35, 1965/66, pp. 304-328; 36, 1966/67, pp. 1-21.
Schäfer, P., "Der Aufstand gegen Gallus Caesar", in: *Tradition and Re-Interpretation in Jewish and Early Christian Literature. Essays in Honour of J. C. H. Lebran*, ed. J. W. van Henten et al., Leiden, 1986, pp. 184-201.
Schwabe, M., "A New Document Relating to the History of the Jews in the 4th Century C.E." (Heb.), *Tarbiz* 35, 1965/66, pp. 304-328; 36, 1966/67, pp. 1-21.
Schwabe, M. and Lifshitz, B., *Beth She'arim, II: The Greek Inscriptions*, Jerusalem, 1967.
Seaver, J. E., *Persecution of the Jews in the Roman Empire (300–438)*, Lawrence, Kansas, 1952.
Seyberlich, R.-M., "Die Judenpolitik Kaiser Justinians I.", in: *Byzantinistische Beiträge*, ed. J. Irmscher, Berlin, 1964, pp. 73-80.
Sperber, D., "Angaria in Rabbinic Literature", *AC* 38, 1969, pp. 164-168.
— "The Centurion as a Tax-Collector", *Latomus* 28, 1969, pp. 186-188.
— *Roman Palestine 200–400: Money and Prices*, Ramat-Gan, 1974.
— "Aspects of Agrarian Life in Roman Palestine I. Agricultural Decline in Palestine during the Later Principate", in: *ANRW* II.8, Berlin–New York, 1977, pp. 397-443.

— *Roman Palestine 200–400: The Land*, Ramat-Gan, 1978.

Sperber, D., *Roman Palestine 200–400. Money & Prices*, Ramat Gan, 1991.

Stemberger, G., *Juden und Christen im Heiligen Land: Palästina unter Konstantin und Theodosius*, Munich, 1987.

Vogelstein, H., "The Development of the Apostolate in Judaism and its Transformation in Christianity", *HUCA* 2, 1925, pp. 100–123.

Vogt, J., *Kaiser Julian und das Judentum*, Leipzig, 1939.

INDEX

Aelia Capitolina 146, 147, 159
Agrippa I 104, 109, 112–13
Agrippa II 113–14, 116–17, 121
Akiba, Rabbi 141, 149, 154
Akra 40, 42, 47, 48, 52, 55, 56, 56–7, 58
Albinus 117
Alcimus 49, 50, 51
Alexander 81, 82
Alexander Balas 52, 53, 66
Alexander Jannaeus 65, 67, 73, 74–5, 76
Alexander the Great 1–2, 6, 7
  Samaritan schism 2–5
  visit to Jerusalem 5–7
Alexandra 92, 94–5
Ananel 92, 93
Ananus II (ben Ananus) 117, 125, 126
Andronicus 38
Annius Rufus 108
Antigonus 81, 82
Antigonus Monophthalmus 8, 9
Antiochus II 18, 32
Antiochus III 16, 21–2, 24, 27, 28–9, 30, 31, 33
Antiochus IV Epiphanes 35, 38, 39–40, 41, 42–4, 45, 47, 48
  "Hellenistic reform" 35–41
Antiochus V Eupator 46, 48–9
Antiochus VI 56
Antiochus VII Sidetes 58, 65, 67–8
Antiochus VIII Grypus 68
Antiochus IX Cyzicenus 68
Antipater 77, 82–3, 84, 85
Antoninus Pius 146, 164, 178
Apamea: peace treaty 33
Apollonius 34

Apollonius ("Mysarch") 40, 41, 46
Archelaus 101, 102, 104–5
Aretas 75, 77
Aristobulus 92–3
Aristobulus I 73–4
Aristobulus II 76–8, 81, 82
Ascalon 20, 21
"Assembly of the Pious" 46
Athronges 101
Augustus 95, 102, 105

Bacchides 50, 51–2
banditry 175
Bar Kochba, Shimon/Simon 148–9
  title of Messiah 149–51
  title of Nasi 151–4
Bar Kochba revolt 145
  causes 145–8
  consequences 158–60
  course of events 154–8
Ben/Bar Kosiba 148
Berenice 18
Beth Shearim 164, 167–8, 182
Bethar 156, 157–8
birkat ha-minim 139–40

Caesar 82–4
Caligula 104, 108–9
canon of books 139
Caracalla 178
Cassius 84–5
Cestius Gallus 122, 123
Chanina ben Chama 168, 170
Chosroes II 190, 193
Christianity: and Judaism see Judaism and Christianity

Index

chronological table 199–204
circumcision 146–7, 159, 160, 164,
    178, 181, 185
Claudius 109, 115
Cleopatra (daughter of Antiochus III) 33
Cleopatra (mother of Ptolemy Lathyrus)
    74
Cleopatra (queen of Egypt) 91, 93
Codex Iustinianus 190
coins: from Bar Kochba revolt 155–6
Colonia Aelia Capitolina 146, 147, 159
Constantine the Great 176–80
Constantius II 180–2, 183
Constitutio Antoniana 178
Coponius 108, 109
curiae 179, 189
Cuspius Fadus 114

Demetrius I Soter 45, 50, 52, 53
Demetrius II 45, 53, 54–5, 56, 58, 68
Demetrius III Eukairus 75
deuterōsis 189–90
Diadochi
    Palestine under 8–11
    political background 7–8
Diocletian 175

economy
    after First Jewish War 131–2
    Hasmonean 66–7
    under Herod the Great 90–1
    Ptolemaic 14
    under Ptolemaic rule 16–18
    Seleucid 28
    in the third century 172–5
"edicts of toleration" 183
Eleazar 121, 122
Eleazar ben Dinaeus 115
Eleazar ben Jairus 128
Eleazar ben Simon 127
Eleazar the Priest 156
Ephraim 55
epispasm 147
Essenes 52, 71, 72
Eupolemus 50

Felix 115, 116
First Jewish War
    beginnings 121–3
    war in Galilee 123–4
    years 68 and 69 CE 124–7
    conquest of Jerusalem 127–8
    end of the war 128–9
    consequences 131–2
Flavius Silva 129

Gabinius 81
Galilee 123–4, 163
Gallus 182
Gamaliel I 125
Gamaliel II 139, 140, 163–4
Gamaliel III 168, 170
Gamaliel VI 187
Gaza 2
Gerizim, Mt. 2, 3, 4, 5
Gessius Florus 117, 121
government
    Hasmonean 65–7
    under Herod the Great 87–91
    Ptolemaic 13–14
    under Ptolemaic rule 15–16
    Seleucid 27–8
gymnasium 36, 37
gynaeceum 180

Hadrian 145, 146, 147, 157, 158–9
Hasmonean dynasty
    Alexander Jannaeus 74–5
    Aristobulus I 73–4
    Aristobulus II 76–8
    government and economy 65–7
    John Hyrcanus I 67–9
    Pharisees 69–73
    Salome Alexandra 76
Heliodorus 34, 35
Heliodorus affair 34–5
"Hellenistic reform": under Antiochus
    IV 35–41
Heraclius 190, 193–4
"heretics' blessing" 139–40
Herod Antipas 101, 102, 103–4, 107

Herod the Great 73
  assessment of 97–8
  events of reign 91–6
  government and economy 87–91
  rise to power 81–6
  succession after 101–2
Herodias 103, 104
Hillel II 179, 183
Hiskia 9
Hyrcanus 22–3, 34–5, 39
Hyrcanus I, John 65, 66, 67–9, 70
Hyrcanus II 76–7, 78, 94
  and the reform of Judaea 81–5

inter-war period (74 to 132 CE)
  consequences of the war 131–2
  Jabneh 137–41
  Johanan ben Zakkai 135–7
  rabbis 133–5
  revolt under Trajan 141–2
  Ishmael, Rabbi 141

Jabneh 137–41
Jason 50
Jason/Joshua 32, 35, 36, 37, 38, 39
Jesus 103–4
Jesus ben Gamala 125, 126
Jesus ben Sapphias 123–4
Jewish revolt 181–2
Jewish wars see Bar Kochba revolt; First
  Jewish War
Johanan ben Zakkai 135–7, 138, 139,
  140
John Hyrcanus I 65, 66, 67–9, 70
John of Gischala 123, 125, 126, 128
John the Baptist 103, 104
Jonathan 51–6, 65, 66
Joseph 177
Joseph ben Matthias (Josephus Flavius)
  123, 124
Joshua/Jason 32, 35, 36, 37, 38, 39
Judah ha-Nasi 164, 168, 169, 170, 175
Judaism and Christianity 175
  Constantine the Great 176–80
  Constantius II 180–2

Julian the Apostate 182–5
Justinian I 188–90
Persian conquest 190–4
Theodosius I 185–6
Theodosius II 186–8
Judas (son of Ezekias) 101
Judas (son of Mattathias) 44, 46, 47,
  48, 49, 50
Judas of Gamala ("the Galilaean") 109,
  110, 112
Julian the Apostate 182–5
Julius Severus 157, 159
Justin II 190
Justinian I 188–90

Laodice 18
Lusius Quietus 141
Lydda 55
Lysias 46–7, 48, 49
Lysimachus 38

Maccabean Revolt
  Jonathan 51–6
  Mattathias and Judas 44–51
  Simon 56–8
Magensia 33
Marcellus 108
Marcius Turbo 141
Marcus Ambibulus 108
Mariamme 86, 94, 96
Mark Antony 93
marriages, mixed 180, 185
Marullus 108
Masada 128–9
mass migration 172–3
Mattathias: Maccabean Revolt 44–6
Mattathias Antigonus 85–6
Maurice 190
Meir, Rabbi 163, 164
Menahem 122
Menelaus 37–8, 39, 40, 42, 43, 47,
  49
Messiah, title of: and Bar Kochba
  149–51
migration, mass 172–3

Mishnah 164–6
mixed marriages 180, 185
Monophysites 188

Nasi, title of: and Bar Kochba 151–4
Nathan, Rabbi 163, 164
Nehemia ben Chushiel 191, 193
Nero 116, 117, 123, 126
Nicanor 49

Obedas 74, 75
Octavian 93, 94
Oniad family 32–4, 38
Onias II 19, 20
Onias III 32, 33, 34–5, 38
Onias IV 49

Panion 24
Parthians 85
Patriarchate 168–70, 175, 179, 187
Patricius 181, 182
Persian conquest 190–4
Pharisees 136
  during First Jewish War 121, 123
  during Hasmonean dynasty 69–73,
    75, 76
  during the time of Herod the Great
    91–2, 97, 98
  and Rabbis 133
  and the Zealots 110
Phasael 84, 85
Philip 101, 102
Philip V of Macedonia 24, 33
Phocas 190
Pilate 104, 107, 108
polis: Jerusalem 36–7, 42, 47
Pompey 77, 78, 82
Pontius Pilate 104, 107, 108
Porcius Festus 116
procurators 108–9, 114–17
provinces, Roman: legal status 105–7
Ptolemaic rule 13
  government and economy 13–14
  Palestine under 15–18
  First Syrian War 15

Second Syrian War 15
Third Syrian War 18, 19
Fourth Syrian War 21–2
Fifth Syrian War 23–4
Syrian War of Succession 15
Tobiad family 18–21, 22–3
Ptolemy (general) 31
Ptolemy (governor) 28
Ptolemy I Soter 7–8, 9, 10–11, 15
Ptolemy II Philadelphus 15
Ptolemy III Euergetes 18–19, 21, 30
Ptolemy IV Philopator 21, 22
Ptolemy V Epiphanes 22–3, 24, 33
Ptolemy VI Philometor 38, 39
Ptolemy VII Physcon 68
Ptolemy Lathyrus 74

rabbis 133–5, 183–4
  Mishnah 165, 166
Ramathaim 55
Raphia 22
"religious edicts" 41–4
revolt, Jewish 181–2
Roman empire: crisis in the third century
    170–5
Roman rule
  legal status of the province 105–7
  procurators 108–9, 114–17
  Zealots 109–12
Rome/Romans 33, 77–8
  alliance with 49–50
  and Herod the Great 87
  and John Hyrcanus 69
  and Jonathan 56, 58

Sadducees 69, 71, 72, 76, 132
Salome Alexandra 73, 74, 76
Samaritan schism 2–5
Samaritans 43, 108, 186
Scaurus 77, 78
Scopas 24
scribes 133
Scythapolis 20, 21
Second Jewish War see Bar Kochba
    revolt

Seleucid rule   27
    government and economy   27–8
    Heliodorus affair   34–5
    "Hellenistic reform"   35–41
    Maccabean Revolt   44–58
    Oniads and Tobiads   32–4
    Palestine   28–32
    "religious edicts"   41–4
Seleucids   19
Seleucus   18, 15
Seleucus II Callinicus   18–19
Seleucus IV Philopator   33, 34, 35
Sepphoris   123
Septimus Severus   171, 178
Severus family   171
Shimon bar Kochba see Bar Kochba,
    Shimon/Simon
Shimon ben Gamaliel II see Gamaliel II
Shimon/Simeon   168, 170
Simon (former slave of Herod)   101
Simon (guardian of the temple)   34, 35
Simon (son of Mattathias)   65, 66
    Maccabean Revolt   55, 56–8
Simon II   32
Simon bar Gioras   126, 128
Simon bar Kochba see Bar Kochba,
    Shimon/Simon
Simon ben Gamaliel I see Gamaliel I
slaves   178, 181, 185, 188–9
social relations: under Ptolemaic rule
    15–18
soferim   133
succession: after Herod the Great   101–2
synagogues   186, 187
Synhedrion   89, 91, 97, 107, 132
Syrian Wars
    War of Succession   15
    First   15
    Second   15
    Third   18
    Fourth   21–2
    Fifth   23–4

Taxation
    under Antipater   85

Hasmonean   66–7
    under Herod the Great   90–1
    by Patriarchs   169
    Ptolemaic   15, 16
    Roman provinces   78
    under the Romans   171–3
    Seleucid   28, 29–30, 31–2, 45–6,
        54–5
    and the Zealots   111–12
Temple cult   132, 133–4, 183–4
Theodosius I   185–6
Theodosius II   186–8
Theodotus   21, 22
Tiberias   123–4
Tiberius Julius Alexander   114–15
Tigranes   76
Titus   126, 127, 128
Tobiad family   18–21, 22–3, 31, 32, 33,
    34–5
Tobiah   17
Torah
    Mishnah   164, 166
    rabbinic Judaism   134, 138–9
    replaced by Roman law   89
    Seleucids   30–1, 36, 37, 41, 43, 47
    soferim   133
    Zealots   73, 111
Trajan: revolt under   141–2
Tryphon   55, 56, 58
Tyre   1–2, 37, 193

Usha   163

Valerius Gratus   108
Ventridius Cumanus   115
Vespasian   123, 124, 126, 128, 131, 137

wars, Jewish see Bar Kochba revolt;
    First Jewish War

Zealots   73, 104, 109–12, 115–16, 117
    First Jewish War   121, 122, 125,
        126–7
Zenon   17
Zerubbabel apocalypse   191, 193

CHRONOLOGICAL TABLE

		Alexander the Great (336–323 BCE) from 323 onwards struggles among the Diadochi		
Ptolemies	*Seleucids*	*Oniad family*	*Tobiad family*	
ca. 301–200 BCE Ptolemaic rule		End of fourth century BCE Onias I		
305–283/82 BCE Ptolemy I Soter		First half of third century BCE Simon I		
283–246 BCE Ptolemy II Philadelphus				
280/279 BCE Syrian War of Sucession				
274–271 BCE so-called First Syrian War				
260–253 BCE so-called Second Syrian War				
259–258 BCE Journey of Zenon			Tobiah	
246–221 BCE Ptolemy III Euergetes		Second half of third century Onias II	Josef (tax-collector ca. 240–218 BCE)	

Chronological table – *contd.*

Ptolemies	Seleucids	Oniad family	Tobiad family
246–241 BCE so-called Third Syrian War			
221–204 BCE Ptolemy IV Philopator	223–187 BCE Antiochus III		
221–217 BCE so-called Fourth Syrian War			
217 BCE battle at Raphia			
204–180 BCE Ptolemy V Epiphanes			
201–200 BCE so-called Fifth Syrian War			
200 BCE battle at Panion	ca. 200–64 BCE Seleucid rule	ca. 200 BCE Simon II.	
	197 BCE victory of Rome over Philip V of Macedonia		
	190 BCE battle at Magnesia		
	188 BCE peace of Apamea		

Ptolemies	Seleucids	Oniad family	Tobiad family
180–145 BCE Ptolemy VI Philometor	187–175 BCE Seleucus IV Philopator	First half of second century Onias III	
		Hellenists	
	175–164 BCE Antiochus IV Epiphanes	ca. 175–172 BCE Jason	
		ca. 172–163 BCE Menelaus	
170 BCE so-called Sixth Syrian War		169 BCE capture of Jerusalem	
168 BCE Second Egyptian campaign, Roman Senate's ultimatum to Antiochus IV		167 BCE capture of Jerusalem	ca. 168 BCE death of Hyrcanus
			Maccabees/Hasmoneans
		6. 12. 167 BCE consecration of the Temple to "Olympian Zeus"	ca. 167 BCE beginning of the Maccabean Revolt
			166–161 BCE Judas
			165 BCE victory over Lysias
	164 BCE vice-regent Lysias		14. 12. 164 BCE reconsecration of the Temple
	163–162 BCE Antiochus V Eupator	163–160 BCE Alcimus	
		ca. 163 BCE flight of Onias IV to Egypt	

Chronological table – *contd.*

Seleucids	Maccabees/Hasmoneans
162–150 BCE Demetrius I Soter	ca. 161 BCE treaty of friendship with Rome
	161 BCE victory over Nicanor
	161 BCE defeat of Bacchides
	161–142 BCE Jonathan
	153 BCE Jonathan High Priest
150–145 BCE Alexander Balas	142–135/34 BCE Simon
145–140 BCE Demetrius II	141 BCE capture of the Akra
	140 BCE Simon sovereign ruler, High Priest and commander of the Army
138–129 BCE Antiochus VII Sidetes	135/34–104 BCE John Hyrcanus I
129–126 BCE Demetrius II	
126–96 BCE Antiochus VIII Gryphus	
111–95 BCE Antiochus IX Cyzicenus	104–103 BCE Aristobulus I
	103–76 BCE Alexander Jannaeus

Seleucids	Romans	Herod the Great	Maccabees/Hasmoneans
95–87 BCE Demetrius III Eukairus			
			76–67 BCE Salome Alexandra
			67–63 BCE Aristobulus II
	64 BCE Pompey sets the seal on the fate of the Seleucid kingdom		63 BCE capture of Jerusalem
		Antipater governor of Idumaea	63–40 BCE Hyrcanus II
			Restoration of Gabinius
	49 BCE outbreak of the civil wars in Italy		
	47 BCE Caesar in Syria	Phasael governor of Judea	Caesar's decrees
		Herod governor of Galilee	
	44 BCE Cassius in Syria		
	from 42 BCE onwards Antony and Octavian	40–4 BCE Herod the Great	40–37 BCE Mattathias Antigonus
	40 BCE Parthians' invasion	37 BCE capture of Jerusalem	36 BCE murder of Aristobulus
	31 BCE battle of Actium	30 BCE Octavian confirms Herod's appointment as King	31 BCE murder of Hyrcanus
	31 BCE–14 CE Augustus		20 BCE execution of Mariamme

Chronological table – *contd.*

Romans	Herod the Great			Maccabees/Hasmoneans
				28 BCE execution of Alexandra
				7 BCE execution of Alexander and Aristobulus
				4 BCE execution of Antipater
	4 BCE Division of the Empire			
	Judaea, Samaria, Idumaea	Galilee, Peraea	Ituraea, Trachonitis, Batanaea, Auranitis	
	4 BCE–6 CE Archelaus	4 BCE–39 CE Antipas	4 BCE–33/34 CE Philip	
	6–41 CE procuratorial province			
	6–9 CE Coponius			
	9–12 CE Marcus Ambibulus			
	12–15 CE Annius Rufus			
14–37 CE Tiberius	15–16 CE Valerius Gratus			
	26–36 CE Pontius Pilate		34–37 CE annexed to the Roman province of Syria	
	36–37 CE Marcellus			
37–41 CE Gaius Caligula	37–41 CE Marullus	39 CE to Agrippa I	37 CE to Agrippa I	

Romans			Patriarchs
41–54 CE Claudius	41–44 CE Agrippa I		
	44–66 CE Roman province		
	44–46 CE Cuspius Fadus		
	46–48 CE Tiberius Julius Alexander		
	48–52 CE Ventidius Cumanus		
		50–92/93 CE Agrippa II	
		50 CE kingdom of Chalcis	
		53 CE Gaulanitis, Trachonitis, Batanaea, Auranitis	
		61 CE parts of Galilee and Peraea	
54–68 CE Nero	52–60 CE Felix		
	60–62 CE Porcius Festus		
	62–64 CE Albinus		
	64–66 CE Gessius Florus		Shimon ben Gamaliel I
68–69 CE Galba	66–74 CE First Jewish War		
69 CE Otho, Vitellus			
69–79 CE Vespasian	70 CE fall of Jerusalem		
	74 CE fall of Masada		74–132 CE Jabneh period
	from 74 CE onwards praetorian province		74–ca. 80 CE Johanan ben Zakkai

Chronological table – *contd.*

	Romans	Patriarchs
79–81 CE Titus	73/74 CE Lucilius Bassus	ca. 80–ca. 120 CE Gamaliel II (in Jabneh)
	73/74–81 CE L. Flavius Silva	
81–96 CE Domitian	about 86 CE Cn. Pompeius Longinus	
96–98 CE Nerva	about 93 CE Sex. Hermetidus Campanus	
98–117 CE Trajan	about 99/100–102/103 CE Atticus	
	about 102/103–104/105 CE C. Julius Quadratus Bassus	
	about 105–107 CE Q. Roscius Coelius Pompeius Falco	
	about 114 CE Tiberianus?	
115–117 CE revolts in the Diaspora	about 117 CE Lusius Quietus	
117–138 CE Hadrian	about 120 CE consular province	
	about 132 CE Q. Tineius Rufus	

Romans	Patriarchs
132–135 CE Bar Kochba Revolt	ca. 132–135 CE Bar Kochba
from 135 CE onwards Sex. Julius Severus	ca. 135–ca. 175 CE Usha period
138–161 CE Antoninus Pius	ca. 140–ca. 175 CE Shimon ben Gamaliel II (in Usha)
161–180 CE Marc Aurel	ca. 175–217 CE Judah ha-Nasi (in Beth Shearim and Sepphoris)
180–192 CE Commodus	
193 CE second year of the Four Emperors	
193–211 CE Septimius Severus	
211–217 CE Caracalla	
212 CE Constitutio Antoniana	
218–222 CE Elagabal	ca. 217–230 CE Gamaliel III (in Sepphoris)
222–235 CE Severus Alexander	
235–305 CE soldier emperors	middle of the third century CE Judah II (in Sepphoris and Tiberias)

Chronological table – *contd.*

Romans/Byzantium	Patriarchs
	middle of third century CE Gamaliel IV (in Tiberias)
	ca. 280–320 CE Judah III
284–305 CE Diocletian	
324–337 CE Constantine the Great	
	middle of fourth century CE Hillel II
337–361 CE Constantius II	358 CE calendar reform
361–363 CE Julian the Apostate	? Gamaliel V
	363 CE beginning of the reconstruction of the Temple
364–375 CE Valentinian I	? Judah IV
375–378 (383) CE Valens and Gratian	
379–395 CE Theodosius I	
	380–391 CE Christianity becomes the official state religion
395 CE Eastern and Western Roman Empire	
	end of fourth century. *Palaestina prima, secunda* and *tertia*
408–450 CE Theodosius II	
	before 429 CE Gamaliel VI
	end of the Patriarchate

Byzantium	Persians
476 CE end of the Western Roman Empire	
518–527 CE Justin I	
527–565 CE Justinian I	
565–578 CE Justin II	
582–602 CE Maurice	
602–610 CE Phocas	
610–641 CE Heraclius	614 CE capture of Jerusalem by the Persians
	617 CE return of Jerusalem to the Christians
	638 CE capture of Jerusalem by the Arabs